the map i draw

Other Works by Heidi K. Brown

The Introverted Lawyer: A Seven-Step Journey Toward Authentically Empowered Advocacy

Untangling Fear in Lawyering: A Four-Step Journey Toward Powerful Advocacy

The Flourishing Lawyer: A Multi-Dimensional Approach to Performance and Well-Being

The Mindful Legal Writer

the map i draw

a memoir of travel as a passport to self

Heidi K. Brown

Text set in Garamond.

This memoir is a reflection of my own experiences, perspectives, and recollections, written with the intention of being honest, authentic, and accurate to the best of my ability. Though I revisited decades of contemporaneous journals and photos during the writing process, memory is imperfect and subjective; other people involved in these stories inevitably may have different perspectives and recall events in ways that diverge from my own retrospection, especially the difficult moments. To protect the privacy of individuals who are a vital part of the most intimate and vulnerable parts of my life story but did not ask to be written about, I have changed names and identifying details where appropriate. This work represents my truth as I understand and believe it, and it is offered with humility, care, and appreciation toward those who intertwined their lives with mine.

contents

acknowledgments

Back in 2000–2001, when I was navigating the trauma of my divorce, an abrupt move from Virginia to New York, and 9/11 layered on top of all that, I lost the ability to read fiction. Instead, I craved narratives of reality—accounts of survival, recovery, transformation—scribed by unfamous people. I wanted to read true stories written by regular humans who had gone through something devastating like I had—even if it was partly or even mostly their own (un)doing, like mine. I needed to immerse in testimonies about how to go on living . . . not just existing but full-on thriving, flourishing, soaring. The genre of memoir saved my life. I am grateful for memoirists whose books I discovered during my roughest time and who showed me a pathway out of the mire.

To turn a memoir manuscript into a book anyone might want to read requires trusting others to give you periodic gut checks that the project is worthwhile . . . that perhaps someone else might benefit from your truths, your learnings from mistakes, your raw unprettiness at times, your epiphanies. I am thankful for readers of early excerpts and drafts of this book, including Clay Edmonds, Flora Midwood, Jenn Liles, and Tracey Campion, plus Caroline Weiss who empowered me to "interrogate" my inner dialogue and dig deeper, Karen Bailey who pushed me to jettison shame and step into strength, Jordana Confino who kept urging, "Do not play small; stand like a starfish and keep going," Kelly Nutty who penned note after note saying, "Light and dark . . . full and empty . . . through it all . . . you're fierce . . . you're a baddy," and Michele Morgan who nudged, "Own it all, girl."

I love my girl power gang: tenacious queen Kelly Nutty, radically radiant Jordana Confino, U2 sister and travel beacon Michele Morgan, coadventurer Jenna Adikes, spirited star Jenn Liles, beautiful soul Julie Seder, empowering butterfly Esperanza Franco, and steadfast sage Shailini George.

Thank you to my brilliant and hilarious cadre of confidants and creativity cheerleaders: Lauren Brownstein, Susan Silver, Todd Flournoy, Kim Hawkins, Christopher Corts, Marjorie Silver, Jodi Balsam, Paula Faulk, Judy Corless, Jenny Bailey, Ketan Soni, Lucinda Heidsieck Bhavsar, Anna Miller, Cecilia Silver, Carole Post, Maryellen Fullerton, Dana Brakman Reiser, Heidi Gilchrist, Gina Alexandris, Patrick Patino, Jen Leonard, Anita Bernstein, and Kendra Brodin.

To my BFF Clay Edmonds, thank you for making me spit out precious coffee or wine laughing *every single day*.

Thank you to my boxing coach and friend Lou who reminds me to breathe and *be* and has made me cherish the firepower of my fifty-five-year-old body.

Thank you U2, for oxygenating the artist in me.

Thank you to my book's glam squad: proofreader Danielle Lange, typesetter and interior designer Suzy Bills, and cover illustrator Michelle Argyle Park of Melissa Williams Design.

To my family—I'm proud of us for alchemizing conflict into new chords of connectivity.

To M—for showing me ride-or-die affection, even if it couldn't last.

And J—the most formative relationship of my life that will never be replicated. Love always.

introduction:
a sticky parking lot in
south florida

(seven years before the pandemic)

I itched.

Fifteen hours earlier, as the sun dunked into the Atlantic, sand fleas infiltrated my carefully constructed layers of DEET spray, Avon Skin So Soft, snowboarding socks, and athleisure. I thought the strata would protect my forty-three-year-old New York skin against, at most, the usual smattering of mosquito bites I sustain during my annual obligatory family get-together in Jupiter, Florida. Somehow a plague of "no-see-ums" (as Floridians call them) maneuvered like ninjas through barriers of diethyl toluamide, Lycra, and Egyptian cotton. The bugs chowed the flesh along my arms and legs. Neither my parents, my brother, his wife, nor my teenage niece or nephew sustained a single bite. The insects' target seemed to prove my parents right.

I'm the rotten one.

I itched.

The soles of my flip-flops stuck to the melting tar of the timeshare motel's parking lot, like black taffy.

I yearned for quiet. Air-conditioning. Solitude. My ears rang from a cacophony of kids cannonballing into the community pool . . . their parents, sporting jarring tattoos of split-tongued serpents and blood-spattered daggers, popping lids off perspiring

1

cans of Budweiser . . . gardeners' leaf blowers blasting the patio
. . . a low-flying biplane trailing a banner announcing two-for-
one margaritas and a gun show.

A pair of tears busted loose despite my efforts to corral them
by scrunching my face to suppress stirring anger I knew, if
unshackled, would only worsen an already fragile family vibe.
Grateful for sunglasses, I didn't want Dad to erroneously assume
my tears represented contrition.

Earlier that morning, I'd left the one-bedroom condo I temporarily occupied with my parents, clutching my laptop, seeking
out the timeshare "clubhouse" where I could access Wi-Fi and
check email. To supplement my paltry mid-level legal writing
professor salary, I juggled multiple summer freelance gigs, including writing briefs for a Washington, DC, law firm and
grading students' practice bar exam essays for a California law
school. I needed to check my essay queue to ensure I provided
feedback within twenty-four hours as contractually promised.
Working from the East Coast, I liked to clear my essays before
students woke up on the West Coast.

Mom and I had planned to take our ritual morning walk
along an oceanfront pathway beneath the shade of sea grape
trees at 9 a.m. before Florida's heat index climbed to its peak and
hovered there for the rest of the day.

I sighed as the clubhouse's dodgy Wi-Fi connection booted,
unbooted, rebooted. Luckily, no essays loomed in my inbox.
But after responding to a few pressing emails, I returned to the
condo eight minutes late. Mom already had changed out of
the workout gear I'd seen her wearing when I'd left forty-five
minutes earlier. Vigorously scrubbing an imaginary red wine
blemish from the Formica kitchen counter, she refused to look
at me.

"Everything okay? Should we go walking now?" I probed.

"It's too late."

I glanced at the clock on my phone. 9:09 a.m.

I scratched an itch on my elbow.

"Sorry . . . I needed to clear my essays. The Wi-Fi wasn't working great. We can go now?"

"Too late."

I scratched an itch on my calf.

I tugged the hem of my leggings to glance at my shin. Red dots commingled with my usual galaxy of freckles.

"I think I got bitten by a *lot* of mosquitos, or something, last night." Scratch.

Mom still wouldn't look at me.

"Mom, what's wrong?"

"All you care about is your work! You're incredibly selfish."

Three nights with my family is usually a hard max. We'd just begun Day Four. Inner fury I'd kept subdued for the last seventy-two hours by serial sippy cups of Spanish red wine began to unfurl.

"Mom, I'm eight minutes late! If you guys would get Wi-Fi, I could check email here instead of having to trudge to that clubhouse constantly. I wish you would be proud of me for working hard, not constantly criticize me."

Sweat droplets trickled my arms and legs, stoking the itch.

The condo's air-conditioning unit powered up like a jet engine, its thermostat set by Dad at an ineffectual seventy-one degrees. Not ratcheted low enough to generate a consistent, quiet stream of cool air, the unit thudded on, off, on, day and night.

Dad stepped through the patio glass door, clutching swimming goggles and a damp towel. A green lizard darted out of his way. Mom sniffled.

He glanced at her. "What happened?"

My rationality elbowed my emotionality. *Don't say a word. Keep your mouth shut.* Frustration prevailed, as usual.

"I was eight minutes late getting back from checking essays, so Mom canceled our walk and now she's upset."

A retired Episcopal minister, Dad rarely swears. "You work too damn much," he growled.

Scratch.

Itch.

Sweat.

Steam.

Throb at my right temple.

Migraine percolating.

Mom sniffed. Her lower lip trembled.

Dad scooted to her side.

Knowing the conversation was over (Mom's rescue choppers cued), I plodded to the bathroom to change into a swimsuit. I peeled sweaty spandex from nettled skin.

Emerging from the bathroom in cutoff jean shorts and a tank top, I showed my parents the constellation of rosy welts dotting my arms and legs. Now dry-eyed and cheery, Mom chimed, "The no-see-ums sure love you. Must be the red wine you drink. We don't have any bites!"

"I think I need to go to a pharmacy."

"Well, first we need to drop off lunch supplies and the coolers at Chris's place."

My brother Christopher, his wife, my niece, and my nephew had road-tripped to Florida from North Carolina and set up camp in a larger timeshare condo for the week. As the childless, single, older sister, I slept on a sofa bed in our parents' space. Before Mom and Dad had purchased the timeshare three years earlier, our family hadn't vacationed together since Chris and I were in high school. Throughout our adolescence, we'd tagged along while our parents ran Vacation Bible Schools every summer on East Coast beaches. My brother and I canvassed boardwalks in T-shirts bearing the logo for Children's Sand & Surf Mission. (The initials CSSM reminded me of the Cyrillic letters CCCP emblazoned across the backs of Soviet gymnast uniforms in the early 1980s.) We handed out yellow flyers advertising Jesus-themed skits to parents holding the hands of elementary school-aged kids. CSSM team members constructed a makeshift amphitheater on the beach each morning using buckets of water and shovels to tightly pack tiers in the sand so kids could sit and watch my dad strum a guitar, my mom slap a tambourine, and camp counselors act out Bible parables.

Thirty years later, my mom craved "happy family" vacation vignettes—scenes she coveted in her friends' grandkid photos. One problem: Our family had no historical blueprint for this type of performative closeness. But out of a sense of familial duty—and an effort to see each other—Chris and I showed up.

My parents and I crossed the pool deck, lugging ice chests to Chris's condo. As we passed my mother's buddies sprawled across lounges, a few diagnosed my splotchy quads.

One noted, "Yeah, sand fleas have burrowed under your skin. You can almost see 'em moving."

My parents finally agreed to drive me to two pharmacies. The clerks seemed baffled by the intensity of my body's reaction to such a common Florida irritant. I spent fifty-six dollars on calamine lotions (sticky and unhelpful) and aloe vera gels (stickier and even less helpful). After more intensive internet searches, I bought tea tree oil and cocoa butter—a stinky combination that brought instant topical relief and reportedly would prevent scarring.

Grumpy, dead tired, and irritated—inside and out—in the back seat of my parents' un-air-conditioned Buick, I crafted excuses to avoid sitting poolside all day in sweltering humidity while strangers stared at my embattled skin and interrogated me about my life in New York. I tried to conjure my happy place: a solo voyage to an unfamiliar land where people don't speak English.

In three weeks, my passport would transport me to Rome for the first time. I planned to speak the Italian I'd studied decades earlier in college and in more recent group lessons in New York, visit the Colosseum, eat *carciofi alla romana* (Roman-style artichokes), and hopefully meet a hot Roman with a name ending in a vowel.

Shiiiitt. Itch. Scratch. *How can I possibly frolic through Italy in three weeks if I look like a measles patient?* I pouted in the Buick's back seat, vinyl upholstery sticking to my rash.

Dad steered the car into the timeshare driveway. Mom hopped out and rushed to the pool to see if her church friends had arrived. Dad detained me in the parking lot. As a fellow introvert, my father doesn't say much, but when he gets mad, usually in response to Mom feeling criticized or disrespected by someone, his blue eyes weaponize.

"You need to get your priorities straight. You need to find God in your life. You're in peril again. You need to find peace in your heart. You're never going to do that through *work*. Or living in New York. You have a hole in you. Maybe it's your lawyer life. Maybe it's the regret, the shame, of your past. Your divorce. Your broken relationships. Something has a hold on you. You need to find your soul. And you're not going to find your soul in Rome."

You're not going to find your soul in Rome.

Unsafe. Run.

When I'm scared, my amygdala does what it's biologically supposed to do. It flashes a warning alert to my nervous system, activating my fight-flight-freeze response. My *brain* frantically yanks the *flight* lever, seeking a rapid stacking of miles between my body and the perceived threat. If my brain were 100% in charge in these situations, it would whip out a mobile phone and credit card, book the first flight home to New York, snap a finger, and hail the closest taxi to extract me from the situation.

My body, however, takes a different tack. It *freezes*. Goes numb. Total paralysis. *Don't move. Don't emote. Don't exist.*

At forty-three years old, I felt confused and rattled that mere words coming out of my father's mouth still had the power to freak me out. To shake me. Similar syllables and phrases had emerged from my parents' lips many times: "You need to be brought to your knees by God." "If you'd give your life to God, you wouldn't be having these relationship problems." And one of the most memorable gems from Mom: "I'm a failure as a mother because my children don't go to church."

None of my accolades matter. Cum laude and salutatorian honors in high school, ranking second in my graduating class. Scholarships and Phi Beta Kappa distinction in college. Law degree. Prestigious law firm jobs. Professor status. Publications. Awards.

None of it is ever enough to deflect the blanket of shame they're still capable of throwing over me, smothering my light.

Knowing I didn't have the audacity for a dramatic early exodus (a much more cinematic and defiant *flight* response compared to my catatonic *freeze* state), I hid the blaze in my eyes behind my biggest pair of sunglasses. My flip-flops carried me back to the pool, balls of liquefied asphalt sticking to rubber soles. I marionetted a fake smile on my face for the strangers. I'm good at that. I've been doing that my whole life.

I watched my mom distribute slices of cake on paper plates—mementos of their forty-fifth wedding anniversary celebration. My brother's kids played Marco Polo in the pool, unjaded voices popping out of chlorine.

I sat motionless as poolside inquisitors peppered me with questions like "What's a single girl like you living in a big dirty city like New York?" and unsolicited assertions like "I'm going to pray a special man enters your life, sweetheart."

Please don't. I'm fine.

Words from a song called "Bad" by Irish rock band U2 (my favorite musical artist) popped like strobe-lit dialogue bubbles in my brain. *Condemnation. Dislocation. Desolation. Separation. Isolation. Desperation.*

Unsafe. Run.

"You're not going to find your soul in Rome."

Dad's words threw down a gauntlet.

Oh yeah? Watch me.

🧳   🧳   🧳

I stayed in Florida one more day. Two days too long. My parents deposited me at West Palm Beach Airport, all smiles, prayers, hugs. Like nothing had happened, as always.

Perfect minister's family.

Sticky, itchy, lonely, angry, I flew home to New York.

I dumped my bags in my apartment's foyer. I stood under the waterfall of a lengthy shower, willing steam to expel every histamine from my inflamed skin. I examined the numerosity and size of my bumps, reapplied layers of oil and ointment, donned soft sweatpants, cranked my air-conditioning, lit every candle I owned, ordered two tubs of vegetable korma from my go-to Indian restaurant, and tuned into a *Law & Order: Special Victims Unit* marathon. While Benson and Stabler solved crimes, I rolled my laptop cursor over a virtual map of Rome. I traced my index finger along the S curve of the Tiber River.

My heartbeat decelerated. Breathing stopped hurting. The vise around my ribs loosened. I stopped wrinkling my nose to avert tears—an emotion-suppressing habit I'd developed since the end of my second long-term relationship.

Under a weighty comforter, I slept ten hours, my bedroom cold as an igloo.

🧳   🧳   🧳

Since my father's scolding in that swampy Florida parking lot twelve years ago, I've traveled. A lot. I've embarked on trips with girlfriends; I've also found a groove voyaging alone. Planning and navigating adventures—booking window seats on international flights, researching artsy hotels, deciphering train schedules, learning at least ten phrases of each unfamiliar language (essentials like "hello," "goodbye," "thank you," "please," "how much does this cost," the numbers one, two, and three, "I like red wine that tastes like pepper and earth," and "may I have the check, please"), changing money, deterring rumored yet undetectable pickpockets at ATM machines, finding nontouristy places to eat without feeling awkward occupying a table solo—each time, I remember and relive snippets and vignettes from prior trips, layering experience onto innocence. I notice things my maternal grandmother Doris—my first travel idol—would have loved.

My dad was partially correct.

I didn't, and I don't, *find* my soul in foreign lands. My soul is not tactile like the wristband from a Rome-Bologna soccer match—a piece of blue-silver ribbon now preserved in a favorite dog-eared book. My soul is not tangible like the sticks of palo santo wood and male-female Inca talisman (with penis *and* breasts) I bought in Peru. Or the sack of rocks I lugged home from a beach in Troncones, Mexico, that transform from dull gray to kaleidoscopic colors when wet. Or the ticket stub from a U2 concert in Dublin—my initial all-access pass into a worldwide fan family. Or the graffiti pictures I've snapped in Amsterdam, Madrid, Belfast, and numerous other locales, stoking artistic rebellion in me—a lifelong rule follower, a dutiful sheep.

My soul is not a reckonable article I need to procure and tuck away for safekeeping. Travel *is* my soul. Or it fires up my soul. It fuels exhilaration and wonder and marvel.

Travel affords me quiet space in a deafeningly loud world. To heal.

To recover from my excruciating divorce from Trey—the most formative pain of my life I thought I'd worked through, but still haven't fully or deeply enough, even though two and a half decades have passed since I left him twenty-five days before my thirtieth birthday.

To expunge a deeply rooted misbelief that I am unlovable and undesirable, reinforced by another eight-year, push-pull, intimacy-starved relationship with Forrest.

To process guilt and shame from years of family conflict over religion, politics, my shattered relationships, my serpentine career path.

To understand why I continue to seek out love that feels like maim.

Through travel, I kindle a fortitude that magnifies into a fierceness even I sometimes can't believe I possess. Exploring unfamiliar cultures anonymously with no one to answer to or tell me what my choices should be. Making mistakes—getting on the wrong train, using the wrong phrase, smiling at the wrong guy, getting occasionally scammed, trying a local delicacy that turns out to be gross, losing electricity, setting off smoke alarms, still sometimes saying yes when I mean no—and realizing the world does not come to an end.

Travel coaches me to stop and acknowledge moments of spontaneous combustion and take it all in. The instances when you just cannot fathom where you are in the world, what just happened, what you just accomplished or experienced, and how you feel exactly in that split second of revelation.

"You're not going to find your soul in Rome," my dad warned.

But my soul is teeming with delight at the mere thought of Rome right now, and I haven't even extracted my passport from its secret location in my apartment yet.

🧳   🧳   🧳

My life's soundtrack includes a lot of U2 songs. Snippets of lyrics and other phrases and sentences the band members have murmured, shouted, or scribbled over the years echo from boom boxes in my brain. I remember five words front man Bono whispered into his microphone at the beginning of each show on U2's 2015 *iNNOCENCE + eXPERIENCE* tour. He posed a question: "Where are we going?" Then shouted, "Everywhere!"

I agree.

Let's go.

1

roma

My knee banged the undercarriage of a wooden desk built for a middle schooler. A loose screw snagged my tights. Scuola Italiana—an Italian language institute for adults—convened at night in a Catholic junior high school attached to Our Lady of Pompeii Church in the Greenwich Village neighborhood of New York City. Mimeographed photos of various popes gazed from four classroom walls upon a motley collection of New Yorkers struggling to conjugate Italian verbs.

I realized I was gritting my teeth. *Why don't these people just do the homework?*

Our teacher, Angelo, turned to me. "Ma, Heidi, che cosa hai fatto di bello oggi?" *But, Heidi, what did you do today that was beautiful?*

Locks of chaotic hair floated around Angelo's smirky mouth and caramel eyes. Acrylic paint smattered his cargo shorts and Adidas sneakers. His words, accent, gestures . . . total mischief vibe.

Man, I know what I want *to do today that is beautiful.*

I responded—in cautious, grammatically uptight Italian— that earlier in the day I began packing for my vacation to Rome and Puglia.

"Puglia! Bella! La mia città natale! Ostuni!"

His birthplace. Of course, I already knew Angelo was born in the Italian region of Puglia, the town of Ostuni. He liked to share details about himself, and I paid rapt attention.

In planning my summer break from my law professor job, having binge-watched HBO's series, *Rome*, I'd scheduled a week in Italy's capital, eager to immerse in the city's historical sites for the first time. For a countryside contrast, midway through the two-week trip, I intended to fly from Rome to Brindisi, one of three airports in the region of Puglia situated in the "heel" of the Italian "boot." Angelo had taught us about *masseria*, whitewashed farmhouses converted by entrepreneurial locals into shabby chic B&Bs, part of the *agriturismo* trend. I'd reserved a room at a masseria in Ostuni—Angelo's hometown—a geographical detail I omitted when I relayed my travel itinerary to the class, not wanting my crush on our teacher to seem embarrassingly obvious.

At home, a canvas suitcase lay flat on my apartment floor. I'd bought the luggage two years earlier for my cross-country move back to New York from Laguna Beach, California, after finally exiting my eight-year relationship with Forrest, a fun but manic Brit who unfortunately loved cocaine more than he loved me. Dark marks evidencing friction with baggage claim conveyor belts bruised the suitcase's silver material. Its zipper pulls cracked and broken, I had to use fingernails to tug its sliders open and closed. The bag had not been handled with appropriate care. Indeed, neither had I. After four years of futile efforts to rekindle a flame of intimacy with Forrest that our "great West Coast experiment" had extinguished, I finally had to admit that sexual problems are unfixable if one party is categorically disinterested in fixing them.

As usual, I overpacked. Sundresses I never wear in New York City. Linen tops and shorts for sightseeing in Rome's summer heat. Sexy going-out outfits. Ankle-breaking sandals wholly inappropriate for tromping around on cobblestones. Sleepwear. Poolside attire for Puglia. Sunglasses. A straw fedora I bought in Turkey. Too many books. My laptop, to edit my legal textbook manuscript—my second book publication—in Ostuni.

An Italian dictionary. A European electrical converter. Toiletries. Passport (and extra paper copies neurotically tucked into my suitcase and carry-on bag). An envelope of euro bills. My social security card, just in case I lost all other identification. *Sono pronta*. I'm ready.

☐ ☐ ☐

I hailed a taxi from my downtown Manhattan apartment to John F. Kennedy Airport. Perennially early, I checked my bloated suitcase, breezed through the Transportation Security Administration PreCheck line, and surveyed restaurant options to grab a glass of wine and a preflight snack. I ordered an overpriced goblet of Barbera and a tuna tartare, which arrived crammed with red onions though I specifically told the bartender they give me migraines. *Non mi piacciono le cipolle rosse*, I planned to recite to every Italian waiter. Plucking little red monsters from chunks of tuna, I texted Mia to check on her ETA.

I'd originally met Mia at a pal's rooftop barbecue in Manhattan. Close in age, both single and travel hungry, we'd instantly bonded, sharing a laugh over a realization we'd had a Tinder date with the same guy—a New Zealand rugby player trying to sleep his way through New York.

Midsummer, I'd bumped into Mia on Bleecker Street in the West Village as I departed an Italian lesson.

"Hey! What's up?" Mia's wide blue eyes and frisky smile implied wild weekend stories.

"I'm heading to Florida to visit my parents soon. Then I'm off to Rome on vacation!"

"Ah, Rome's my favorite place! Who are you going with?"

"Just me."

"By yourself? Wow. Well, hey, if you want a travel buddy, I'm always game."

While I desired to do most of my first trip to Rome alone, I conceded it probably would be good for me to have a girlfriend along for part of it, to force me to go out at night and actually interact with other humans. A plan gelled. Mia would join me for a long weekend, leaving me plenty of time to explore Rome my way and then bounce onward to Puglia.

⚏ ⚏ ⚏

No return text yet from Mia.

I paid for the Barbera and picked-over tartare and headed to the gate. Minutes before Alitalia agents began inviting the first cadre of passengers to board the plane, Mia rolled into the waiting area like a VIP. Shiny blonde hair gleaming beneath a straw fedora similar to mine. Backless halter dress. Ankle boots.

Every man in the vicinity—Italian, American, old, young—swiveled to stare at her. She plopped a slim tote bag onto the floor near my overstuffed carry-on, snatched my boarding pass from my hand, and strode to the agent desk.

To my initial relief, Mia's charms were unavailing in her efforts to convince airline personnel to reconfigure seat assignments to place us together. My preferred flight plan included popping melatonin and Advil PM, leaning my head against a window shade, and attempting to sleep for at least a portion of the eight-hour overnight journey. Sleep-deprivation migraines plague me. The last thing I needed was a raging headache compounded by blistering Roman sunshine on Day One of this Italian adventure. Undeterred however, Mia spent the bulk of the boarding process maneuvering, cajoling, finagling, and bartering with other passengers to move me from my window seat on the opposite side of the plane to the aisle seat next to hers. Not wanting to seem like a lame trip mate, I acquiesced. But unable to prop my head against a solid surface, sleep eluded me.

Excitement at hearing the pilot's melodic voice welcoming us—in Italian—to Rome's Fiumicino Airport overrode a dull ache at my temples. In the taxi line, I pulled the address for Hotel Bernini Bristol from a pink folder with gold lettering stating, *Obviously Brilliant Ideas.* My mom buys packets of sparkly novelty folders at the Dollar Store and gives them to me for Christmas and my birthday.

"Piazza Barberini, per favore," I said to the Roman taxi driver.

"Prego."

The driver attacked the *autostrada* like a Formula One racer. Lingering haze from his last cigarette drifted into the back seat as he swore and gestured at careening gasoline trucks and Smart cars. He spoke in rapid Italian, cursing traffic thwarting his efforts to deliver us to the hotel in record time. As he punctuated shouts of "Che cazzo!" (Italians' version of the F-word) with passionate hand gestures, I grinned and peered out the window. Aqueducts, arches, and obelisks constructed two millennia ago loomed. Fallen ancient columns lay in green grass near pine trees with leaf canopies shaped like parasols. Statues of various Roman emperors blurred as the taxi boomeranged around the Colosseum, looped Piazza Barberini, and planted us on the doorstep of the Hotel Bernini Bristol. I scanned the piazza, looking for the Triton Fountain, a masterpiece (a *capolavoro*, or "chief work," in Italian) by Baroque sculptor Gian Lorenzo Bernini I'd seen on the hotel's website—a merman kneeling on a shell supported by four dolphin tails, blowing into a conch like a trumpet. Reconstruction scaffolding unfortunately blocked the fountain from view.

Too early to check in to our rooms, we dragged our luggage into a muggy restroom and rummaged for sightseeing clothes. Mia stripped to a leopard-spot silk bra and pulled a clingy black sundress from her carry-on bag. I regretted my travel choice of comfy T-shirt bra that had faded from magenta pink to gray-beige. *Greige.* I felt greige next to glamorous Mia. I pulled shorts and a sleeveless top onto my sweaty body and wrangled my wild hair with my fedora. We entrusted our bags to a concierge and bounded into sunshine.

A veteran of Rome travel, Mia already knew the city's layout. In espadrilles, she marched across Piazza Barberini. I scampered after her. My throbbing skull screaming for coffee, I convinced her to duck into a café.

"Un espresso, per favore," I asked the barista. I usually soften the assault of strong coffee with milk, but mirroring the Romans, I consumed a thimble of pure caffeine in three sips, standing against a glass case displaying *cornetti* (Italian croissants) and almond brioches. Watching patrons flick pastry crumbs off tailored jackets and designer blouses, I wondered how Romans stay so thin.

Ah, cigarettes.

At the café doorstep, a man with salt-and-pepper facial scruff lit a woman's cigarette with the click of a silver lighter. She exhaled a stream of smoke from one side of her mouth. The man kissed her on both cheeks, grabbed a Vespa helmet from a chair, whispered, "Ciao, amore," touched her hip, and strode away.

I want all my mornings to start like that.

In my first eighteen minutes on the streets of Rome, I saw six couples kiss. I tried to remember whose lips had last grazed mine.

Mia's espadrilles were on the move again. Navigating Rome's maze of cobblestoned alleys, we passed leather goods stores, *enotecas* (wine shops), and bodegas selling tricolored penis-shaped pasta and aprons bearing photographs of Michelangelo's statue of *David*, intricately chiseled genitalia prominent.

As we turned a corner, I heard thundering water. A panorama of bright white sculptures refracted sunshine into a glistening clear-blue pool. Sparkles of copper—coins of countless currencies—glinted beneath the water's surface.

Fontana di Trevi. The Trevi Fountain. The word *trevi* derives from the Latin *trivium*, meaning *three streets*.

Muscular, bearded Oceanus, the god of fresh water, perched one foot on a massive clamshell. Burly Tritons—mermen—gripped the manes of sea horses, one agitated, the other tranquil. Water bounced off rocks, like diamonds and crystals plunging into the pool.

I felt like I'd been tasered. I'd never seen a fountain so dramatic.

The boom of the water competed with the many languages sloshing around me. Vendors hawked selfie sticks; others heaved gelatin toys into the air that whistled as they hurtled back to Earth, slapping flat on cobblestones. Mia pressed through the throng to the water's edge and corralled two male tourists to join her in a selfie.

I felt jittery, like I'd touched an electric fence. I tried focusing on concrete things or people I could see—to reground. Three pairs of security officers in different uniforms: a duo in green camouflage, fingers poised on machine-gun triggers; a second dyad in dapper dark blue, red stripes bifurcating each pant leg, white leather belts strapped diagonally across their chests, gold buttons and buckles shimmering in sunlight; another twosome in light-blue fatigues, pistols holstered around bulging quadriceps. Their six sets of brown eyes scanned the sea of humanity for potential threats. In a lady's arms, a Chihuahua licked pink gelato from a waffle cone. A street musician squeezed Andrea Bocelli arias from an accordion. A church faced the fountain, its bowels reportedly storing the embalmed hearts of twenty-two of the Catholic Church's 266 popes, its facade decorated with sculpted angels and an architectural ornament called a mascaron (a face), allegedly a portrait of one of Louis XIV's mistresses.

I smelled grapefruit in the perfume of French girls standing arm in arm next to me. Heard laughter of Italian children playing hide-and-seek behind their father's knees. Tasted espresso lingering on my tongue. Felt tiny, yet also Roman-goddess-vibey.

I need to live here. I feel like I have lived here. Like I belong here.

I scrutinized the ripples of muscle chiseled by the fountain's sculptors to depict the strength of Oceanus, the mermen, the horses. Stared into the blinding white of the marble and travertine. Blinked away the glare, closed my eyes, and imagined slipping beneath the water's surface. Deep cleanse. Fresh start.

I opened my eyes to find Mia wriggling, gyrating, itching to move on.

Next stop on our high-velocity tour agenda: the Villa Borghese, one of the largest public parks in Europe, Rome's "green lung." *Polmone verde.* Mia and I darted up a hilly boulevard lined with luxe hotels and art galleries and raced down the Spanish Steps, named for Spain's Embassy to the Holy See—the oldest embassy in the world—located in the piazza at the base of the staircase. (The term *see* derives from Latin for *seat*, and refers to the pope's jurisdiction as bishop of Rome.) We scooted along a shopping avenue toward the Piazza del Popolo (named for the "people" but also the poplar tree). As we blew past store windows curating Italian couture and ready-to-wear fashion, a small sign pointing toward a street called Via Margutta caught my eye. I recalled reading something about Pablo Picasso once living and painting there in the early 1900s—my favorite artist, though I wish he hadn't been so awful toward women. Reportedly, out of the seven women who occupied the most prominent roles in the painter's romantic life, two died by suicide and others battled severe depression. Mia raced onward. I followed but made a mental note to explore Via Margutta solo when I had more time.

A grand archway led us into the Borghese Gardens, a labyrinth of trees, pathways, and fountains. Like at Trevi, sounds of water—trickles, splashes, gushes—echoed throughout the park. In a marvel of intelligent engineering spanning over five hundred years—from 312 BCE to 226 CE—Romans built a network of aqueducts to channel fresh water from the countryside to populated urban areas. Still today, fresh, cool, sanitary drinking water abounds in Rome. Gargoyle mouths and ornate spigots pour potable water into stone troughs positioned at alleyway corners in the city center and throughout parks and piazzas. Tourists, nuns, and businessmen queue to refill empty bottles with clean water streaming from gaping lips of sculpted fish heads, Medusas, and cherubs.

I'm an Aries, a fire sign. Water sometimes feels menacing, or extinguishing, to me. It didn't always. As a kid, during our family's Bible beach mission trips, I'd frolicked in the Atlantic Ocean without hesitation. My brother and I bodysurfed waves, getting tossed upside down, little shoulders slamming into hard sand. We shrugged off mild jellyfish stings. Stepped on horseshoe crabs. Even saw occasional sand sharks the length of our forearms. Before puberty, I don't remember being afraid of the ocean, or anything really—besides disappointing my parents. At some point though, Chris and I developed a palpable fear of bodies of water. Oceans purportedly full of stingrays and hammerheads just waiting to slice or dismember us. Riptides beyond our power and control. Rivers and lakes teeming with snakes and eels. Decades later, I'm still a complete chicken about swimming in anything other than a chlorinated swimming pool in which I can see the bottom. Why did growing up stoke our fears instead of assuage them?

The tides coursing through Rome's granite and marble prodded me to notice the ubiquity of water in the city and consider its nobler purpose—not to destroy but to replenish. Cleanse. Empower. A hydrocurrent surging through ancient aqueducts underground, below my feet, capable of recharging instead of drowning me. A power source with no off-button. I'd only been in Rome a couple of hours, yet everything about the city screamed energy, movement, anticipation, electricity, grit, edge, a stirring. *Want to stagnate? Go somewhere else.*

Mia kicked off her espadrilles and climbed *into* a fountain, sundress hiked to her thighs.

"Can you snap a picture of me?" she asked, arms forming *V* for victory, index and middle fingers flashing peace signs.

Quizzical tourists stared, shaking their heads. *Crazy Americans.*

We abandoned the Villa Borghese, zigzagging our way through *viali* (avenues), *vie* (streets), and *vicoli* (alleys) toward Campo de' Fiori. The piazza—whose name translates to *field of flowers*—bustled with vendor stalls selling fresh-cut tulips, fruit juices, olive oils, spices, and naturally, more penis-shaped pasta. I tried translating handwritten tags advertising salamis, sausages, and hams. A young butcher wearing a paper chef's hat grinned as I deciphered *palle del nonno*. Balls of grandfather. Grandfather's balls. The knobby salami resembled a lumpy pine cone.

Restaurants flank the four sides of Campo, each identified by placards decorated with laminated photos of greasy pizza and pasta dishes, or carts showcasing plastic reproductions of meatballs, artichokes, and mozzarella orbs. Men with slicked-back hair wearing shiny black pants and white shirts with sleeves rolled to their elbows stand at the entrance of each trattoria, beckoning passersby with, "Ciao, ragazzi! Ciao, bella! Vieni qui a mangiare!" One gently touched my wrist, pulling me with a flirty wink toward his establishment, gesturing at an empty table.

"You break-ah my heart if you don't dine-ah here, bellissima principessa," he murmured.

Despite the hard sell (which I hate), I smiled when he called me "beautiful princess" (which I didn't hate, though he obviously said that to everyone).

"No, grazie." I wanted authenticity for my first Roman meal.

Hunger rumbling, Mia and I aimed toward the hotel to check in, shower, and change into dinner clothes. Passing through Piazza Navona, we paused for a full minute at the Fountain of the Four Rivers—*Fontana dei Quattro Fiumi*, another Bernini sculpture—constructed in 1651. Water gods depicting the Nile (representing Africa), the Ganges (Asia), the Danube (Europe), and the Rio de la Plata (America), dominate the fountain's four corners. Ganges's foot outsized my head.

A few more twists and turns funneled us to the doorstep of the Pantheon, an imposing cylindrical structure with a domed roof. Twenty columns of varied colors and textures support an entryway portico. The architecture elicited a vivid memory of a prominent icon from my past.

I spent four years of college and three years of law school at the University of Virginia. On school grounds, a rotunda sits at one end of a green meadow known as the Lawn, the nucleus of UVA's "academical village." UVA's Rotunda—designed by Thomas Jefferson—witnessed my transition from seventeen-year-old teenager to adult. The dome watched over me as I studied languages and foreign affairs, met and fell in love with Trey, had sex for the first time, rejoiced over good grades, moped over less-good ones, forged female friendships, flirted then tangoed with alcohol, eventually walked down the Lawn in cap and gown, and graduated. Twice. Once from college, with high distinction. A second time from law school, with zero distinction.

Until I stood in Rome's Piazza della Rotonda, I never fully appreciated the Roman roots of my university's most famous symbol. UVA's Rotunda was completed in 1826; the Pantheon was over 1880 years old. Latin letters etched across the pediment of the Pantheon's portico read *M· AGRIPPA· L· F · COS · TER-TIUM · FECIT*, meaning *Marcus Agrippa, son of Lucius, built this structure when he was consul (a chief diplomat) to Rome for the third time*. I remembered from HBO's series, *Rome*, that Agrippa was a boyhood friend of Octavian, great-nephew of Julius Caesar. Octavian eventually became Caesar Augustus. Agrippa, a fierce military leader, served as his lieutenant.

In contrast to the flash white of the thick calf muscles of the Ganges god in the Fountain of the Four Rivers, and the ice-white flowy beard of Oceanus in the Trevi Fountain, the Pantheon's ashy palette—pewter-gray concrete slabs against a backdrop of layered rusty peach—gave off a more ominous air. One of gravity. Urgency. Mandates. Quests. Again, like at Trevi, I felt an electric surge. As if Agrippa were gripping me by both shoulders, murmuring, "I see you. You're meant to be here. Let Rome help you find your way."

Craving a shower, a meal, and our first glass of wine, Mia and I sped back to the hotel. We dragged luggage wheels through hallway carpet pile and found our rooms.

When I'd first started planning the trip, I'd researched a few boutique hotels that looked artsy and interesting. Modern, bohemian, quirky, cheerful places with groovy light fixtures and plush bedding. Hotels with literary themes, ironic typewriters, intentional graffiti on indoor walls. But Mia knew the Hotel Bernini. She'd stayed there before. Walking through the humdrum halls of our home for the next few nights, I thought about how, for forty-three years, I'd deferred to the preferences of more assertive voices—parents, boyfriends, husband, friends. *It's time to stop defaulting to that.* For extroverted, energetic travelers like Mia, hotels perhaps merely serve as convenient places to time out at night. For me though, the four walls surrounding me when I sleep, wake up, sip coffee, write in my journal, ease into the day, elevate the romanticism of the adventure. Entering my room—unremarkable, bland yet functional—I made a decision: *From now on, I'll prioritize accommodations-ambiance.*

I tugged a tapestry curtain aside to survey the view. My window framed Via del Tritone, a wide boulevard fringed with flower stands and *tabaccherie*—tobacco shops selling bus, tram, and lottery tickets; postage stamps (called *francobolli* in Italian); and international SIM cards. The wail of sirens—different from American fire trucks and police cars—sounded like the backdrop of an international spy movie.

I hung clothes in an armoire. I stashed my computer and passport in the hotel safe, pressing the numerals of Trey's birthday into the keypad as my passcode . . . reflex habit, though I hadn't seen him in twelve years and had invested eight years with Forrest in the interim. I plugged my phone into a European converter to charge. Texted my parents so they wouldn't catastrophize and call Interpol: LANDED IN ROMA. ALL GOOD HERE.

I warred with the shower nozzle to switch the water flow from handheld spigot to overhead rainfall, reminding myself that *C* meant *caldo*—hot—not cold. The bar of soap approximated the size of a lozenge, but it lathered. I slid into a sheath dress and strappy sandals with chunky rubber heels and attempted to dry my hair with a beige tube attached to the bathroom wall. The contraption emitted a faint whisper of air. Dab of eye makeup. Tousle of still-damp hair. Ready for Roman nightlife.

Mia waited in the lobby, again looking like she'd just stepped off a yacht. Sleek hair. Another tight wrap dress. Gold gladiator sandals laced around tan calves.

We zigzagged through side streets until we found Bottega Maccheroni, a trattoria in Piazza delle Coppelle (*coppelle* are cupels, or shallow, porous containers used for refining gold or silver) topping Mia's list of restaurants specializing in her favorite pasta dish: *cacio e pepe*, spaghetti tossed into a scooped-out wheel of pecorino cheese (*pecora*: sheep), stirred to let melted cheese attach to the noodles, then plated and sprinkled with fresh-ground black pepper.

Maccheroni's bistro tables already overflowed with gorgeous Romans, guys fingering tresses of hair and napes of necks of girlfriends, ladies pressing cigarettes between red lips, children posing questions in singsong Italian, their parents responding with "Sì, amore" and a reassuring caress. I try but can't remember being touched like that as a kid.

I approached the maître d' stand and requested—in Italian—a table for two. The host responded in English, "In one hour, you can sit outside."

He gestured toward an *enoteca* next door and suggested we have an *aperitivo*, a predinner drink, while waiting.

We parked ourselves on barstools circling wine barrels near a row of Vespa scooters in shades of sherbet: lime, raspberry, lemon, blueberry. The enoteca proprietor placed a handwritten wine menu on our barrel and offered us a drink.

"Buonasera, signorine. Sono Giovanni. Qualcosa da bere?"

I liked that he used the honorific *signorina* (miss) instead of *signora* (ma'am).

I recited my wine preference line. "Buonasera, Giovanni. Mi piacciono i vini rossi con il gusto di pepe e la terra." *Good*

*evening, Giovanni. I like red wines with the taste of pepper and
earth.*

He laughed. "Ma, certo. Di dove siete? Svezia?"

"Siamo americane." *We're not Swedish; we're Americans.*

I rambled in bumpy Italian about how we'd just flown all
night from New York and were excited to be in Rome. Giovanni
disappeared and returned with four wine glasses—tastings of
Nero d'Avola and Sangiovese—and two plates of aperitivo snacks.
Crunchy bread with pâté, burrata (mozzarella filled with cream),
ripe tomatoes. I opted for the Sangiovese.

Sipping wine, as Mia and I mapped out a plan for the next
two days, I watched couples finish meals and climb onto Vespas,
ladies clutching elegant handbags and their lovers' waists.

When Maccheroni's host waved us back, Giovanni hugged
us, kissed us on both cheeks, and implored us to return to the
enoteca another night.

Ushering us to an outdoor table, a waiter delivered wine
glasses etched with a reveling Bacchus—the god of grape har-
vests, winemaking, wine, ritual madness, and fertility.

I love Bacchus's first four claims to fame. Hard pass on
Number Five.

🏛 🏛 🏛

I've never felt an overwhelming urge to have kids. Dating Trey
throughout my last two years of college and all three years of
law school, marrying him two weeks after my twenty-fourth
birthday, we'd agreed to wait another five years to even think
about procreating so I could establish myself on the law firm
partnership track. Like clockwork, around my twenty-ninth
birthday, Trey was ready for a mini-Trey. I wasn't. But I stopped
taking birth control pills. I painted our guest room yellow. I read
What to Expect When You're Expecting because, if I was going to
do this, I was determined to be awesome at it. We picked out
cool names. On a business trip to Los Angeles, feeling woozy,
I trotted to the Pink Dot convenience store on Hollywood's

Sunset Boulevard and bought a pregnancy test. Hours later, at a work-related happy hour, I stealthily dumped apple martinis into planters at the Mondrian Hotel. I flew home, retrieved my car from airport parking, drove to the closest mall, bought a pair of blue baby booties, tucked them into a gift bag, and that evening announced to Trey he was going to be a daddy.

A couple months later, at an OBGYN appointment, a technician pushed a sonogram wand inside my body like a novice race car driver clumsily operating a Porsche's stick shift. It hurt. They couldn't find a heartbeat. The ferocity of my own pulse threatened to rupture my eardrums. A distant voice scheduled a D&C surgery—to "remove the tissue." (I still hate the words those initials represent: dilation, curettage.) Trey's bewildered brown eyes stared at me from the edge of the examination table.

They botched the procedure. I bled for a week. Needed steroids to expel the *rest*. Despite doctor's orders to refrain from intercourse until my body (and heart) healed, Trey needed sex with me *ten days* after my surgery. I let him.

My miscarriage, though emotionally wrenching and physically wrecking, had been a poorly packaged gift. A sulfuric whisper of smoke from a match that lit a spark of a flame that grew into an untamable conflagration that destroyed my marriage. And set me on a quest to understand why I've long ceded access to and esteem about my body to others.

While I still have trauma flashbacks to the miscarriage—mostly during certain invasive medical procedures—I have never wished for a different outcome. And I've never wanted children since.

🏛 🏛 🏛

A sip of Chianti wrapped a shroud over that memory, tucking it away again.

Mia sampled Maccheroni's *cacio e pepe*. I ordered linguini with sautéed mushrooms, which arrived blanketed with parsley, not my favorite. Other than my red onion aversion, I'm really not a picky eater. But parsley tastes and feels like a mouthful of grass clippings.

Jet lag kicking in, wine blurring our banter, we paid our bill, downed a complimentary *limoncello*—lemon liqueur—and headed home.

As we retraced our steps through the Piazza della Rotonda, moonlight bounced off the Pantheon. A street musician began singing "One" by U2. Reportedly, Bono wrote the song about fractured relationships while the bandmates struggled to record their album *Achtung Baby* in Berlin in 1990, nearly breaking up over creative differences after fourteen years together—since they'd formed the group as mere teenagers. I'd once painted the song's lyrics into a collage of papier-mâchéd ticket stubs, photographs, and matchbook covers—an art project a therapist suggested might soften some of the sharp edges of anxiety while I tried to figure out how to finally leave Forrest. I didn't know how to admit to the world—my parents, my friends—that I'd failed again. A second long-term relationship, tanked. This one eight years instead of the twelve I'd clocked with Trey.

In the beginning, I thought Forrest and I had hit the compatibility jackpot. Intellectually harmonious, we read books on our couch in our Manhattan apartment every weekend, our adopted dog Rowan asleep at our feet, an inseparable unit, us against the world. Forrest included me in every outing with his pals and public relations clients. Wanted me as his social wingman. Prioritized me over his family. Texted me ten times a day. Called me *honey-bunny* in his gritty British accent. Slept with his arms around me every night. Then we moved to California and everything changed. Cocaine touched his nose; he stopped touching me. I hauled myself to aerobics classes, honed my thirty-six-year-old body into shape, bought ridiculous lingerie, toys, body paint, contorted myself into a caricature of what he seemed to want me to be: sexier, edgier, wilder, cooler, more adventurous. *Please touch me. I'm dying.*

It confused me. Trey had wanted sex all the time. Zero to sixty in five seconds. Few words of affirmation. No foreplay. Just climbing on my sexually naive body whenever he was stirred. I guess I . . . we . . . thought that's what he—my husband—was supposed to or entitled to do. It hurt.

All of it hurt.

It took me a long while to realize that what happened in both scenarios dented and destabilized my psyche. Trey watered seeds of self-consciousness about my body—originally planted by my mom—but quenched his corporeal needs with it anyway. Forrest withheld touch and let me believe it was my fault. When my relationship with Forrest began to falter, I thought maybe I deserved it—a sex-starved relationship as punishment, karma, for quitting my marriage, abandoning Trey, embarrassing him, running away to New York, detonating my life, my career, my reputation in the messiest way possible just to get some time to myself; to let my body heal from the miscarriage, from the surgery aftermath; to learn how to amplify my voice instead of trying to communicate through telepathy; to stop feeling ugly, fat, broken, hungover, too emotional, too needy, too insecure, too much, too little. Unlovable.

The accent of the musician singing in front of the Pantheon— something other than Italian, maybe Spanish or Portuguese— added sultriness, seduction, to the words I'd listened to Bono sing over and over. Agrippa's phantom hands slipped onto my shoulders again. *I see you. A fighter, like me.*

A pizza box snapped open and closed in my face. Two Roman *ventenni* (twenty-year-olds) flapped a cardboard carton, strings of melted mozzarella stuck to its lid, offering Mia and me a slice.

Mia laughed and blurted, "Hey, where can we find the best gelato?"

The boys wore Roma soccer jerseys, skinny jeans, and Adidas sneakers, their hair styled in wavy faux mohawks. They cautioned us to never buy gelato from a shop displaying puffy pastel pillows of frozen dessert piled high in overflowing tubs. The best gelato—real artisanal gelato, they advised—is kept in small metal canisters with lids. They told us to hunt for a gelateria with no confection visible through the store window.

"Ciao, ciao, ciao, ciao, ciao!" They ran off with their pizza box.

On the way home, we found a gelateria that met the boys' criterion. Ambling toward the Bernini Bristol, I spooned dollops of green *pistacchio* and beige *nocciola* (hazelnut) from a small cup, *una coppetta piccola*. Mia licked a waffle cone of *melone*. We said good night at the hotel elevator and agreed to meet in the lobby at 8 a.m.

I pulled my dress—damp from humidity and sweat—over my head and plunked it in a pile of dirty airplane clothes, beginning to doubt whether I'd brought enough outfits to sustain a full week in Rome and another in Puglia without a laundry machine. Slipping into a cotton T-shirt and pink-striped boxers, I washed my face and slid between cool sheets. Turning out the light, I heard a *scratch, scratch, scratch* in the wall. Exhaustion trumping curiosity about its source, I lost consciousness and dreamed of making out with Agrippa.

Hours later, the *scratch, scratch, scratch* woke me up.

When I was twelve years old, a boys' boarding school hired my father as its chaplain. My parents, my brother, and I moved into faculty housing—a three-bedroom stucco cottage squeezed between the school library and the dining hall where we ate breakfast every morning and dinner each evening. For five years, my family basically lived in a fishbowl. I plodded through my teens—and hit puberty—surrounded by three hundred cute prep school boys who were reluctant or afraid to talk to me because of my dad's role at their institution, or maybe they just thought I was a nerd. An early introduction to avoidance and rejection by adolescent crushes that rotated on a weekly basis.

One year, maintenance guys chopped down a rotting tree in our yard. Unbeknownst to us, a displaced family of opossums infiltrated our home through a hole in our basement wall. One evening, my brother and I were fully immersed in an episode of the late 1980s TV show *Magnum, P.I.* when a chunky marsupial with a long pink tail jumped onto the couch, the corner of a Snickers wrapper in its mouth. Leftover Halloween candy. We screamed. My parents came running. Our shrieks must have summoned the brood. Another opossum poked its head around a radiator. Another bounded down a staircase. Wielding a broom, my dad opened our back door. My mother, brother, and I raced outside. Dozens of boarding school boys had just been released from evening study hall. They hooted in laughter as my family wriggled and writhed, freaked out over our close encounter with wildlife inside our home. Not our most poised moment. We were the butt of teenage jokes for weeks.

Since then, I've never been a fan of mice, rats, or rodent-like species. I broke a two-year lease on my second New York apartment, a third-floor walk-up in Chelsea where I recovered from my divorce from Trey, because baby mice had invaded a bag of dog food beneath my kitchen sink. I can spot a rat on a New York subway platform from twenty yards.

Scratch, scratch, scratch.

Is the sound coming from an animal stuck inside the wall? I peered beneath the hotel bed. I stood up and swept the tapestry curtains aside. Finding no interlopers *in* the hotel room, I decided to pretend I'd heard nothing. I showered and headed downstairs.

Mia had researched a bicycle rental shop. We planned to bike the Appia Antica—an ancient Roman road engineered in 4 or 5 BCE that once extended 330–400 miles from Rome to the port of Brindisi, in Puglia. A stretch of the original route weaves through an urban park in Rome, closed to vehicle traffic on Sundays. Tourists and residents bike or walk the path, stopping at ruins, museums, catacombs, and trattorias.

I sipped a lukewarm cappuccino in the hotel lobby while Mia borrowed a highlighter from the front desk clerk and marked a short walking route to the bike rental shop on a paper map.

We found the shop easily, spotting its signature red bicycle welded vertically to a metal stand on the storefront sidewalk, rear wheel jutting high in the air. The shopkeeper entrusted two rugged mountain bikes into our care. We promised to return the bikes by 4 p.m. or forfeit our deposit.

As I began situating my phone, wallet, and lip balm in a fanny pack attached to my bike's handlebars, Mia took off, rocketing down a steep hill. I murmured *grazie* to the shopkeeper and pedaled after Mia.

She swung a right turn onto a main avenue, curled around the Colosseum, and veered onto another busy roadway leading toward the Appia Antica. The New York City spinning classes I'd attended religiously twice a week for two years—reserving Bike #26, a stationary bike bolted to a cement floor, traveling nowhere—had done nothing to prepare me for this madness. I quickly learned to squeeze the Roman all-terrain bike's handlebar brakes with enough force to avoid slamming into Fiats, then just as resolutely pump the pedals—quadriceps burning—to keep up with Mia's white Capri shorts as she wove around three-wheeled trucks toting flatbeds of flowers. I crossed my fingers and hoped I wouldn't sustain a brain injury from succumbing to peer pressure to forgo safety helmets.

Mia whizzed around turns, crossed multiple lanes of traffic, and barreled toward the Appia Antica's entryway. I swallowed a flicker of annoyance—a familiar sensation of abandonment—and tried to keep up.

When I was eighteen and a half, Trey drove me home from college for winter break to meet his parents. His mom, who cooked

my first tastes of gourmet food—*penne alla vodka,* steaks in bour-
bon glaze, Spanish paella—teased that I'd likely end up a "sports
widow" given her son's obsession with any activity involving a
ball. Tennis, baseball, golf, basketball. For the next five years, I
showed up to all Trey's flag football games and softball matches—
fast-pitch and slow-pitch— strutting to the stands in cutoff jean
shorts and tight tank tops, begging for attention, approval. *Look
at me. I'm Trey's girlfriend! I'm cute enough for the team's star athlete, right?* When I graduated from law school a month after we
married—my father had walked me down the aisle, then turned
around to perform our marital rites—I sat on bleachers and
studied for the bar exam, memorizing legal rules from flash cards,
cheering for my athletic husband as he threw touchdowns and
smacked home runs with the aluminum bat I'd bought him for
his birthday.

The first few months of our marriage, thinking he'd be proud
of me for pinching pennies before I obtained my bar license and
my first-year law firm associate salary kicked in, I ate nothing but
homemade bread every day for lunch. I baked it in an electric
bread maker we received as a wedding gift. I sat on a barstool at
our kitchen counter, practicing bar exam multiple choice questions, dipping hunks of toasted sourdough into pools of olive
oil and balsamic vinegar. The carbs stretched my waistline. At
night, in bed, Trey poked my belly and joked, "What's this?" He
told me he thought he'd married a woman who "would never let
herself go."

I stowed the bread machine in a linen closet and joined a
gym.

I tried taking up golf and tennis, sports presumably Trey
and I could do together for decades. He attempted to teach me
how to properly swing a golf club, a tennis racket. Got impatient
with my awkwardness.

I started running instead. Alone. Slow and steady. I didn't
hate running.

On one occasion, Trey decided to go jogging with me in the hills around our house. After a few minutes, he told me I was too slow. He ran ahead.

I *hate* being abandoned.

Mia hooked a hard right turn into the entryway of a park and shot down an incline covered in bark and leaves. I edged down the slippery embankment, clenching the brakes, squeaking to a stop near a sign labeled *Appia Antica.*

The Appian Way consists of large boulders placed in soil by Roman slaves 2300 years ago. Tall pointy cypress trees shaped like popsicles provide a modicum of shade. Strata of stone, brick, and mortar—each layer symbolizing a generation or two of humans who've lived and died—border a single lane, weeds poking from seams. Headless and armless statues sculpted millennia ago cling to crumbling pedestals.

Away from vehicle traffic, my bike tires bumping along boulders, I slowed, relaxed, and inhaled fresh air. I tried decoding Latin inscriptions on arches and pavilions without crashing.

Mia shot ahead again. When her bike hit a jagged rock and jackknifed, sunglasses flew from their perch on her hat. She kept going. A few jounces later, her hat fell to the ground.

I collected her jettisons, but I decided to stop trying to keep up. *This is your adventure too. Go at your own pace.*

I decelerated. Snapped a photo of a triptych frieze of ancient Romans draped in robes. Paused to pet a fluffy white dog sniffing lavender whose one blue eye and one brown eye reminded me of my dog Rowan—a mutt mix of Australian shepherd and Alaskan malamute I'd adopted with Forrest.

Eventually, I caught up with Mia.

We walked our bikes down a dusty side road, hunting for a restroom, and discovered an osteria. *Osteria* derives from the Latin word *hospes,* meaning *guest, visitor, host, stranger, foreigner.*

In Italy, osterias (historically, wine bars that have evolved in modern times to serving simple seasonal menus) are less formal than trattorias (a term derived from *trattare* or *trarre* in Italian, meaning *to treat*), which offer authentic regional or local dishes, which in turn are less fancy than *ristorantes.*

Leaning the bikes against an orange tree, we sat at a wrought iron table. Rosemary shrubs in terra-cotta pots held floral table-cloths in place. A curvy waitress with bountiful bosoms greeted us with two cold Peroni beers and a carafe of *acqua naturale*, cold tap water. She returned with *panino* (sandwich) triangles: thinly sliced eggplant, shockingly red tomato slices, and caramelized onions pressed between crispy slices of toast. A third offering: cold risotto tossed with chunks of ham, crunchy celery, and egg.

Retrieving the bikes, we pressed onward, following signs toward *le catacombe*—mass burial sites of early Christians extinguished by polytheistic Romans. I noticed a placard with the words *luogo sacro*, meaning holy place, accompanied by an image of what looked like two people wearing pink and blue lederhosen—shorts and tank tops—with a line crossing through the outfits. I glanced at my skorts, uncertain about the dress code.

The ticket line for catacomb tours extended thirty people deep. We stationed the bikes against a brick flower box.

Apparently, like many rules in Italy, the no-shorts-or-tank-top edict was subject to interpretation, a suggestion more than a prohibition. Tourists in cutoffs, Bermudas, and culottes emerged from underground, resurfacing through a stone archway. Mia headed toward the exit hole in the earth.

"C'mon. If they ask us for tickets, we'll just play dumb."

I have a strong aversion to playing the "clueless American" card. I like adventure, but intentional scofflaw stuff bugs me. I resolved to work out competing inner desires—loosen up my rote rule compliance *and* resist deference to stronger personalities—later. I followed Mia, pressing *down* the stairway against a tide of people ascending to open air. Tourists barked at us in multiple languages, gesturing toward the daylight behind us. We descended merely ten stairs before an Italian docent pointed at the exit and admonished, "Girate e lasciate." *Turn and leave.* I pivoted and ran up the steps.

Skipping the catacombs, we resumed cruising the rustic Appian promenade.

"How long do you think it will take us to get back to town?" I asked Mia, starting to fret about returning the bikes to the rental shop on time.

"Dunno. Let's go a little further."

I decided to temper my habit of overthinking everything. *Relax and enjoy the ride. It doesn't really matter in the grand scheme of things if the bikes are late. If the bicycle shop is closed, the hotel must have storage. Just ride. You're in Rome. On the Appia Antica. A public works project launched by Roman censor, Appius Claudius Caecus. The artery which some historians say, at least in part, inspired the expression, "All roads lead to Rome." The trail on which Caesar's military troops marched.*

After twenty minutes, Mia turned around. We backtracked, exited the park, crossed multiple highway lanes, circled the Colosseum, pedaled up a final hill, and returned the bikes minutes before the shop closed.

We retreated to our hotel rooms for power naps before dinner. I nestled my head into my pillow and closed my eyes. *Scratch, scratch, scratch* within the walls.

🏛 🏛 🏛

A lone palm tree swayed over the Spanish Steps, a 135-stage staircase connecting twin bell towers of the Trinità dei Monti church with the Piazza di Spagna below. Tourists and Romans congregated on landings—smoking, kissing, laughing. At the bottom of the steps, Mia and I passed a fountain shaped like a sinking boat (Fontana della Barcaccia), then meandered Via Condotti (named after *dotti*, ducts or channels transporting water to the Baths of Agrippa—a public bathing house). Along the stylish street in Rome's high-end shopping district, storefronts showcased brands like Valentino, Prada, and Gucci. Windows displayed platform combat boots with steel grommets, metallic handbags, puffy neon vests.

We encountered another fountain, a carving of a muscular female wolf nursing two plump infants. The children: Romulus and Remus, twin sons of Mars, the god of war, who forced himself upon Rhea Silvia, a "Vestal Virgin"—a priestess of Vesta, the goddess of Rome's sacred hearth and flame—exempt from societal expectations to marry and produce heirs. The legend goes: One of Rhea's power-hungry and jealous male relatives imprisoned the priestess and condemned her twins (presumed competitors to his political trajectory) to death-by-drowning in the Tiber River. An empathetic servant placed the babies in a basket (like the story of Moses-and-the-Nile in the Bible) and set them afloat down the stream. A she-wolf, Lupa, rescued them. The boys grew into natural leaders. But they argued. Romulus wanted to establish the city of Rome on the Palatine Hill; Remus preferred the Aventine Hill. (Rome boasts seven hills: Palatine, Aventine, Capitoline, Quirinal, Viminal, Esquiline, and Caelian.) Unable to work out their geography dispute, Romulus killed Remus and founded Rome.

Mia and I located Antica Enoteca, a rustic wine bar on Mia's *cacio e pepe* hit list, and opted for a table outside rather than sitting in its steamy interior. Mia ordered her usual. I chose *rigatoni amatriciana. Piccante.* "Spicy," the waiter promised with a smile, running a hand through tousled blond-brown hair. My dish introduced me to a new word and taste: *guanciale.* Pork jowls. The world's crispiest bacon. A mouth-watering addition to zesty red pepper and sweet tomato sauce.

Pleased that we'd consumed nearly every morsel on our plates, our waiter offered three choices of *digestivo*: limoncello (the lemony after-dinner drink we'd sipped at Maccheroni—sweet, citrusy, and summery), grappa (a brandy distilled from vine stems, seeds, and grapes that, depending on the quality, can taste either like smoky cognac or lighter fluid), or *amaro* (an herbal liqueur in flavors like pine, anise, mint, or wood). As we mulled our choices, two dark-blue BMW motorcycles with white reflective letters spelling *carabinieri* eased onto the street where we sat.

Italy has seven police forces—five national and two local. The carabinieri are Italy's badass military police force. Their name originates from a French word, *carabinier*, which means "soldier armed with a carbine."

The two motorbikes rolled in slow motion past our table, streetlight glinting off the riders' shiny boots and the word *carabinieri* draped across their shoulder blades. Red stripes ran the length of their blue-black jodhpur pant legs, matching the scarlet of their brake lights and a coat of arms emblazoned on the motorcycles' rear compartments. When the wheels reached a spot ten feet beyond our table, the driver on the left rotated his head toward us, the eye screen of his helmet raised. Both officers paused. In unison, they planted one boot on the ground, propping up the bikes. The driver on the left stared at me. Olive skin. Dark eyebrows. Intense eyes. No smile.

He and I blinked. Mia's blonde hair whipped across the table as she swiveled toward the carabinieri. The driver on the left broke his gaze. The officers' boots lifted from the ground, again in synchrony. The motorcycles shifted forward. Mia shot out of her seat, the white of her jeans a comet trail behind her. She began chasing the men. Noticing her, they pulled their motorcycles to the sidewalk.

I planted forehead to palm.

The carabinieri dismounted their bikes, balancing helmets on hips. Mia gesticulated back and forth between the motorcycles and me. The taller of the two men engaged with Mia, laughter animating his mustache. I wondered how they were communicating; Mia spoke barely any Italian. The other one— slim, six feet tall, shaved head—stared at me again, his face slightly obscured in shadow. His lips a straight line.

The carabinieri restraddled their motorcycles. Mia skipped back to our table, blue eyes wide as euro coins.

"Why didn't you come talk to them?" she ribbed me. "I was trying to get them to give us rides on their bikes!"

"Oh geez, seriously?" My face flushed. I unstuck hair from my sweaty neck.

"Did you see how gorgeous they were? They get off duty in a half hour and are going to meet us at the Pantheon for a drink."

I ran my finger around the rim of a mini-flute of amaro the waiter placed before me. *Why am I annoyed? Mia is just trying to have fun. I haven't met anyone the slightest bit intriguing in a long while. Why am I resisting this?*

I'd deleted every dating app from my phone. Most nights, cocooned in my downtown New York apartment, tired from a day of teaching, writing, and working out, I'd order Indian or Thai food and burrow into my couch to watch crime shows or read travel memoirs. My last attempt at a romantic con-nection—initiated by a blind date arranged by a law professor girlfriend—sent me racing back into my introverted safe house, slamming and bolting the door for a while. The ink on the guy's divorce papers from a twenty-year marriage barely dry, he rel-ished in fighting about everything from the best bagel flavors to the proper amount of cracked pepper to sprinkle on steak. His assertiveness about restaurant choices and after-dinner night-cap locales had seemed vaguely chivalrous at first, but quickly turned into verbal tirades and bullying. I'd worked too hard to extricate myself from three consecutive toxic law firm bosses to tolerate yet another aggressive, demeaning jerk. I'd rather be alone. When I broke it off with a nice but firm "This just isn't a good match for me," he wrote in an email, "Your two exes must think you are the *biggest bitch* in the world." Reading those mean words, I vowed never to share my long-term relationship history with anyone that quickly again.

Mia finished a neon-yellow limoncello and ordered another one. "Come on. It'll be a blast!" she prodded.

I knew she was right. I needed to make more of an effort. *You're in romantic Rome with a vivacious friend who successfully facilitated a date for drinks with two hot carabinieri officers. Lighten up. Be fun. Be like Mia.*

We counted euros for the check and placed intricate paper bills into a jeweled cigar box. Mia readjusted her black tube top and led the charge to the Pantheon.

Moonlight ricocheted off the monument's dome.

"Ha, I think that's them!" She waved at the tall mustached one. He recognized us and grinned. Shaved Head scanned the crowd—like a periscope. The guys had changed out of their uniforms into dark jeans and pullover shirts bearing European brand icons I didn't recognize. We converged at a corner of the piazza's fountain, an obelisk rising from its center point, gargoyles spitting water from mouths below dead eyes.

We exchanged awkward double kisses, chins and bodies colliding. I never know whether to start left cheek or right cheek and inevitably smash the wrong body part.

"Io sono Roberto," the mustached one said, pointing to his chest.

"Luca," said the other, touching my shoulder as he said his name. "How long are you here in Roma?" he asked—his *r*s lingering longer than the rest of his consonants.

Still unsmiling, he surveilled the piazza.

Mia and Roberto communicated in English and mime, which made them both laugh. She indicated she would be in Rome for one more night.

Luca looked at me. "E tu?"

"Sono qui a Roma fino a Mercoledì." *I am in Rome until Wednesday.*

They asked if we were up for a nightcap or would rather meet the next day. Mia looked at me.

"Domani mattina presto, facciamo un giro del Colosseo." *Tomorrow morning early, we are doing a tour of the Colosseum,* I explained.

Luca stepped in. "Is late now. Tomorrow evening, we meet you both for dinner in Trastevere?" Trastevere is one of Rome's twenty-two *rioni* (administrative divisions).

Thankfully, Mia acknowledged that drinking more at that moment was a bad idea given our early wake-up call. We agreed to link up with the guys on the Trastevere side of the Ponte Sisto, a bridge crossing the Tiber River, at 8 p.m. the next evening.

More cheek kisses. "Ciao! Ciao!"

As Mia and I strolled back to the hotel, she exclaimed, "Double date with studly carabinieri officers!" She laughed and high-fived me.

I finally smiled and laughed too. I've always been intrigued by guys with risky jobs: firefighters, pilots, soldiers, boxers.

I fell asleep, tuning out the *scratch, scratch, scratch* in the walls.

🏛 🏛 🏛

I met Mia in the hotel lobby. We hailed a taxi to a tour office near the Roman Forum. Mia stared out the window on the ride over, her usually glowing complexion a tad greenish.

Ah, limoncello hangover.

Two Brits, an extroverted American couple, and a solo Australian lady composed our tour group. Our guide, a peppy Dutch woman named Dani with short pigtails poking from a straw hat advised we refill our water bottles at every fountain we passed. "Today's gonna be a scorcher."

Mia winced.

Dani herded us across a wide avenue past burly men dressed in gladiator gear and spray-paint artists setting up their wares.

"Don't snap photos of the gladiators," Dani cautioned. "They'll badger you for money."

We stepped around a woman prostrate in prayer on the hot sidewalk, head and shoulders covered by a wool scarf, wrinkled hands holding a broken Styrofoam cup containing a few euro coins. She murmured Bible verses in Italian.

Flashing laminated credentials and handing a ticket collector a stack of passes, Dani led us past a long line of sunburned tourists through a VIP gate into the Roman Forum.

The Forum is the size of approximately five football fields. Paved pathways channel tourists around walls, beams, and foundations of long-crumbled yet formerly majestic structures, many bearing Latin inscriptions and carvings. Lone columns and trios of pillars jut into the sky. Remnants of ancient statues and toppled arches lie in grassy patches. Dani gave us a few seconds to absorb both the grandiosity and humility of our surroundings—the contrast of the Roman Empire's former dominance with its subsequent demise, the inevitability of wear and tear as time passes, the unavoidability of change. I imagined toga- and tunic-clad Romans walking in leather sandals along the same cobblestones where my feet stood.

Dani led us to a structure called the Temple of Vesta and further explained the trade-off granted to the priestesses of Vesta, goddess of the hearth: In exchange for stoking a sacred fire, vestal virgins earned a special dispensation to reject the traditional assumed life path of marriage and motherhood. Laughing, I snapped a photo to text to two college girlfriends with the caption FOUND OUR NEW HOME. Standing at the temple's circular base, I felt a twitch of electrical current again. Of the female kind.

After a tour of the ruins of the House of the Vestal Virgins—ancient Rome's version of a sorority house—Dani urged, "Drink some water, take twenty minutes to wander, then we'll reconvene here."

Eager to distance myself from English speakers for a bit, I separated from the pack, searching for ancient graffiti. Dani had suggested we look for unsophisticated Latin and Greek carvings in stone—markings by civilians, prisoners, and plebes rather than commissioned architects and artists.

I found the Temple of Antoninus and Faustina, the most romantic rubble in the Forum. Emperor Antoninus Pius built it to honor his late wife, Faustina. Reportedly, Antoninus was a good emperor. Among other accolades, he supported the arts and sciences, including financially rewarding teachers of rhetoric. Like me.

Dani corralled our group and ushered us out of the Forum toward the Colosseum, into the fast-track line, past a logjam of tourists dabbing perspiration with handkerchiefs and bandannas. We entered the amphitheater conceptualized in 72 CE by Emperor Vespasian and dedicated in 80 CE by Emperor Titus. For context, Dani explained that a sequence of seventy emperors had governed Rome, beginning with the first one, Caesar Augustus—Agrippa's buddy, Octavian. Through a lengthy and strategic seventeen-year process after his great-uncle Julius Caesar was assassinated on March 15 (the Ides of March) in 44 BCE, Octavian eventually assumed leadership of Rome's republic and gradually transitioned it into an empire. The Roman Senate bestowed the title *Augustus* upon him (meaning *venerable* or *revered*, coming from the Latin *augere—to increase* or *to exalt*), but Octavian called himself "Princeps Civitatis," or "First Citizen" to perpetuate the facade of the republic. The reign of emperors spanned until Romulus Augustus was deposed in 476 CE; Rome fell to Germanic barbarians, launching the medieval era and tolling the end of the Western Roman Empire.

Inside the Colosseum, I ran my fingers along letters etched into columns fashioned two millennia ago. We passed glass cases housing skulls and bones of bears, boars, and wolves slaughtered by *bestiarii*, specially trained warriors. Dani pointed out trapdoors where rabble-rousing entertainment directors released animals into the arena to maul, maim, and kill criminals and slaves—or vice versa—before a bloodthirsty Roman audience. The interior architecture reminded me of a sooty honeycomb, tourists scurrying like bees in and out of nooks and alcoves.

The tour complete, Mia and I thanked Dani, left the Arch of Constantine (dedicated to the first of Rome's polytheistic emperors to convert to Christianity) behind us, and headed toward the Tiber River. Modern graffiti—some romantic ("Ti amo"—*I love you*), some rebellious ("Non ascoltare l'autorità"—*Don't listen to authority*)—tagged walls along the riverbank. The Tiber's greenish-brownish water—the color of a kale smoothie—flowed beneath stone bridges. We followed the river's curves, then cut inland toward the hotel to rest before meeting the carabinieri on the pedestrian bridge, the Ponte Sisto, at 8 p.m.

Grateful for a couple hours alone at the hotel to rejuvenate, I read and wrote in my journal, then showered and dug through my suitcase for a black silk-polyester halter top with a plunging cowl neck my mom bought at a secondhand store and gave me for Christmas. I held the wall-mounted blow dryer within inches of my skull and waited until my hair finally dried enough to run a curling iron through it.

My girlfriends who'd learned the art of dating in their twenties—rather than stepping into the scene in their forties like me—seemed to enjoy the dance of first dates: choosing a rendezvous spot, curating the perfect outfit, deciding whether to show up slightly early or slightly late, the will-we-or-won't-we seesaw over whether to kiss (or more), who follows up with a next-day text . . .

First dates fluster me. The anticipation of that initial glance of recognition, the awkward ordering of drinks, the decision whether to eat, who pays, how much information to disclose about past relationships. I blush, red splotches exploding like land mines along my cheeks and neck. Lots of guys have pointed out my blush. When they do, my face flushes an even deeper red. Like a third-degree burn. I wish someone had sat me down in my teens and twenties and explained, "Dating isn't a test to see whether *you're* worthy of *them*. It's about letting someone into your orbit, your airspace, for a duration of time to assess whether they're interesting enough for *you*."

I don't know how to go on dates with strangers and decide whether we're compatible enough for a second get-together. I know how to meet someone in the wild and fall in love in ten seconds. And then contort myself into their idea of perfection.

I'd met Trey when I was seventeen during my first year at the University of Virginia. He was the older fraternity brother of my first college boyfriend (a partner in a sweet studious relationship that never proceeded physically beyond third base). Trey and I started dating my second year of college, his last year at the university. At eighteen, I knew from the instant he pressed his lips to mine while we danced atop a radiator in his fraternity house to Modern English's "I Melt With You" that I would marry him. (My parents married within a month of college graduation; I'd always assumed that's what I was supposed to do.) Trey was my first major *everything*.

The first six months, we spent every hour together outside of class—meals in the university dining hall, football games, fraternity parties, wine tasting in the hills of Charlottesville, Virginia, riding around in his Ford Fairmont without seat belts, just my body fastened to his. He wrote me cards, gave me stuffed animals, and bought me adventure novels by authors like Clive Cussler he knew I loved. Then he graduated, secured a job, and moved to Northern Virginia two hours away. For the next five years—as I toiled through four more semesters of college and six of law school—we spent summers, weekends, and school holidays together. But every time I drove myself back to Charlottesville—in my beat-up 1983 Mazda RX-7 hatchback, my first car purchase, which Trey helped me negotiate—to dive into French, Italian, Russian, and foreign affairs classes, juggling my desire to land good grades and cultivate female friendships, I ached. I worried Trey's popularity at work, his coed softball teams, his golf tournaments, his close-knit family, would make him realize he didn't need me. That I was just a replaceable accessory.

Visiting me at school, he often teased me—casually—about my appearance. Joked that my teeth looked like yellow Chiclets.

My skin was so freckly, unlike his golden-olive complexion. My 34C boobs already saggy. My belly not flat. My breath not peppermint fresh enough. I believed him. I was accustomed to this. Throughout my adolescent and early adult years, my mom hadn't exactly instilled confidence in me regarding my looks. Before church on Sundays and breakfasts and dinners in the boarding school dining hall, while she radiated glamour in her stilettos, flawless makeup, and frosted blonde highlights, she'd urge, "Run a brush through that mop of hair. Put some blush on. Change into something colorful that flatters your figure."

I don't remember hearing, "You're beautiful."

I can't *unremember* the self-esteem paper cuts. They accumulated.

Even now, decades later, when I look in a mirror, I immediately see the wrinkle, the blemish, the extra curve. I have to force myself to look again.

Six years into our marriage, twenty-five days before my thirtieth birthday, I left him. I still can't believe I did that. Three months later, I left everything else—our two beagles, most of my worldly possessions, my law firm job where I probably would have made partner in another year or two, the acceptance and approval of my friends and family—and moved to New York with practically nothing. I cried every day. I wanted to die. Or take it all back and pretend I hadn't lost my mind over the miscarriage, over Trey wanting me to get pregnant again—on schedule, his schedule. Pretend I hadn't screwed up my life, my reputation, by drunkenly kissing a law firm client in a sketchy bar after a holiday party, simply because he told me I looked pretty—a colossal mistake that fast-tracked my unraveling.

For months after I ran away to New York, I continued paying my share of our Virginia house mortgage out of guilt, shame, Trey's artful rhetoric, and my lawyer's incompetence, yet simultaneously tried to finance a fledgling New York fresh start. Desperate for money, I landed a new job in a law firm on the thirty-ninth floor of Tower Two of the World Trade Center. I stared out my office's waffle windows at sailboats circling the Statue of Liberty, wishing I could escape on one of them. I flinched each time my new boss—the second in a series of three volatile personalities who dominated my professional life for two decades—screamed into his speakerphone in the office next to mine.

Five months after I separated from Trey, I stood in a purple bridesmaid's dress mentally gearing up to witness my brother marry his long-term girlfriend in the same church where Trey and I'd wed. I was barely holding it together. My mother gave me a once-over as we walked to the wedding chapel and blurted, "Suck in your stomach."

I sobbed the entire ceremony. Before I departed for New York, my mom—still oblivious to my visceral need for even an ounce of reassurance—threw one more jab: "Well, if you're so miserable, why don't you just beg Trey to take you back."

I didn't go back. New York kicked me around like a hacky sack for a bit, its version of tough love for many newcomers. Finally, after a full year, I stood up to my lawyer and Trey, stopped the financial hemorrhaging, and signed divorce papers, which landed in my mailbox on the Fourth of July, my independence day. I also stood up to my hot-tempered boss when he yelled at me for stapling a document the wrong way and told me I'd better get my act together and make my job my "number one priority."

"It's not my number one priority. *I am*." A blush erupted on my cheeks.

The shock of being contradicted (and my purple face) seemed to tap a hidden vein of empathy in him. He calmed down. Sat down. We had our first real conversation, commiserating about the brutality of divorce; he was on his third. He directed me to Human Resources who granted me a temporary leave of absence to catch my breath and figure out my life. In late August, I cashed in some frequent flier miles and flew to Greece to join a few new Manhattan friends on a girls' trip to Athens and Santorini. I sat on a balcony at an island hotel called Homeric Poems, wrapped in a blanket, staring at the dark Aegean Sea, wind battering my cheeks, finally feeling the anvil of anguish crushing my rib cage begin to lift. *You* are *going to be okay. It's all going to be okay.* My friends flew home a day earlier than I did. Still a bit naive about travel and forgetting to book a hotel for my last night, I slept on a bench in the Athens airport, flew to Frankfurt, Germany, and boarded a connecting flight to the United States. Midway across the Atlantic, the pilot diverted the plane to Gander, Newfoundland, in Canada.

9/11 happened during my flight. The Twin Towers, my office, gone.

Canadians fed, clothed, and took care of me (and six thousand other stranded passengers from thirty-nine redirected planes) for five days. Once I eventually got home to the rubble and burning metal smell of downtown New York, my city's grief smacked me out of my divorce depression. I no longer felt entitled to feel sorry for myself. *People get divorced. Yes, it hurts. It sucks. It feels like death. But I'm alive. I wasn't in the South Tower. And I was tremendously lucky to be on a different plane.*

🏛 🏛 🏛

I never returned to the law firm, which relocated to Midtown (and thankfully didn't lose anyone that tragic day). Instead, I grieved 9/11 staying up late watching Osama bin Laden documentaries on CNN, writing (journal entries, snippets of my first legal textbook, reflective essays about my marriage and my upbringing), and taking walks down the West Side Highway past dump trucks hauling twisted metal debris away from the World Trade Center disaster site.

A few months later, slowly, for the first time in my adult life, I went on a handful of dates with boys I met by going about my daily life as one of millions of New Yorkers trying to make sense of our post-9/11 existence. A cute South African painter who asked me to dance at a nightclub and invited me to picnic on the floor of his Tribeca art studio. An obnoxious lawyer who bought me a drink after a St. Patrick's Day parade and announced he'd only meet up on weekdays, reserving his weekends for doing ecstasy with his friends. A former NFL football player who followed me out of a corner grocery store, handed me a bouquet of tulips, and kept referring to himself in the third person. Each time, I blushed. They teased. I just wanted to kiss them or fool around so they wouldn't focus on my red face.

Ten months after 9/11, a male friend from back home in Virginia set me up on a blind date with his former college roommate, a charismatic Brit I'd heard stories about for a decade.

Forrest.

Three hours into our first meetup, clinking shots of tequila in the hazy depths of an underground speakeasy bar in Manhattan, Forrest stared at me with aquamarine eyes and said, "You're adorable, and I want to spend as much time with you as possible."

We spent the next eight years together.

Two modes of romantic operation feel normal to me: feeling like I've been hit by an eighteen-wheeler of love and I might die if I don't see the guy again; or curling up on my couch alone in sweatpants, glass of Spanish Rioja in hand, TV tuned to *Law & Order: SVU*.

I'm weird in the in-between.

Sweat coated the small of my back on the walk with Mia to the Ponte Sisto—a stone pedestrian bridge named after Pope Sixtus IV that connects Rome's city center to Trastevere, an artsy neighborhood of bistros, bookstores, and bodegas. At the midpoint of the bridge, street musicians strummed electric guitars connected to portable amps and sang American pop songs with European accents. Roberto and Luca awaited us, as promised, at the Trastevere end of the bridge. Kiss, kiss, *baci, baci*. Roberto wore a shirt with letters spelling *Cortina* across his chest, a ski town in Northern Italy, he explained. Tattoos covered his right forearm, mostly dates in Roman numerals, memorializing major events in his carabiniere career, we later learned. Luca's face and biceps glowed with a summer tan. A thin silver chain hung around his neck, tucked into his polo shirt. No smile yet.

Golden light flickered from lanterns along a waterfront quay—the Lungotevere—bordering the Trastevere side of the Tiber. We descended a staircase from Ponte Sisto leading to a bar at the river's edge. Luca gestured toward a low whitewashed wood table. He chose a chair across from me. Roberto sat across from Mia. A waiter delivered a bowl of unshelled peanuts and four orange Aperol spritzes. Roberto and Mia used crayons and a paper placemat to draw a map of the United States. Mia animatedly pointed to a blob on the map meant to identify New York City, scribbling an *X* to mark Lower Manhattan and give the guys a geographical sense of our home base.

I asked Luca, "Come stai stasera?" *How are you tonight?*

"But why do you speak Italian?" he asked, in English. He grabbed a peanut and pressed its shell into the textured grain of the table.

"I think Italian is the most beautiful language. Also, I don't want to seem like the kind of American who won't try to learn or speak anything but English. I studied French for a long time in school. But I really love Italian."

He stared at me and popped a shelled nut into his mouth. He scanned the bar like he'd surveilled the Pantheon's piazza. He seemed on constant alert.

"Siete carabinieri?" *You are carabinieri?* I asked.

Roberto, peppering English with words in Italian and spirited hand gestures, explained that Luca was his *comandante*, and today they'd arrested a band of drug dealers in a sting operation. Mia looked at me and mouthed, *Hot.*

The guys paid for the spritzes. We climbed the staircase to street level and walked deeper into Trastevere, stopping at a trattoria. A short older man in a green rugby shirt greeted us, slapping Roberto's and Luca's shoulders. The three men exchanged cheek kisses. Nothing sexier than grown men unabashedly displaying public affection. The man, another Giovanni, beckoned us toward an outdoor table. Luca grabbed the chair next to me.

Giovanni asked me, in Italian, what I liked to drink. I practiced my line about peppery, spicy, earthy wine. The guys and Mia ordered beers. I leaned back in my chair and felt Luca's hand graze my shoulder.

"Mi dispiace." *I'm sorry*, he said and pulled away.

I smiled at him. He *finally* smiled at me, one corner of his mouth lifting higher than the other. His arm trailed back onto my chair.

"What would you like to eat?" he asked.

"I want to try something authentic and Roman."

The boys ordered an enormous margarita pizza. Luca requested gnocchi in a red sauce for me. Mia continued her daily taste test of *cacio e pepe*.

Roberto and Mia played deejay on his phone, mixing Rush and Bruce Springsteen tunes. Periodically tending to his few other restaurant patrons, Giovanni mostly lingered at our table, smoking, cracking jokes with the guys. He poured a steady flow of Chianti into my glass. Luca relaxed into his chair, often quiet, content to let Roberto and Mia entertain us. As Giovanni closed his eyes and danced at the end of our table to a Bon Jovi song, Luca ran his fingers along my knee. Hot, buzzed, and blushing, I sipped my wine and held his hand.

You're not going to find your soul in Rome, my dad had said. This moment felt like a giant neon arrow flashing and pointing at my soul. Five individuals laughing like we'd known each other for a decade. The taste of tomato spice and wine in my mouth. Symphonic accents swirling around me. Ancient cobblestones beneath my feet. A beautiful, quiet, confident, accomplished man intentionally touching me in a way that felt good, affectionate, welcome.

A bottle of limoncello appeared on the table. I needed ice water. I joked to Luca that one of my immutable American traits is: I like *ghiaccio* (ice). Luca stood and led me by the hand into the empty interior of the restaurant to an ice machine behind the bar. He looked like he wanted to kiss me. I wanted to kiss him. He hesitated.

Roberto and Mia barreled into the bar sloshing shots of limoncello. I noticed a poster of the New York skyline. An outdated one. The Twin Towers still loomed at one end. I pointed to a high-rise building.

"Abito quasi qui." *I live almost here.*

Luca took my hand and put his other palm on my waist. He kissed me lightly, then more intently. We sat on a leather banquette sharing a glass of ice water, watching Roberto, Mia, and Giovanni dance to a Madonna song, passing the bottle of limoncello. I wondered if Mia would feel up to catching her nine-hour transatlantic flight in the morning. *Energizer bunny. She'll be fine.* Luca caressed my sweaty back. Kissed my neck.

The lack of air-conditioning inside the restaurant making us sticky and dizzy, we returned to the outdoor table.

No check ever appeared; no money changed hands with Giovanni.

As the guys walked Mia and me back toward the Tiber, Luca asked, "You're definitely not leaving with your friend tomorrow, no?"

"No, I'm in Rome for two more nights, then I fly to Puglia for a week."

"What are you doing tomorrow?" Again, each *r* hung in the air.

"I have a Vatican tour most of the day with a guide."

He handed me a thick business card embossed with cursive letters, his formal title "Tenente." Lieutenant.

"Call me, or if your phone doesn't work without Wi-Fi, have the Vatican guide call me at this number at the end of your tour. If I am finished with work, I will come pick you up. If I am still working, I will come get you at your hotel later, and we can have a nice dinner together. Would that be okay?"

I smiled. "Sì."

He kissed me again. We hugged. As our bodies pulled apart, we noticed Roberto and Mia making out. We laughed. I liked hearing Luca's staccato laugh. Like a burst of firecracker pops.

The guys hailed a taxi and put us in it. We waved.

"Okay, you were right," I admitted to Mia. "That was a *pile* of fun."

High on endorphins from kissing a guy, in *Rome*, of the rush of feeling someone's touch, his interest and attention, I smiled and listened to Mia interrogate the cab driver about his last visit to New York. I looked out the window. Ancient columns seemed to jive and sway.

Mia and I exchanged sweaty hugs at the elevator bank.

"Thank you for your excellent wingwomanship. I never would have met Luca if you hadn't pushed me," I conceded.

In the morning, a gift bag containing a parcel of penis-shaped pasta hung from my doorknob. An accompanying note from Mia: "Have a blast with your sexy Roman carabiniere stud!"

When I arrived at the Vatican, I immediately wanted to *be* Elena, the tour leader. Bronzed skin, kohled eyes, black wavy hair tucked behind each ear, beguiling accent. She counted eight of us, distributed headsets so we could hear her alluring voice over the din of tourist chatter, and led us into the Vatican Museums to start the day.

Elena masterfully steered us around throngs of sightseers gridlocked in the museum's hallways, hustled us past rows of headless discus throwers, and huddled us before a child-size marble sarcophagus. She vividly illuminated the storyline carved onto the stone tomb. I clung to her side, watching her artfully suppress irritation at the members of our group defying her instructions to move out of the way to allow a squadron of high school students to pass without further clogging the human traffic jam. She murmured into our headsets, "As I said three times already, it's important we stay together as a group because if you stray too far from me, your headset will stop working and you'll be lost forever."

She nudged us like ducklings into strategic positions in subsequent rooms where we could have the best, the closest, the most interesting angle of each tapestry, each painting, each sculpture embodying scenes from Caesar's reign or Mark Antony and Cleopatra's love affair.

I paused in front of a severed marble toe the size of my torso. *Was this attached to a giant body once? Or had a Roman artist simply obsessed over capturing every divot of a toenail, every wrinkle of a cuticle, every whorl and ridge of a toeprint in a block of stone?*

We moved into a long hall. I looked up and saw a ceiling fresco framed in ornate gold. Angels with 3D wings, like I could reach up and grab them. Biblical tableaux. Birds and saints.

Panels the size of movie screens covered each wall, evoking seas and lands in what looked like cobalt-blue and emerald-green thread, pastel embroidery adding topographical context and shading—water, mountains, valleys. Gilded letters spelled *Corsica, Sardinia, Campania*. Elena's voice whispered through the headset: "We are in the Gallery of Maps. And I know you're thinking the maps are woven tapestries or rugs. But they're not. They are frescoes *painted* on wall panels in the late 1500s."

Maps.

I am geographically challenged. I have deplorable directional instincts. Someone could offer me a million dollars to quickly state whether my New York apartment's windows face east, west, north, or south, and I would 100% get it wrong.

Maps comfort me. They symbolize opportunity, adventure. Getting lost without *being* lost. Whenever I plan a trip, I spend hours tracing my fingers over online maps, trying to memorize each new city's layout; how long it might take to walk from my hotel to a street art district; where I might find a grocery store or a wine shop; where I can go jogging near a river or in a park.

Galleria delle Carte Geografiche. Gallery of Maps. *This might just be my favorite room on the planet.*

I wanted to yank the blue-green map of Sicily off the wall, roll it up, haul it home, lay it over the hardwood floors in my apartment, throw two squishy pillows on it, lie down with a chenille blanket and a travel memoir, and stay there forever.

Reluctantly, I obeyed Elena's directive to move onward. I yearned to stay behind, enveloped in those maps.

Elena rounded us up in the next room, directing our attention to one painting, pointing out different workaday activities pursued by men dressed in togas and tunics in the image. Some of the characters conversed about the day's news. Others reclined on staircases. A few gossiped in small groups. Another handful debated politics, religion, societal values. Most of the figures wore bright oranges, blues, reds. Elena drew our focus to a bearded man standing at the scene's left side, in a pea-green tunic—the blandest color in the piece's palette.

"This man right here is Socrates. Many Greeks made fun of him for being unattractive," Elena explained. "Here, he's engaging in his inquisitive question-and-answer patter, the Socratic Method we reference today. He's asking his fellow Athenians what they think about topics like justice, freedom, morality. Socrates was a humble man and didn't believe he knew all the answers. He enjoyed asking questions to expand his own knowledge and that of his fellow citizens."

Hold on a second. For a solid twenty years, I'd been mad at Socrates for inventing the Socratic Method—the relentless question-and-answer technique used, and often misused, by law professors in American law school classrooms. I still have nightmare flashbacks to traumatic Socratic classroom experiences: blushing; my mind going blank; not being able to string a coherent sentence together, though I'd done all the assigned reading and outlined all the legal rules in my notes; feeling stupid and embarrassed. In my experience, the Socratic Method had been a weapon of educational destruction when mishandled by professors who enjoyed proving their intelligence by making first-year law students feel dumb. When I quit practicing law and switched to full-time law teaching, I began writing and publishing articles about how the teaching tactic of "cold-calling" first-year law students—putting them on the spot without advance notice or training, grilling them about the day's assigned reading, pressing them to answer convoluted questions about complex legal statutes or case law, surrounded by eighty peers—was not conducive to inclusive learning. Some students—introverts and naturally quiet ones—need time to think, to vet and test ideas, theories, opinions, before sharing them aloud, especially in front of an (often competitive) audience while learning the unfamiliar language of law.

Wait a minute. Socrates was a nice, humble guy? People made fun of him for being unattractive? I think I owe Socrates an apology.

If Elena is right, which she seemed to be about all things thus far, Socrates modeled intellectual humility, not superiority, as an educator. I felt a creative tug. *Maybe I'll research and write about that when I get home.*

Elena guided us into the Sistine Chapel where elderly Catholic priests shushed the crowd, intoning *"Silenzio, per favore"* every five seconds. Michelangelo's work, of course, gripped me, but the Gallery of Maps and Elena's disruption of my long-held (mis)perception of Socrates dominated my thoughts.

Quickly passing through St. Peter's Basilica, we burst outside, sunshine drenching our already hypersaturated senses. Elena noted the Vatican's Swiss guard, young military sentinels recruited between the ages of eighteen and thirty who possess Swiss citizenship and complete training with the Swiss Armed Forces. Beginning in the Middle Ages, monarchs had enlisted Swiss mercenaries, renowned for military professionalism, as special protective units. The dress uniform of the Vatican's security detail, the only Swiss guard still in existence, has a Renaissance flair—blue, orange, and red striped pantaloons, puffy jackets, boots, black berets.

As our tour group dispersed, I asked Elena if she would mind calling Luca for me on her Italian cell phone. I gave her his business card, calligraphied letters spelling his name.

"Certo!" she smiled. "Allora . . . " My favorite word in the Italian vocabulary. *Allora* means *so* or *therefore*, and is often used to introduce a thought still being formed. It's a word of possibility. Getting from here to there. Six letters suggesting, *I'm not sure what's next, but it promises to be fun.*

"Ciao, sì, ecco Heidi," she said into the phone and handed it to me.

"Are you having a beautiful day?" Luca asked me.

"Sì, yes!"

"*Brava.* I am at work now, so I will pick you up at your hotel tonight at 8 p.m., okay?"

"Okay!"

"Ciao, bella."

I returned the phone to Elena, thanked her, and wound my way through landmarks I was starting to recognize, back to the Bernini Bristol.

Luca called my hotel room's landline at 7:45 p.m. and bumped our arranged pickup time to 8:45. I waited in the lobby, sweating again in jeans and a black tank top. I noticed a Smart car loop Piazza Barberini and screech to a stop between two taxis idling in front of the hotel, Luca's clean-shaven face in the driver's seat. He pressed the passenger door open. I jumped inside. "Ciao, bella," he said, shifting the tiny vehicle into gear, then placing his hand on my thigh. No smile yet.

I buckled the seat belt. He raced through back alleys and one-lane streets, mere millimeters separating the car's doors from hydrants, bicycles, Vespas, humans. The vehicle jarred to a stop in a cobblestoned square, front bumper wedged against a terra-cotta planter.

Luca unfolded himself from the two-seater car. He opened my door. Restaurant owners greeted us with boisterous Italian salutations and cheek kisses, inviting us to a candlelit table inside. Someone handed me a flute of prosecco. A waiter delivered a two-tiered platter of oysters, clams, mussels, octopus, and translucent shrimp. Luca touched his prosecco glass to mine.

White wine and champagne always get me looped too fast without a velvety buzz, unlike glorious red wine. I sipped the prosecco anyway, not wanting to be rude, but realizing how much I defer to others to write all my scripts.

Luca brushed his fingers along my bare arm. "So, bella, why are you alone?"

Seriously. Where do I even start with that one?

I blinked. "Um. È complicato." *It's complicated.*

His thin lips opened, white teeth gleaming, as he finally smiled and laughed, another staccato burst, like a surprise. He rested a hand on my wrist. The prosecco seemed to relax him a bit.

He described his job as a squad leader in the carabinieri. Arresting drug rings. Dealing with shootings. Investigating currency fraud. He lived in the military barracks. Grew up in Genova, where his mother and sister still lived. He didn't mention a father.

We shared a whole baked fish, more prosecco. After a dessert of cinnamon gelato, the restaurant proprietor hugged and kissed us forcefully, as if our leaving devastated him. As we walked to the car, I realized, once again, I never saw any currency or credit card change hands.

Luca zipped the Smart car through serpentine streets, eyes fixated on the road, hand on my kneecap. He pulled into a parking lot, weeds poking through cracks in concrete, and extinguished the headlights. He got out, opened my door, reached for my hand, backed me against the car, and kissed me. Palms on my hip bones. His mouth tasted of cinnamon. He pulled away. Looked at me. A laugh, again like popcorn. He grasped my hand and led me across the parking lot to a marble wall with a regal green door. A young couple took turns pressing their faces against a brass keyhole in the portal. They moved away. Luca encouraged me to place one cheekbone against the door and look through the small aperture. In the night sky, I saw the dome of St. Peter's Basilica fully illuminated, perfectly framed within a telescoping corridor of shadowy tree foliage. Luca hugged me from behind and pressed his face against mine, kissing my cheek. Another soul-stirring moment. Historical intrigue, mindful architecture, beauty, romance, physical touch.

We pulled away from the peephole to let other couples have a turn at the semisecret vista on the Aventine Hill. Luca and I walked hand in hand toward a half-crumbled wall of brick and stone. He lifted me up to sit on the ruins and hopped up next to me. We stared at the Tiber, our legs dangling. He laid me down, his hand on my spine, his mouth trailing my cheek, my lips, my neck. A ridge in the mortar scraped my back.

He kissed me under the starlight. In the car. In the hotel elevator. As we fell into bed, his mouth released a torrent of words and phrases—nouns and verbs and adjectives and adverbs he'd kept contained all evening. A tumble of Italian, English, lots of exclamations of "Dimmi!" *Tell me!*

His body was pure muscle on frame. He lay in my bed, sheets tangled around a chiseled quadricep. Buttery skin. Abs like Michelangelo's *David*. Military dog tags on a silver chain resting on his chest. I began to play with them, tried to read them. He took them out of my hand, hiding them behind his neck.

We slept intertwined.

I awoke to the *scratch, scratch, scratch* in the wall. Blurry-eyed, I watched Luca button jeans over tight boxer briefs. Studied his serious face as he checked his phone.

"Tesoro, darling, I must go to work for just a short while. Afterwards, I will take the rest of the day off, which I have not done in a long, long time." He smiled. "I will pick you up at ten, and we will spend the day in Fregene together."

"Okay," I murmured. He kissed my lips and left me. The hotel room looked like a crime scene. Bedsheets and furniture askew. Last night's clothes a trail from the doorway. I'm glad I'd at least had the foresight to hide Mia's penis pasta in my suitcase.

The clock read 6:04 a.m. I ached. In five thousand good ways.

I grabbed my phone and typed Fregene into a search engine. A beach town about an hour's drive from Rome.

I dozed until nine, then showered and dressed in a black cotton miniskirt, a ruffled white T-shirt, and sandals. I tucked a black bikini and sunscreen into a tote bag and scooted to a café near Piazza Barberini where the barista taught me the translation for coffee "to go." *Portare via.*

I slurped a last sip of coffee, tossing the too-hot plastic cup into a garbage bin just as Luca's Smart car stuttered to a stop in front of the hotel, passenger door flinging open. Luca scolded someone through his phone as I slid into my seat. He pursed his lips, miming a kiss in my direction, eyes hidden behind aviator sunglasses. Muscles in his tan legs flexed as his Adidas sneakers alternated clutch, brake, and accelerator pedals. He put his phone down, smiled at me, and said, Ciao, tesoro." *Hi, darling.*

He turned on the radio. Italian pop music blared. Ignoring most stoplights and traffic signals, he wagged a hand at drivers who honked at him as he threaded the two-seater through cars, trucks, and motorcycles. I tried to convert kilometers per hour into mph to calculate how fast we were going when we hit our stride on the autostrada, but I gave up. *Fast.* That's how.

Exiting the highway, Luca hung a sharp forty-five-degree angle onto a side street. We hit a bump, sending us airborne for an instant. One hand on the steering wheel, the other on my leg, he spun the car into a parking spot. A one-story white-washed building stood between us and the Tyrrhenian Sea. Lounge chairs and umbrellas bearing a beach club's logo dotted a beige shoreline. Skinny palm trees swayed in sync with a rip-pling Italian flag. A red wooden boat marked *Salvataggio* (res-cue) lazed near the flagpole. Like at the restaurants we'd dined in so far, men in charge greeted Luca as if he'd just returned from war. One man steered us toward two lounge chairs resting in soft sand; another placed bottles of cold acqua naturale and a tray of cantaloupe and toothpicks on a wooden table between the chaises.

I walked toward the clubhouse to change into my swimsuit, sneaking a glance at Luca chatting with the guys. He stood like a professional athlete. Earned arrogance. All sinew, like a lion.

Another phone call for Luca provided a welcome distrac-tion as I reclined on the lounge chair next to him and removed my shirt, sucking in my stomach. My skin looked even frecklier and whiter in sunlight next to his unblemished oliveness. He put his phone away, stabbed a chunk of melon with a toothpick, and tucked the bite into my mouth. He leaned over and kissed me. He laid his forearm on the wooden table between us so he could graze my hand as we both fell asleep, lone sunbathers on an empty beach.

Late afternoon, a breeze picking up, the melon plate empty, we dressed and headed toward the clubhouse. He ordered a bot-tle of white wine. I escaped to the restroom to survey my ap-pearance. Decent color in my cheeks. I wiped traces of eyeliner from beneath my eyes and pushed salty hair off my face with my sunglasses.

A man in an ecru linen suit and camouflaged dress shirt de-livered our wine. He joined us at a patio table, lighting a thin brown cigarette.

"Piacere," the stranger said to me, kissing my hand. *A plea-sure to meet you.* He tossed a thin novella onto the tablecloth. A lemon-yellow Vespa beamed from the book cover. The author's name: Alessandro Spolvi. Luca flipped the book over and showed me the author's picture. The gentleman who'd just kissed my hand.

"Mi piacciono i libri," I said. *I like books.*

"Ma, sei americana?" He perked up.

"Sì. Anch'io scrivo libri." *Yes, I'm American. And I write books.*

The author maintained eye contact with me while carrying on conversation in demonstrative Italian with Luca. I understood about 30 percent of their exchange.

"Come stai?" Luca asked me. "You okay?"

"Non capisco niente ma mi piace." *I don't understand anything but I like it.*

They both laughed.

We shared the wine. Ate pistachios. The sun set. Closed beach umbrellas against the backdrop of the sea reminded me of the pointy shape of cypress trees. Luca's fingers played with mine. I watched his mouth form lyrical sentences, listened to his bursts of laughter at the author's jokes I didn't quite understand. A familiar pinch of worry began to crimp my insides. My flight to Puglia in the morning . . . overlapping with Luca's scheduled trip to visit his mother and sister in Genova. *Would this feeling of possibility, this spark between us, vanish?*

Stop. Don't overthink. Don't fast-track to the future. Don't cling to the intoxication of connection, the lightning strike of infatuation. Just enjoy this instant.

At sundown, we hugged the author goodbye, pressing cheeks to cheeks. Luca drove us back to the hotel. We skipped dinner. Fell into bed.

"What time is your flight to Brindisi tomorrow?" he asked, his fingers drawing curlicues on my sternum.

"Eleven."

"I'll send my guy, Paolo, to take you to the airport. I would take you myself, but I must go to the office tomorrow before I leave for Genova. When you come back from Puglia next week, I will arrange a hotel here for your last night in Italy, and we will be together, *insieme.*"

He slept. I replayed every detail of Fregene, our repartee with the author, Luca's entrancing accent, his taut body on mine, how expressiveness supplants his quiet vigilance when we entwine in bed.

I awakened to Luca leaning over my pillow to kiss me good-bye, his carabiniere dog tags bumping my chin.

"I will call your hotel in Puglia tonight, bella."

I rolled over to try to go back to sleep. *Scratch, scratch, scratch* in the walls.

Luca's driver friend, Paolo, a sweet older man, arrived on time with an enormous van to transport me and my luggage—penis pasta stashed between swimsuits and dirty clothes—to Fiumicino Airport. Before he drove off, Paolo pressed a casino chip—a luck talisman, he said—into my palm. "Per amore," he winked.

Walking through the airport, I passed a mobile phone vendor.

"Quanto costa?" I pointed to a flip phone with a thirty-day subscription for an Italian number with unlimited texts and phone calls. I paid the sales clerk and raced to my gate to find an outlet to charge the phone.

"Pronto." Luca's serious voice boomed through the receiver.

"Ciao! It's Heidi! Ho comprato un telefonino italiano!"

"Brava, tesoro!" I loved hearing his stutter laugh again. He promised to call and text me on my Italian phone in Puglia, and reiterated the plan to see each other in a week when I returned to Rome for one night before heading home to New York.

I settled into the leather of the Alitalia airplane seat, my body a twist of emotions. The velvety memory of Luca's mouth on my skin. Being desired by someone that confident, physi-cally strong, professionally powerful, seemingly in control at all times—except when he let himself enjoy being close to me, releasing his pent-up deluge of words, the passion he seemed to muzzle all day. A hopefulness that perhaps this could turn into, be, something real. My brain already doing its silly thing, fast-forwarding—*Could I teach from Rome? Write from Rome?* A slap-smack of fear . . . *You're not cool or sexy enough for him. You're not going to find your soul in Rome.*

Stop. Shut *up*. You're wrong.

I *am* Rome.

As the plane rocketed toward Brindisi, I knew that, no matter what happened with Luca, Rome had transfused my blood. Infiltrated my bones.

I thought, *Someday, not just yet but someday, I'll be tough enough to prevent any man, anyone, from ever again robbing my power and standing between me and my essence. The Roman warrior-goddess, the muse, the artist, the vestal virgin, the poetess, the Aries, the fighter, the pugilist, the growing rebel—in me.*

2
puglia . . . and roma,
ancora

My plane flew a pretzel loop over the Adriatic Sea and landed at Brindisi Airport. Masseria Cervarolo—the farmhouse converted into an inn where I planned to spend the next six days reading, editing my legal textbook manuscript, and sunning like a Pugliese artichoke—sent a driver to retrieve me from baggage claim. All business, in a dark suit and mirrored sunglasses, he opened the passenger door of a black Mercedes. I felt fancy.

The sedan coiled along dusty roads flanked by cactus plants, twisty olive trees, and grapevines. I caught my first glimpse of Puglia's *trulli*, stone huts with cone-shaped roofs resembling gnomes' hats.

A driveway funneled us toward a sprawling structure of white limestone, wrought iron gates, balconies, and five trulli. The sixteenth-century masseria's name—Cervarolo—derived from the Italian word for female deer, a doe. *Cerva*. A golden retriever greeted the Mercedes, fluffy tail in frantic wag. The hotelier, in head-to-toe linen—the apparent uniform of the stylish mid-forties Italian male—followed. He helped the driver wrangle my heavy suitcase from the trunk.

"Benvenuta, signora! Sono Rafaello. But, it is just you, signora?" Rafaello peered into the Mercedes window, searching for a travel companion. My email correspondence had unequivocally reserved a room for one person.

"Sì. Da sola. Io. Una." I reconfirmed my status as solo traveler. Rafaello rolled my suitcase through pebbles toward a small office on the masseria's ground floor. A shallow reflecting pool centered an interior courtyard. Green glass bottles of varied girths decked each step of a stone staircase ascending to a row of guest rooms. The dog plopped down in a shady corner of the courtyard, one paw dangling in the reflecting pool.

Rafaello requested my passport, querying once more whether anyone would be joining me. It seemed quite possible that, in the five-hundred-year history of the masseria, I was the first female traveler to trek to this Ostuni hideaway alone. I couldn't tell if that rendered me cool or tragic. I decided, the former.

Rafaello ferried my suitcase up the stone stairs. Succulents in painted flowerpots fringed my room's rustic doorway. I smelled lavender. Rafaello placed an oversized key in a lock and nudged the door open. A crocheted quilt lay at the foot of a double bed. Reclaimed timber nailed to the wall served as a headboard. A book of poetry sat on a nightstand next to a water pitcher repurposed as a lamp's base. A window with lacy curtains and white shutters framed a view of walking paths, olive groves, wildflowers, and a swimming pool shaped like a gourd.

Perfetto. I smiled, happy I'd trusted my budding hotel research skills and persisted in venturing to a place I knew little about.

I hung dwindling clean clothes in a wooden wardrobe; changed into a swimsuit; grabbed a book, sunglasses, and the Italian phone; and headed to the pool to refresh. Duets and trios of lounge chairs dotted a green lawn. A family of five—blond, built like Olympians—sat beneath a trellis braided with pink and orange bougainvillea, sipping lemonade, laughing, and speaking German.

A pair of ladies, skin baked to a shade of brick, leaned elbows against chaise cushions, smoking cigarettes, pert nipples exposed. They greeted me with "Bonjour."

"Bonjour," I responded. I looked around to see if anyone else was sunbathing topless. Not the Germans.

As I swam, I listened to the German family tease one another . . . the French ladies speculate about meat dishes on the dinner menu . . . a bird cheep . . . a wind chime jingle.

Reclining on a lounge, I grabbed the Italian phone and noticed a text from Luca:

BELLA, COME STAI? *Beautiful, how are you?*

The cheap flip phone required me to press each button once, twice, or thrice to choose the correct letter of the alphabet to craft a response, which I painstakingly did, until I realized I couldn't access a strong enough cell signal near the pool to transmit. I closed my eyes and fell asleep, bumblebees buzzing in a nearby flower bed.

I woke up to sounds of guests arriving at the poolside bar for a sunset aperitivo. The pop of a cork stirred me like one of Pavlov's dogs. Wiping sleep from my eyes, I moseyed to the bar and ordered a Pugliese wine by process of elimination, choosing the name of a grape I didn't recognize: *Verdeca*. The only audible English came from two Scots, a couple in their fifties with broad smiles. They raised their glasses toward me in a toast. The wine tasted of green apple, cucumber, lemon. Crisp, cold. A blue-eyed bartender topped off my drink before I glided back to my room to shower and change for dinner.

I lingered in the stone shower, keeping an eye on a long-legged spider in the corner. Having noted the upscale attire of the masseria guests at happy hour, I pulled a long clingy sundress from the armoire—three shades of blue merging in bands of pretty tie-dye. I'd bought the dress in Akumal, Mexico, but rarely found occasion to wear it at home. Standing at my bedroom window, I eked enough of a cell phone signal to reply to another text from Luca. I started writing "I miss you too!" in Italian, but remembered my teacher Angelo explaining that the verb *to miss*, in Italian, is a reflexive one. Italians basically say, *You are missing to me*. I worried I was demanding *You miss me!* instead of what I really meant to convey. I switched to English.

A tad self-conscious about dining solo my first night in such intimate surroundings, I wandered the grounds of the masseria to sneak a peek at the seating arrangements before entering the dinner area. I ambled through olive trees, branches twinkling with white lights, past the trulli. Candles and lanterns gave the dining patio—situated in a former citrus grove—a dusky glow. Sprigs of garlic and shallots hung from ropes along a stone wall. Ceramic roosters holding butter, salt, and pepper sat on wooden tables covered in white linens. The Germans, the French, the Scots, and other guests I hadn't met yet occupied seats. A maître d' swooped toward me, gesturing to an empty table set for two.

"But you are alone? Sei da sola?" he asked.

Yes. Alone.

He pulled out a chair. I sat. The Scots waved. The other guests smiled at me, then resumed conversations. I love eating alone but wished I'd brought a journal or a book to dinner. Sometimes when I stare into space just trying to take it all in, people mistake that for loneliness and kindly try to intervene.

The menu described a collection of farm-to-table pluckings from the land surrounding the masseria. A waiter offered me tastings of *Negroamaro* and *Primitivo*—two Pugliese red wines. The latter—thick and jammy—tasted like definite hangover. I preferred the lighter traces of allspice and clove in the Negroamaro.

I dipped a chunk of fresh bread into olive oil. I sampled bites of golden beets and goat cheese arranged on crisp lettuce leaves. I bit into ravioli hand folded around artichokes and asparagus, dribbled with butter, sprinkled with toasted sage. For dessert, the waiter brought a small vial of grappa and a slice of raspberry tart. The Scots and French relocated to chairs around a firepit. The Germans listened to their children tell stories. I grabbed my grappa and wound my way through the paths, up the stone staircase, back to my room. A landline phone rang as I entered. I answered, "Pronto?"

"Signora, there is a gentleman calling for you," Rafaello indicated.

"Oh! Grazie!"

I heard Luca's voice . . . his syncopated laugh. "Bella, come stai?"

I filled him in on the day's events: the flight from Rome to Brindisi, the driver, the pool, dinner.

"But you are there with friends, no?" Another one, mystified by the prospect of intentional solitude.

"Friends will meet me here later this week." A semantic dodge. Not a total falsehood if I made an effort to manifest new acquaintances at the masseria. Either way, intimating I had travel buddies joining me seemed easier in the moment than explaining my happiness vacationing alone—reading, writing, resting, processing my life.

Luca sent me off to sleep with *baci, baci, baci*.

🛵 🛵 🛵

A breakfast bell clanged.

I lazed in bed for an hour, hoping most of the inn's lodgers were early risers and I could appropriate the last half hour of morning mealtime for myself. Hearing splashes from the pool, I extended one leg from beneath the covers and nudged a shutter open with my foot. Guests already had begun claiming lounge chairs for the day. The Scots sprayed one another's backs with sunscreen. The French ladies puffed Gauloises. The Germans took turns leading one another in calisthenics—jumping jacks, high knees, push-ups—on the lawn.

I found the breakfast area inside a cavernous farmhouse kitchen. The waiters had arranged a place setting for one—for me. A family of Italians occupied one end of a communal table. Curly-haired children licked apricot jam from toast. The parents and I exchanged *buongiornos*. I placed my room key, tied to a wooden placard with the masseria's logo—a sun hand-painted in white and black—on my napkin. A waiter asked if I preferred a caffè americano, an espresso, or a cappuccino.

"Cappuccino, per favore."

I walked to the buffet and piled a blue ceramic plate—also stamped with the masseria's sun logo—with scrambled eggs, prosciutto, fresh sourdough bread, a spoonful of peach jam, a slice of broccoli frittata, and a small mason jar of yogurt. Handwritten cards explained the differences among *prosciutto crudo* (pork cured with salt, aged one or two years, then sliced paper-thin), *prosciutto cotto* (cooked instead of aged), *speck* (denser ham cured with spices like juniper and bay leaves, then smoked and aged), *mortadella* (classified as a sausage and comprised of ground pork and pork fat), *capocollo* (a mashup of the words *capo* [head] and *collo* [neck], taken from those parts of the pig, seasoned and salted, stuffed into a natural casing, and aged for up to six months), and *bresaola* (the beef form of *capocollo*).

The cappuccino arrived in a steaming bowl. The waiter also brought a tumbler of fresh-squeezed clementine juice. As the breakfast room emptied of waiters and guests, I constructed a few sandwiches—crusty bread, prosciutto, and cheese slices—in case I felt like doing my own thing for lunch.

For the next two days, I repeated this routine, sleeping as late as possible until the breakfast bell rang, lingering in bed reading, arriving last for the morning meal. I lounged poolside all day, editing pages of my book manuscript. Rogue ink from my blue pen mixed with sunscreen on my legs. I rinsed the temporary tattoos with pool water and floated on my back. New couples arrived at the masseria. I remained the lone American and the only solo traveler, which I liked. Not hearing American accents made the trip feel more exotic, far away from everyday life, clearing my mental chalkboard. Like shaking an Etch A Sketch toy.

The phone signal spotty in my room, each day around happy hour, I climbed an additional flight of stairs to a rooftop lookout with panoramic views of Puglia, and called or texted

Luca. Determined to converse through static and dropped calls, the extent of our conversation became, "Mi manchi." *I miss you.* Direct translation: *You are missing to me.*

I like when someone tells me they miss me.

In the long-distance phase of my relationship with Trey— my last two years of college and three years of law school—I yearned for him to tell me he missed me. Ever logical, he reminded me how his parents endured six months apart each time his father shipped out for Navy tours; in his view, our weekdays apart weren't "that big a deal." Even so, I missed *him.* Five days of separation felt like an eternity, his breeziness intensifying my wistfulness. I'm a world-class *wister.*

"Ci vedremo presto," Luca reassured. *We will see each other soon.*

One evening, as I approached my dinner spot, which the waiters now seemed to enjoy decorating with *single* place settings in increasingly creative explosions of color, the Scots leaped to their feet, beckoning me to their table. "Join us!" they pleaded.

Appreciating the invitation, I acquiesced. The wife quickly shared, "I'm a professor in Scotland. We're dying to know what you're writing at the pool every day!"

A waiter moved my chair and silverware to the Scots' table and delivered a bottle of Pugliese wine. The couple explained they'd traveled to Ostuni to celebrate their anniversary. They inquired about my book project. We talked about teaching and travel amid bites of fettucine in a sauce of basil and tomatoes picked that morning from the masseria's garden. Thin-sliced grilled eggplant. Portobello mushrooms. A final course of limoncello meringue.

"What's your plan for tomorrow?" the husband asked.

"We're driving to town to see the historical sights, if you'd like to join us," the wife offered.

I'd been nervous about renting a car in Italy. I hadn't driven one in several years. My dog Rowan passed away at fourteen years old two weeks before my move back to the East Coast from California. Forrest and I had broken up. I'd landed a new teaching gig at a law school in Manhattan. I'd been planning to drive Rowan across the country, but when she died, I sold my convertible and bought a one-way plane ticket to New York. When I boarded the flight, I realized I carried no keys—no car, no office, no home—an interesting temporary state of limbo. Like the word *allora*. Between here and there.

In Puglia though, I hadn't realized how tied to the masseria I'd be without wheels. I welcomed the Scots' offer to explore Ostuni together.

The next morning, after breakfast, we drove to La Città Bianca—the "white city"—earning its name from sun-bleached architecture. White stone cathedrals, white fortified walls, white palazzi. We strolled cobblestones, passing men in striped tank tops playing checkers, bakery windows displaying elaborate cakes, pots of geraniums hanging from balconies. The Scots insisted I experience my first taste of blood-red Campari (Italy's refreshing herbal and fruity liqueur, in the category of a *bitters*, yielding flavors of orange peel and rhubarb) and soda, served with a sprig of lavender.

We exchanged more stories of academia, of global adventures.

"So, is there a man . . . or someone . . . in your life?" the wife asked.

"Sort of. I don't know yet." I recounted the play-by-play of how I met Luca.

We returned to the masseria in time for an afternoon cooking class. The chef placed paper toques (from the French *tuque* and Arabic *taqa* for *hat*) on our heads and distributed wooden cutting boards, orbs of yellow dough, knives, and small spoons. In half Italian, half English, he modeled how to roll the dough into snakelike tubes, cut each strip into half-inch bits, and use the curve of the spoon to press each piece into orecchiette—ear-shaped pasta.

With a new batch of dough, we learned how to make *tar-alli*—Puglia's traditional cracker, the size and form of a bite-sized donut with the texture and crunch of a pretzel. The chef rewarded our efforts with glasses of chilled pink Negroamaro rosé wine.

My six days in Puglia passed quickly. As I plowed through manuscript edits in the sunshine, my skin turned light gold.

My last day at the masseria, I exchanged email addresses with the Scots, promising to visit Edinburgh or possibly orchestrate a teaching exchange. I texted Luca before hopping into the Mercedes for the forty-minute ride back to Brindisi Airport: "Non vedo l'ora di vederti stasera!" *I can't wait to see you tonight.*

Too early for my flight—as always—I bought nail polish remover and pink lacquer in an airport cosmetics shop. I liked learning and pronouncing the new vocabulary. *Smalto*, for polish. The sales clerk pronounced *acetone*, for remover, as if it rhymed with rigatoni.

Luca texted an apology that his work schedule prevented him from picking me up at Rome's airport but relayed he'd send Paolo, his driver, again to transport me to a hotel where Luca had "arranged a room" for my last night in Italy.

🛵   🛵   🛵

The hotel lobby seemed more Atlantic City, New Jersey, than Rome. Fake ficus trees. Gaudy mirrors. Aging bellhops in disheveled tuxedos. As I checked in, the concierge asked for my credit card. I realized I'd misunderstood Luca's intent regarding the hotel: He'd reserved a room in a place owned by his acquaintance, but apparently I'd be covering the cost. I wished I'd stuck with my original idea to book a room for us at a boutique hotel with an artsy vibe, but I'd gotten excited about feeling romanced, taken care of. Maybe his concept of hotels was like Mia's: function over form. Either way, I needed to get more information about his housing situation and why we couldn't just stay at his place. "I live in the military barracks" had better not be code for "I live with my wife and three kids."

A bellhop led me *underground* to the room. Like, subterranean. Submarine. No windows. Dark wood. A mirror . . . on the *ceiling*.

Claustrophobic within minutes, I texted Luca to report my arrival, and after he confirmed he'd meet me at the room at 8 p.m., I headed outside to visit Oceanus, the river god, at Trevi Fountain again, find a gelateria, and spend my afternoon getting purposefully lost. I wanted to deepen the bond I'd begun with Rome, let it speak to me like it had started to six days earlier, raise my vibration. I wanted to feel its electric shock again, make sure I hadn't imagined our magnetic connection.

The throng of tourists at Trevi too packed for me to infiltrate close enough to stare at the muscles of the Tritons, I pressed onward, past the Pantheon into Piazza Sant'Eustachio where I'd noticed an artisanal gelateria I wanted to try. A German-sounding name: Günther. The gelateria's founder hailed from South Tyrol—a region called Alto Adige in Northern Italy near Austria. I entered and requested una coppetta piccola, a small cup, of the darkest chocolate available. *Cioccolato fondente*, from Venezuela. No added sprinkles. No chocolate chunks. No caramel. No nuts. No *panna* (cream). No biscotto (cookie). Just two scoops of plain, creamy, superdark chocolate. I passed the sales clerk three euro coins. He handed me the coppetta and a pink plastic spoon. As I walked through Piazza Navona past tarot card and palm readers advertising divinations in multiple languages, I wondered how the Italians conjure the consistency and texture in gelato that is so much more tactile, dense, and substantial than airy American ice cream or vapid frozen yogurt.

In Campo de' Fiori, I resisted pressure from gregarious juice and spice vendors to stop and shop. I breezed past boutiques along Via dei Giubbonari (*giubbonari* meaning *jackets*), crossed a small park called Piazza Benedetto Cairoli (named for an Italian statesman), and entered a district known as the Jewish Ghetto. I noticed sunlight glinting off brass squares inlaid in cobblestones in front of an apartment doorway. I stopped and looked down. Inscriptions in the brass listed names, birthdates, the word *assassinato* (masculine) or *assassinata* (feminine) and the date and location where the individual seized from that exact spot in 1943 was ultimately killed during the Holocaust. I'd always naively assumed the term "Jewish Ghetto" derived from World War II. But Rome's Jewish Ghetto is regarded by historians as the oldest in the Western world, dating to 1555 when Pope Paul IV—bent on bolstering Catholic dominance—ordered its construction and forced Roman Jews to live solely within its bounds, revoking many of their civil rights. On October 16, 1943, Nazis stormed the neighborhood and extracted over one thousand Roman Jews from their homes, transported them by train to Auschwitz, and murdered nearly all of them. Reportedly, only sixteen survived.

I forced myself to move, still staring at the ground, hunting for more brass plates affixed in cobblestones—like bezeled gems—fronting doorways of shops, restaurants, and apartments, noting names and ages of people snatched from those spots. Identical surnames on clusters of inscriptions memorialized entire families abducted at once.

Such violent historical madness contrasted sharply with the upbeat modern-day aura of the Ghetto's main street—Via del Portico d'Ottavia. Kosher restaurants advertised deep-fried artichokes (*carciofi alla giudia*, Jewish style—an alternative to carciofi alla romana, Roman style, which are sprinkled or stuffed with herbs and braised in olive oil and water). Placards boasted catchy slogans like "La vita è troppo breve per mangiare carciofi sbagliati." *Life is too short to eat the wrong artichokes.* Gelato shops and cafés buzzed with patrons. Hebrew, Latin, and Italian words commingled on stone.

At the end of the Ghetto's boulevard, I encountered a set of unfamiliar ruins: peeling layers of fresco clinging to a lingering arch and columns, peach-colored plaster, brick and stone strata serving as durable evidence of bygone bloodlines. The Portico d'Ottavia. A structure built by Caesar Augustus (formerly Octavian) to honor his sister, Octavia. She'd had a son named Marcellus with her first husband, a senator named Gaius Claudius Marcellus. Later, in another strategic political alliance, she'd married Mark Antony (his fourth wife before he ran off with Cleopatra). A fish market and a library once occupied Octavia's portico. I stood before the edifice, pondering why I'd never heard of it. To me, its rustic beauty outshines Rome's more famous icons.

I descended a pedestrian ramp, following a pathway through downed columns, toward the Teatro di Marcello, an ancient theater devoted to arts and music, named for Octavia's son, Marcellus. Beside the theater, a trio of still-standing columns—part of another patinaed ruin—halted me. These columns shot high into the sky, connected by a lingering cornice, vestiges of a temple. Remains of the Temple of Apollo Sosianus, named for Apollo (the Greek god of archery, music, dance, truth, prophesy, and more) and Gaius Sosius, a Roman general, politician, and buddy of Mark Antony. Sosius rebuilt the temple after workers wrecked its first rendition while constructing the Teatro di Marcello.

The three columns garnered less attention from passersby than the more exalted structures nearby. But something propelled me toward them. Standing in a nondescript triangle of soil, grass, and pebbles, staring at the three pillars, I sensed another electric jolt. Again, I felt tiny but expansive at the same time. A recognition of the massiveness of the universe and the reality I'm just one blip in a timeline of millennia of humans passing through that same cross section of longitude and latitude. But also a supercharge of motivation that I can, and must, do something worthwhile and big with my life. Like, it's time to stop resisting, time to let the blood of epochs of **defiant women pump through me. I felt confused about the influx of female energy while standing** at a spot dominated by males: Apollo, Gaius Sosius, Marcellus.

Maybe it was Octavia.

🛵　🛵　🛵

Ironically, dressed in a black minidress and peep-toe wedges, I sat in a dank hotel room at 8 p.m. *waiting for a man.*

And still at 8:30 p.m.

At 8:45 p.m., I gathered my handbag to buy myself a drink—at sea level—when I heard a knock at the door. I opened it.

Luca said, "Sei rosa." *You're pink.*

As he shifted me backward toward the bed, I grabbed his jacket lapels to catch my fall.

🛵　🛵　🛵

Luca whisked me to a rooftop bar, ordered two glasses of prosecco before I realized what he'd said to the waiter, then asked about my Puglia trip. His buzzing phone interrupted us. While he took the call, I asked the waiter if he could bring me a glass of Sangiovese instead. The waiter nodded and said, "Certo!"

Luca finished his call, turned to me, kissed my mouth, and said, "I want to be honest with you. I want to start this relationship with no secrets."

Um. "Certo."

"I have two children. Twin girls. They live with their mother in Malta. We are not married. We're not together anymore. I just didn't want to hide that from you."

His phone rang again.

I considered whether his disclosure meant I should tell him about my divorce twelve years earlier from Trey. About the subsequent long-term situation with Forrest. My two primary relationships had gone from zero to sixty in five seconds. At forty-three, I still had no idea how much or little personal history to share on a first, second, or third date. I didn't want to obscure or mis-imply anything about my past. But I also wasn't sure what exactly was relevant to the present.

That night, Luca slept while I stared at his bare trapezoids in the mirror on the hotel room ceiling. At dawn, he bolted awake.

"I must go to work now," he whispered, teeth grazing my neck. "But I will pick you up at ten and drive you to the airport."

He left. I switched on a bedside lamp. I pulled the sheets down to my hips, assessing my body in the ceiling mirror. *I'm not rosa . . . pink. I have tan lines. I'm also looking somewhat fit.* After twelve days in Italy eating fresh vegetables and meat free of the preservatives and hormones stuffed into American food, my stomach looked flatter than usual. I rewrapped the sheets tight against my chest, tired yet content. Readiness to go home began intertwining with wistfulness about leaving. I thought about how wistfulness—a sense of longing—or the act of *wisting* (if I invented a new action verb) feels romantic to me, but probably stokes my bad habit of clinging, attaching to men in unhealthy ways, seeking to make intimate tableaux last as long as possible, at whatever cost.

I showered and changed into my last clean outfit. As I zipped my suitcase, I discovered Luca's watch lying on the floor beneath the bed. I tucked it into my handbag to return to him. As I paid the hotel bill, I vowed to control—or at least have substantial input into—hotel reservations in the future.

Luca's Smart car zoomed to a halt in front of the hotel on time. I unsuccessfully tried not to be dazzled by his full carabiniere uniform. I handed him his watch. His face all-serious again, he touched my knee, floored the accelerator, swerved onto a sidewalk to scoot around a milk delivery truck, and raced toward Fiumicino Airport.

Instead of dropping me at the international departures entrance, he drove to a separate depot, whipped the vehicle into a no-parking zone, grabbed my luggage, and escorted me inside to a special check-in area. He asked me for my passport and spoke in hurried Italian to a ticket agent.

"You can depart from here instead of waiting in the regular lines."

"Okay," I responded, a tad dizzy.

He pecked my cheeks, quickly surveilled our immediate surroundings, then kissed my lips. "Ciao, bella. Download WhatsApp on your phone when you land in New York. I will see you very soon." He turned and strode away, fluorescent airport lights refracting off the metal hardware of his uniform.

My heart pinched. I felt tended to, yet at the same time, easily shipped off.

🛵   🛵   🛵

In a taxi home from JFK Airport, new to the international texting platform WhatsApp, I accidentally downloaded a fake German version first. A couple clicks and taps later, I successfully messaged Luca. It was past bedtime already in Rome, but he responded immediately, spelling "sweetie" as "sweety," and filling my screen with kiss emojis.

Over the next several weeks, as New York summer ebbed and a new teaching semester drew near, I recovered from jet lag, finished editing my book manuscript, prepared syllabi and materials to teach a fresh batch of first-year law students, and communicated with Luca over text and the occasional live phone call. He wrote to me every night as he went to sleep in the carabinieri barracks in Rome. Each morning, messages from him awaited, like UN MONDO DI BACI PER QUANDO TI SVEGLI. *A world of kisses for when you wake up.*

During our short time together in Rome, we'd talked about seeing each other again in September or October, and the possibility of my spending Thanksgiving week with him somewhere in the world. My law professor job afforded much more flexibility than his 24/7 carabiniere job. I told him I'd happily fly to Rome on a Thursday night, stay for a long weekend, and journey back home on Monday to tackle the rest of my workweek. He had trouble understanding how or why I'd fly 8,600 miles round-trip for three days together. I assured him I could and would.

August melted into September. One day, I opened my apartment mailbox and found a package containing three homemade CDs of Italian pop songs Luca thought I'd like, and a notecard imprinted with a vintage photo of carabinieri motorcycles against a backdrop of the Colosseum. A message in meticulous handwriting: "Sweety, I really hope to see you again as soon as possible. The time we spent together has been fantastic—like you!! Waiting to see you again, I send you a big kiss. Ciao bellissima, Luca."

I found an Italian bookstore in uptown Manhattan called Rizzoli and purchased three novels by Dan Brown—author of *The Da Vinci Code*—translated into Italian. I wrapped them, along with prints of photos I'd taken the night of our dinner with Roberto and Mia in Trastevere and our beach day in Fregene. I spent a sack of money to ship the package to Luca's office in Rome.

One night in mid-September, bored on my couch watching crime shows, I researched flights to Rome. My teaching calendar indicated the law school would be closed for a set of Jewish holidays, providing some travel leeway. I texted Luca and proposed a weekend date in late September to fly to see him.

He wrote: BUT TESORO, IT IS SO FAR FOR YOU TO COME FOR JUST A SHORT TIME.

I responded: I FEEL LIKE WE SHOULD SEE EACH OTHER THOUGH. I DON'T WANT US TO LOSE MOMENTUM OF WHAT WE STARTED IN ROME.

Me, always worrying about the future instead of appreciating the present.

I wanted to see him.

I traded Delta miles and credit card points for a plane ticket. The instant the image on my laptop screen transformed from rotating "transaction in progress" wheel to a glorious announcement from Delta, "Congratulations! You've booked your trip to Rome," I realized the prospect of another liaison with Luca drove only one degree of the zap of excitement I felt. Completely separate from him, the notion of a new adventure mere weeks away brightened my worldview. I sprang from bed each morning, reinvigorated toward work. My punch combos in boxing lessons packed more power and purpose. At dinners in neighborhood restaurants, my friends snapped their fingers in front of my eyes, trying to garner my attention as restaurant servers awaited my food order. *Snap, snap.* "Dude, focus! What is with that dazed grin on your face?"

Luca said eventually he could get me on the security list to stay in his room at the carabinieri barracks, but for now, we should stay at a hotel. Desiring sexier accommodations than the last two places we'd slept, I browsed travel blogs curating Top Ten lists of boutique inns in Rome offering more intrigue than dull corporate brands or dated B&Bs. Scouring photos, poetic descriptions, and straightforward consumer reviews of lodgings ranging in price from reasonable to outrageous, I settled on a B&B called the Ariadne Inn near Piazza Barberini and Mia's Bernini Bristol.

Of course, the romance part heightened the trip's allure; I upgraded my lingerie and invested in sexy suede ankle boots. But the boldness, the thrill, the zest, of another voyage—jetting off to my newfound favorite European city for a whirlwind three days—felt just as energizing. Rebellious. Empowering.

On my way to JFK, I joked on social media: "Heading to Rome for the weekend! Don't tell Mom and Dad . . . "

I boarded the flight, unsuccessfully tried to sleep, and swatted away one sticky thought: Luca hadn't offered to pick me up at the airport, nor had he proposed sending his driver Paolo this time.

Determined to act like a local, I researched public transit—a train and a subway, the *metropolitana*—from the airport to Piazza Barberini. Landing at Fiumicino, I scanned yellow signs hanging from airport ceiling beams, searching for the word *treni* (trains). I spoke Italian to a man behind the Leonardo Express ticket desk. He responded in bored English and slid a rectangular ticket through a glass partition toward me. I asked, "Devo convalidare?" *Do I need to validate this ticket?*

I'd heard horror stories—potentially urban myths—of tourists charged astronomical fines for boarding trains without first validating tickets at designated machines. The agent took the ticket, poked a hole in it, and pushed it back to me. "Convalidato."

I snagged a window seat on the train and watched farmland shift to *urbana*—apartment buildings, T-shirts and underwear drying on balcony clotheslines, satellite dishes—as the train whipped toward Rome's Termini Station. From there, I easily maneuvered the metropolitana subway and popped aboveground ground right in Piazza Barberini. I glanced toward the Triton Fountain. No scaffolding!

Carrying merely a weekend duffel bag, I climbed a gentle hill and found the Ariadne Inn. The hotelier checked me in five hours early and handed me a key. I hoped a shower instead of one of my heavy-duty migraine pills would fend off the sleep-deprivation headache germinating behind my eyes. I texted Luca. He said he'd pick me up at the hotel after work, around 7 p.m. I slid into the king-sized bed, stretched like a starfish, and napped.

My head pulsated when I woke up—rhythmic punching against the bone at the base of my neck, the arch of my nose, the cavities behind both eyes. I forced myself out of bed to capitalize on an afternoon in Rome alone. No travel companion. No Luca. No tour guide. Just me.

I walked to the Trevi Fountain to get my geographical bearings. Oceanus did not wreck me like he had the first time. I changed tactics. Skipping all tourist hot spots, I chose twists and turns in my walking path based on whichever street names

(*Crociferi* [crucifers, people carrying crosses], *Delfini* [dolphins], *Polacchi* [Polish]) intrigued me. I landed in a small courtyard with a behind-the-scenes view of my three columns. I studied the grooves in the stone and seams where someone a long time ago had mended fallen marble and concrete with metal rods. The flaws, the brokenness, the bruises of history, made the structures even more interesting, more evocative. Not boring perfection or a superficial cover-up. The patched-together columns reminded me of Japanese *kintsugi*—how artists repair fragmented pottery by fusing pieces back together using molten gold or silver, accentuating the cracks, giving the fractures the most pivotal role in new art's creation. I thought of my own scars. A three-inch gash behind my knee caused by thirty feet of rubber-coated wire dog leash shearing off my skin when one of the beagles I'd shared with Trey took off after a rabbit; instead of going to the doctor for stitches, we slapped gauze on the wound and went to Trey's softball game. I contemplated internal scars. Is organ wear and tear from sorrow and grief visible to a doctor's eye in open-heart surgery?

Moving on, I found a *panetteria*, a bread shop. I pointed at a small sandwich in a glass case. "Uno, per favore." A clerk placed the sandwich in a wax paper sleeve. I sat outside on a stool and took a bite. Two rounds of flattened dough, slightly salty, a thin slice of mozzarella, another of prosciutto, plus a layer of something tangy yet sweet. Fig, perhaps. Mouthwatering.

I progressed to the Piazza della Rotonda and stared at the Pantheon to test whether I felt any more prods from Agrippa. Nothing new. My headache worsening, tourist chatter interfering with my mojo, I returned to the hotel.

I fell into bed again, slept until 6 p.m., then showered and dressed. Black jeans. Slouchy shoulder-baring black top. The new suede boots. Luca called the hotel phone. Apologized for bumping my pickup time by another hour. I was beginning to *hate* his job. He asked if I'd brought a jacket.

Fighting disappointment and a familiar feeling—unprior-itized—I opened the door to the hotel minibar and grabbed a bottle of Sangiovese by its neck.

The doorbell *finally* buzzed. I buried annoyance at his re-curring lateness. He hugged me, slid hands to my hip bones, pressed me against the windowsill, kissed me.

"Sei bellissima." *You're beautiful.* "You brought a jacket?"

I pointed at a thin white leather jacket lying on the bed. I'd tossed it into my suitcase as an afterthought. Two years into my life in New York—a year after my divorce from Trey and the trauma of 9/11 . . . the start of my relationship with Forrest—my style began transitioning from preppy, uptight Virginia lawyer to edgier New York wannabe-artsy-writer. I'd discovered a store called Runway. Began splurging on jeans embellished with pink crystals, green corduroys cuffed with brass grom-mets, T-shirts with sleeves resembling floral tattoos. And a sleek, cropped white leather jacket, six-inch zippers at each wrist.

"Perfetto. Andiamo," Luca said, grabbing my hand.

We squeezed into the hotel elevator the size of a phone booth, kissing, descending to the ground floor. Luca opened the building's heavy front door. He gestured toward a Harley David-son motorcycle. Chrome tailpipes gleamed in streetlight.

Holy shit.

Luca opened a compartment at the Harley's haunches. He handed me a black helmet too big for my head. He slid it over my hair, pulling the chin strap as tight as it would go. The globe flopped over my eyes. His own helmet fit snug on his shaved head. He straddled the bike. Released a heavy kickstand. Revved the engine. Motioned for me to climb behind him.

I flung a suede boot over the leather seat, wriggled forward, and wrapped my arms around his waist. He reversed the motor-cycle out of a parking space. Gunned the accelerator. As wheels hit cobblestone, the helmet jostled, covering my eyes and nose, then seconds later, jerked backward, exposing my forehead to

the elements even with the visor closed. The Harley sped up. I
closed my eyes and hung on. Wind whipped into the helmet. My
eyes watered.

Luca swayed the bike left and right. I leaned into him. He
reached his left hand back and squeezed my quadricep like *I've
got you. Don't worry.*

I thought, *I'm riding on the back of a motorcycle of a hot carabiniere officer, zooming by the Colosseum on a September night in
Rome. All the hard moments . . . the ones of despair and distress . . .
the ones that felt like a rusty saw hacking at my abdomen . . . shifted
my DNA around to clear a path for this one.*

I kept my eyes open as much as the wind and unpredictable oscillation of the helmet would allow. We threaded street
after street until Luca steered the bike into Piazza Navona and
parked. He helped me dismount. I felt wobbly. Windblown. A
bit numb. Unsexy.

I mentally recalibrated: *Stop it. You* are *sexy.*

Taking off the helmet, I wiped mascara from my cheeks.

Luca held my hand as we walked past the Fountain of the
Four Rivers, past Ganges's enormous foot, toward a restaurant
with an empty outdoor table.

We shared steaks and salads, exchanging stories of our respective lives since our August liaison. Afterward, we circled Piazza Navona on foot, my arm looped through his. I watched
his brown eyes canvass the crowd. My head jackhammered. A
combination of migraine, overconcentration on trying not to
fly off the back of the Harley, and not enough wine. I craved sex
and sleep. After a quick ride back to the hotel, Luca secured the
bike outside. In the elevator, he bit my upper lip, then the lower
one, took the room key from my hand, opened the door.

Shoes ricocheted off the floor. Jeans flew inside out across a
footrest at the edge of the bed. Lacy bra floated across a striped
pillow. His frugality with words again transformed into a surge of
speech. Italian. English. "Tutto tuo . . . " *All yours . . .* Adrenaline,
dopamine, a cocktail of other hormones, temporarily eclipsed

the pain ravaging my head. I liked seeing his rare smile emerge afterward. "Bella," he said.

He leaped up and found his phone. Set an alarm.

Th-thud. Headache flooded back like a tsunami. I pulled soft sheets over my body and turned on my side, pinching the bridge of my nose. I just needed to fall asleep, and the headache would hopefully fade away. Luca extinguished the bedside lamp and slid toward me.

"Buona notte, bella." Kissed my neck. Pressed his warm frame against mine.

🛵 🛵 🛵

His alarm jarred like a siren. He dressed quickly and left for work, promising we'd meet for dinner later. I swallowed half a migraine pill and went back to sleep. I absolved myself from any guilt about missing out on sights and sounds of the outside world, even the Roman version. The mission of this trip was romance and sex. Cultural horizon broadening could wait.

Around 5 p.m., Luca called to tell me an incident involving two fatalities required the attention of his entire team. Unsure when he'd finish the investigation, he urged me to go eat dinner without him and assured he'd join me as soon as he could.

"I am so sorry, tesoro," he said. "I will run to you as soon as I can."

"It's okay," I reassured. My skull still felt like it had been smashed with a mallet, and frankly I didn't mind spending more one-on-one time with the city, seeing if its whirring energy could smooth the jagged edges of my physical pain.

The cool September night air immediately dialed down the intensity of my headache. I zigzagged alleys, trying to remember how to get to Piazza delle Coppelle—the piazza with the enoteca where Mia and I drank wine with Giovanni while waiting for our table at Maccheroni. I couldn't find it. I kept wandering. I stumbled upon an outdoor trattoria with an aesthetic I liked. Handwriting on a chalkboard menu. Votive candles and fresh flowers on each table. A waiter approached with a smile. I held up one finger.

"Un tavolo per una persona, per favore?" *A table for one person, please?*

"Due?" *Two?*

"No, un tavolo per una, per favore," I repeated.

The waiter brought me a menu in English, and I asked him to please exchange it for an Italian one. Even if I made a rookie culinary blunder (such as mistaking *polpo* [octopus] for *polpetta* [meatball]), I swore to only speak and read Italian when exploring Rome alone. Studying and practicing other languages makes me happy, piques my curiosity about word origins, allows my brain to shift away from ruminating about unfinished work projects and instead play with puzzle pieces: verb conjugations, accents, proper pronunciations. Languages are arts-and-crafts supplies to me.

I'd researched Italian translations of food vocabulary I'd try to avoid: eel (*anguilla*), liver (*fegato*), horse (*cavallo*). I ordered a large bottle of acqua naturale and a small carafe of house red wine to keep the timpani in my head from daring to thump again. The waiter brought a basket of focaccia bread, a vial of olive oil, and a ball of burrata mozzarella the size of my fist. My second course—a bowl of rigatoni with peas and *salsiccia* (sausage)—and sips of the vino *rosso* made me feel almost human again.

Winding back toward the Ariadne Inn, I landed in Piazza delle Coppelle. Of course. Because I'd stopped looking for it. I spotted Giovanni smoking outside the enoteca and reintroduced myself. He insisted I sit and have a drink with him. I listened to Italian couples debate, a chorus of overlapping voices. I understood every seventh word. *Allora. Ma, dai. Amore. Sei pazzo.* (So. But, come on. My love. You're crazy.)

The flip phone jangled in my handbag. Luca explained he and his team were still tracking down witnesses and collecting evidence related to the incident, but he would come to the hotel no matter what time of night when he finished work.

At 2 a.m., the phone vibrated beneath the covers.

I ran down a spiral staircase to open the heavy hotel door to Luca's frown and apologetic eyes.

"Tesoro, I am so sorry," he murmured.

I hugged and kissed him. I didn't know how else to convey I didn't care how late he was. I'd been useless all day anyway. I just wanted to sleep next to him.

He undressed and fell into bed, squeezing me.

I woke up before he did. I lay as still as possible, worrying any slight move would jostle him awake and send him scurrying to his phone. I rejoiced—quietly—that my headache finally had vanished. I felt his brown eyes on me. We smiled and stared at each other. We lounged in bed for another hour before his sense of duty kicked in. He checked his phone.

"Tesoro, do you like football? We have been invited to the soccer match between Roma and Bologna this evening, but we don't have to go."

Oh my God, *finally a real plan.* "I would absolutely *love* to go."

"Okay, first, I will go home to shower and change. I need to go visit the widow of an old friend this afternoon. Will you come with me?"

"Yes!"

He picked me up two hours later in his Smart car. We drove to an apartment complex with a drab exterior—Soviet-esque, colorless. He held my palm in one hand and a cherry tart in the other as we entered the building. Elevator doors opened directly into an elegant flat, gold-framed portraits lining walls, tasseled curtains, velvet-tufted settees and sofas—like a scene from a Marie Antoinette movie. A diminutive woman with black-gray hair coiffed into a bun, dressed in a wool suit and lace-up heels, greeted Luca with many kisses. He smiled wider than he'd previously seemed capable. The woman welcomed me as well, grasping my hands and kissing my cheeks. She beckoned us into the ornate living room. A silver tea set rested on a marble coffee table. Biscotti dotted with confectioner's sugar sat on floral china.

"Parli italiano?" the woman asked me.

"Sì, un po'." *Yes, I speak a little Italian.* "Provo." *I try.*

She spoke to me in slow Italian, asked me how I liked Roma, where I live, what I do for work. When I stumbled over verb conjugations and vocabulary, she assisted. Luca sat next to me, hand on mine, smiling at the exchange.

She turned to him and asked about his role with the carabinieri. From their gentle dialogue, I deduced that her husband had known Luca well but had died a few years ago, and Luca checked in on her often. Luca explained he'd received two job offers in different lines of work. Security forces. Oil industry. I'd snuck a peek at his dog tags as he slept and finally discerned he was thirty-eight years old, five years younger than me. He'd served in the carabinieri for almost twenty years. He could retire soon and pursue a second career.

The lady turned to me and said, "He will never leave the carabinieri force. *È la sua vita.*" *It is his life.*

I nodded.

We said goodbye to the woman, promising to visit again.

"Insieme," she said, smiling, pointing at the two of us. *Together.*

Luca dropped me at the hotel so he could return home and change clothes again for the soccer game. He explained we'd be sitting in a VIP box with some of the players' wives.

Yikes.

I cobbled together the most VIP-esque, soccer-player-wife-worthy outfit I could from the contents of my weekend duffel bag: skinny black jeans; low-cut black top; strappy black high-heeled sandals; my longest, dangliest faux-diamond earrings; and a fancy man-size platinum watch I'd bought myself after Forrest and I split, Rowan died, and I sold my car to move back to New York. I topped the outfit with the white leather jacket, dabbed red gloss on my lips, and trotted down the hotel stairs to meet Luca outside. He wore a pin-striped dress shirt and a tailored suit. Shiny Ferragamo shoes.

Luca's dashboard radio blared Justin Bieber songs as we raced toward Rome's Olympic Stadium, the *Stadio Olimpico*. He invented a parking spot, reversing the Smart car up a muddy hill. I hoped the parking brake would hold; the vehicle seemed precariously positioned.

A ticket collector tied silver ribbons around our wrists, *Roma* embroidered in blue. As we entered a VIP dining area, waitresses in sleeveless tuxedo shirts handed us crystal glasses of prosecco. Tables overflowed with arrays of cheese, a palette of yellows, creams, and whites. Luca gripped my hand as important-looking men in designer suits jockeyed to greet him. He introduced me to one gentleman saying, "Insegnante, a New York." *Teacher, in New York.*

As we transitioned into the seating area of the open-air arena, the crowd chanted, "Roma! Roma! Roma!" Fans waved burgundy-and-ochre flags, some bearing the image of Rome's symbol—the she-wolf nursing twins Romulus and Remus. Luca guided me toward the VIP box. I took a seat at the end of one row. Two women in skin-tight leather pants and fur vests, bedecked in jewels, smoky makeup, manes of hair framing faces of silken skin, welcomed us.

As Roma battled Bologna on the field, I realized my face hurt from smiling. Luca sang the Roman anthem along with the crowd, teaching me the words. The players' wives clasped my hands in joy each time one of their husbands scored a goal. I took it all in. Inhaled the night air. Imprinted the blur of waving flags into my brain. Closed my eyes and listened to the exuberant chants—vowels and consonants swirling around me like musical notes.

Rome beat Bologna 4-0. One of the players' wives gestured to my camera. I handed it to her. She snapped a picture of Luca and me, stadium bleachers in the background, his head pressed against mine. We looked relaxed, content. *Insieme*. Together. I even sort of looked glam, skin glowy, highlighted hair thick and wavy, a hint of cleavage. His dress shirt unbuttoned one notch lower than an American guy would wear it.

Justin Bieber's song "Be Alright" played on our drive away from the stadium, lyrics alluding to long-distance love. I chuckled to myself, realizing I was philosophizing a Bieber song. I thought of a line from an Oasis track—the one that implies we probably shouldn't rely on the musings of rock 'n' roll bands to make major life decisions. Like I do with shiny red flags, I ignore that advice. I love placing my life in the palms of a rock 'n' roll band, reading lyrics like tea leaves.

Luca pulled into a pizzeria. He ordered two Peroni beers, fried mozzarella, and a large pizza. We indulged. Packaged the leftovers.

He stuffed the cardboard pizza box into the tiny refrigerator in my hotel room, grabbed my shoulders, tossed me to the bed, crawled toward me, and stripped off my clothes. His belt buckle pressed into my flesh. Our antics pulled the bed away from the wall, trundling us toward the middle of the room, which made us laugh.

At 6:30 a.m., his alarm blared. We awkwardly clocked foreheads trying to kiss in the dark.

I'd assumed he'd drive me to the airport. He said he couldn't. He had a nonnegotiable meeting with his *capitano*.

"Nessun problema," I shrugged off the mistaken presumption. "Voglio provare il treno ancora." I said I wanted to act Roman and take the train again, back to Fiumicino.

After a quick tight hug, Luca left. I turned on a lamp, grabbed the cardboard box from the refrigerator, and ate cold pizza. I tried to brew a mug of Nescafé instant coffee using a plug-in kettle, but after one sip, I dumped the undrinkable liquid in the bathroom sink. I packed my duffel bag, pushed the bed back to its proper spot, checked the room (reminding me how Trey and I used to check hotel rooms "for bunnies" after I accidentally left the first stuffed animal he'd given me in a motel on a football game road trip, rendering me devastated and guilt-ridden), closed the door behind me, and descended the hotel staircase.

At a café near the metropolitana station, I exchanged two euro coins for a foamy cappuccino and sipped it standing at the counter like the men in Armani suits, Vatican priest vestments, and orange sanitation worker uniforms. I boarded the correct metro to Termini Station, paid the fare for airport transit, watched commuters use the *validare* machine, punched my ticket, and hustled onto the next train bound for Fiumicino.

I heard the conductor announce—in Italian—that this train was indeed *not* the cheap commuter rail I thought I had boarded, but was a special faster mode of transit, and therefore more expensive. Anyone holding a commuter pass would need to pay the fee difference, and of course, a fine. A bead of sweat trickled down my neck. I'd spent my last euros on the coffee and subway token. I wasn't sure if the conductor would accept a credit card. I began panicking a bit.

You haven't intentionally done anything wrong. Just relax.

Thirty minutes of worrying later, ten minutes out from the airport, a Trenitalia agent entered the door to my train compartment, his face frozen in a scowl. He asked to see the ticket of a man in an overcoat and fedora seated at the far end of the carriage from me. The two men began arguing. The passenger waggled his paperwork back and forth in the official's face, gesticulating, spittle flying. The man clearly had the wrong ticket (as did I) and was incensed at having to pay the differential and a fine. The verbal warfare continued for ten glorious minutes as the train approached and then stopped in the airport station, automatic doors opening. I grabbed my duffel and scampered off the train.

Waiting at the gate for my flight, I checked the flip phone. No messages from Luca. I texted him: Ciao, tesoro. Thank you for a beautiful weekend. I hope your work goes well and that we can see each other again soon.

I didn't hear from him before my plane took off for New York.

🛵 🛵 🛵

My reentry into day-to-day life less bumpy than prior trips, I transitioned back into my routine. I taught my classes. Exercised. Explored new downtown restaurants with my friends. Luca's sweet nighttime and morning texts still arrived pretty regularly the first couple weeks I was home. My girlfriends bugged me to download the latest dating apps, but I resisted. I still hated the anxiety of first dates and remained convinced Luca and I were either in, or at some point could cultivate, a real relationship. Many nights, I ordered sushi or rotisserie chicken, watched *Law & Order: SVU*, played around with flight configurations to Rome for Thanksgiving, and researched summer teaching opportunities at American universities with Roman outposts. *I can totally make this work.*

Within a month, Luca started missing a day of communication here and there, claiming phone malfunctions or Wi-Fi problems. My brother and his wife came to New York to visit me at the beginning of November. At night, while they slept in my queen-size bed, I lay on my couch staring at my phone, willing it to deliver a new message from Italy. None came. At breakfast, when I confessed I was bummed Luca seemed to be backing away, my brother tried to give me a reality check. "The relationship is kind of unsustainable anyway, him being so far away."

By Thanksgiving, Luca went radio silent.

🛵 🛵 🛵

Maybe he met someone else. Maybe his intense job and the oceanic distance between us made the whole thing a nonstarter for him. Maybe he never wanted anything serious. Maybe he just wasn't that into me.

Whatever.

I'm glad I had my time with him. I'm glad I took a chance on our spark. I'm glad I learned a bit more about what I like and don't like—even in unimportant decisions like prosecco and hotel vibes.

From time to time, when rearranging stuff in my apartment, I come across a photograph I snapped the first night Luca rode by my table on his carabiniere motorcycle and turned his head in slow motion to look at me. And the snapshot of us at the Stadio Olimpico soccer match. Memories of those electric moments still stir my soul. Rome and Luca showed me I am a *tesoro*. A treasure.

And my dad was wrong.

3

vancouver

The wheels of my suitcase clicked along sidewalks and edges of curbs as I hunted for street signs leading me to Skwachàys Lodge—an Indigenous-run hotel in Vancouver, Canada. Pronounced "skwatch-eyes," a name given by the Squamish Nation to memorialize the original land footprint of salt marshes and underground springs, the hotel houses a fair-trade Indigenous art gallery, low-cost residences for local artists, and eighteen regular hotel rooms.

Stepping around unhoused folks sleeping on pavement, I noticed people openly buying, selling, and doing drugs in doorways—hypodermic needles tumbling to the ground. Arriving at Skwachàys Lodge, I found the front door locked. I rang a doorbell. A tall man—olive skin, creases near temples framing chestnut eyes, long black-gray ponytails resting on regal shoulders—greeted me, opening the door. He reached for the handle of my bag.

"You must be Heidi. You're here for two nights, correct? We have you in the Water Suite."

Painters, designers, and material suppliers from the Vancouver community collaborated on the design of each Skwachàys room, bringing themes like Feather, Air, Poem, Drum Circle, Earth, and Moon to life through choices of furniture, textiles, and wall decor.

"I see from your reservation request that you're interested in a sweat lodge ceremony," the proprietor stated. "The elder is available at two thirty tomorrow afternoon if that suits you."

"Yes, that would be awesome. Thank you."

I was excited for a do-over of my first sweat lodge experience now that no acute relationship drama clouded my thinking.

        ⌁   ⌁   ⌁

A decade earlier.

Still wrestling with whether, and how, to leave Forrest and our intimacy problems for good—exhausted by several years of fruitless and humiliating attempts to crack a conundrum I'd finally comprehended wasn't mine to solve—I'd left our dog Rowan in his care and flown to Cancun, Mexico. I'd boarded a two-hour shuttle to the village of Akumal for a three-day "spiritual" retreat.

A hippie named Andreas with unruly hair rang a gong to summon ten retreat participants—surfers, musicians, restaurant workers, nomads, and me—to our first midmorning yoga class. Though I was unfamiliar with the Sanskrit words he used to describe the initial series of yoga poses we'd be practicing, his buttery voice reassured me I could handle this, whatever *this* might entail.

I unfurled a borrowed rubber mat in a far corner of the yoga loft near an open window. Classmates undulated bendy bodies through sun salutations. A beach dog sauntered into the studio, trotted over to me, downward-facing-dogged, curled up on my mat, and fell asleep.

The least experienced yogi in the room, I fumbled my way through the ninety-minute class. Andreas occasionally stopped at my mat to press warm hands into my hunched shoulders and rigid spine, nudging my tense body to relax into proper angles.

After a quick wardrobe change, our group piled into a van. Destination: *temazcal sweat lodge*. Like Andreas's Sanskrit phrases, I lacked a clear understanding of what those three consecutive words meant or to what I had consented. The retreat organizers had marketed *temazcal* as a "transformative" experience. This thing with Forrest was either going to resolve soon or I needed to muster the courage to leave. "Transformative" sounded worth a try.

The retreat van pulled into a rutted driveway shaded by a canopy of jungle vines. A compact silver-haired Mexican gentleman greeted us. Women in embroidered peasant blouses and flowy skirts poured water from clay pitchers into matching mugs. A few of the yogis washed down green-and-blue pills with sips of water—some sort of drug, I supposed, to enhance the advertised transcendence of the experience. A girl with a French accent opened her palm, offering me one. I declined. I needed to face whatever we were about to do head-on.

Humidity hung in the air like gelatin as guides led us through draperies of plant life. In a clearing, I noticed a grouping of small structures shaped like halved tennis balls layered in woven wool blankets. I smelled sage. *Wait a minute.* At hearing the terms *sweat* and *lodge*, I'd envisioned something like an outdoor sauna, maybe a tad on the rustic side, *sure*, or maybe something log cabin-y. The rounded huts in the Mexican jungle were no bigger than Volkswagens.

The silver-haired man led us toward the domes. Two helpers tended to a kiln nearby, heating stones. An assistant tugged a corner of a tasseled rug draping the front of one lodge, revealing an arched entrance.

Ten of us are supposed to cram inside that thing? No. Way.

My stomach twitched. A pinch of panic. One of the yogis—a blonde Californian who'd moved to Akumal a decade earlier to open a bakery next to the yoga studio—noticed my bugging eyes.

"It'll be okay. You'll be fine, I promise," she murmured, grabbing my elbow.

The helpers placed a bowl of hacked aloe chunks inside the hut. My comrades shed outer clothing layers. The French girl stripped down to bikini bottoms, bouncing as she waited her turn to enter the dome. One by one, the yogis crouched to their knees and crawled inside.

I tried to rally a sense of adventure. *Trust the universe. You're not going to die in the middle of a Mexican jungle. You've been seeking clarity every day for two years on what to do about Forrest. Maybe a Mexican sweat lodge will finally yield the answer, or a method to leave with the least amount of trauma. Be brave. Get in the hut.*

The helper held the rug flap open for me. I kneeled, edged inside, touched my forehead to the mud floor and scooted clockwise, as instructed. I squeezed into a vacant spot between the French girl and the Californian. I didn't want anyone else's skin touching mine, but that desire seemed delusional given the cramped quarters. The silver-haired man—now shirtless and evidently our shaman—entered and positioned himself near the arch. The flap closed. We sat lotus style in darkness for a moment. The flap opened again as the helpers, wearing heatproof gloves and wielding shovels, piled hot stones in the center of the hut. The shaman ladled water from a wooden bucket onto the stones. Droplets sizzled and crackled as they landed. Steam billowed, gluing my contact lenses to my eyes. The air thickened. I couldn't see anything or anyone. My lungs strained. My heart thudded. My eyes welled with tears.

I hadn't cried in so long. Well, for a whole entire week.

I grabbed the Californian's knee. "I don't think I can do this," I whispered, my words melting into mist, tears intermingling with sweat.

"Just breathe. Five counts in. Five counts out," she coaxed. "You're okay. I've done temazcals a zillion times. You'll be all right."

She placed her hand on my sticky back, pressing, releasing slightly, then pressing again, reminding me that I, indeed, knew how to inhale and exhale. Haze spiraled toward a chimney—an exit—in the roof.

Okay, there's a hole in the roof and that front flap opens. You're not trapped. There's air in here. Breathe in, breathe out. You're also not trapped with Forrest, you know. You can leave. You're not going to die if you break up with him. Remember . . . nothing will ever be as bad as leaving Trey. That was pure agony. You survived.

The shaman began to chant. Invited us to repeat refrains. I breathed—five counts in, five counts out—and tried to join in. As water from the shaman's ladle splattered on the rocks, vaporizing into puffy clouds, he sang about fire . . . water . . . wind . . . earth. He recited poetry about purification. He passed the bowl of aloe chunks. Through the fog, I saw the Californian miming that I should take a piece of aloe and rub it into my skin. I did.

After numerous rounds of chanting and aloe rubbing, the shaman directed us to curl into fetal positions on the ground. I sensed bodies shifting, though I couldn't see much. The French girl climbed over me and shoved her way out of the hut. I inched into precious empty territory she left behind. I closed my eyes, coiled into a ball on the surprisingly cool earth, rubbed aloe into my back and shoulders, and hugged myself. I started to feel floaty, detached from my surroundings. As the shaman and the others chanted, I focused on one word: *clarity, clarity, clarity.* Please God, just one ounce of clarity about what to do about Forrest. *It's okay to leave him you know. You've tried everything, every dumb, mortifying, degrading trick to fix your sex life. You deserve intimacy. You cannot . . . should not . . . will not . . . live without it. It's okay for you to move on. You can simultaneously love him and leave him. You're not a failure. You're also not a bad person. You don't need to be ashamed of craving touch, especially from someone you love.*

Eventually, the flap opened. Light streamed in. Blurriness segued to lucidity. The yogis unfolded from child poses, wriggled out of the hut, and galloped like gazelles past ferns, vines, and cacti toward a natural swimming hole. A *cenote*, a derivation of a Mayan word for a sacred well—a sinkhole created by collapsed limestone exposing groundwater. The others leaped, cannonballed, and dove into the shimmering blue green. The French girl splashed the others who floated on their backs, smiling and laughing.

I reached the edge of the cenote. Normally, I'd start fretting about whether snakes or piranha or barracuda or eels or flesh-eating spiders or other jungle creatures potentially lurked in there, just waiting to puncture my skin. I jumped in. The water felt soft, chilled but not chilly. I dunked below the surface. I swam in circles for a few minutes, then stroked toward a stony landing. I slipped trying to gain a foothold on mossy rocks, but eventually secured sufficient grip to pull myself from the water. I was the only temazcal partaker not lingering in the cenote, but I didn't care. I was proud I'd stayed in the sweat lodge. I hadn't bailed out. A helper handed me two warm towels. I wrapped both around me, pressing the pads of my feet into smooth stones.

Forrest is never going to end the relationship; he won't be the "bad guy." You're the brave one. You will be okay. You will be better than okay. You are going to roar.

Eager to see my "Water Suite" at the Skwachàys Lodge, I followed the ponytailed man through a gift shop—displays of macramé dream catchers, wispy feathered jewelry, handmade soaps, and pottery—to an elevator. My room's furnishings prompted me to look up the word for a "person obsessed with trees." (It's *dendrophile*.) Whittled timber composed the desk. Tree stumps doubled as nightstands. Lumber inlaid with polished river stones served as the bed's headboard. Abstract images of orca (representing *community*) and salmon (signifying *survival*)—in metallic grays and oranges—splashed color onto white walls.

Starving, I headed back outside. Rain drizzled. On the hotel's doorstep, I passed two guys engaged in a transaction that seemed to be going awry. They argued, slurring words. Crumpled currency floated to the pavement. I sidestepped them, crossed two avenues, followed a sidewalk along a row of restaurant doorways illuminated by flickering gas lanterns, and ducked into a wine bar. A waiter informed me the kitchen had already closed for the night. But he ushered me to a table near a window. Brought me a glass of regional red wine from a bottle that had definitely been open too long. Syrupy texture. Flavor of overripe raisins.

I hate raisins.

My grandmother Doris, who taught me to read when I was three years old and whom I called Mommom (my mom's mom), loved telling a tale of how I arrived home from kindergarten one day and announced, "I ate *four* raisins," like I'd made some grand societal sacrifice.

I sipped the wine anyway, then ordered something different from the Okanagan Valley, a Vancouver winemaking region. I stared out the window and thought about Mommom.

☃ ☃ ☃

I loved all four of my now-deceased grandparents, but I'd had the closest bond with Mommom. She had curly jet-black hair and feisty hazel-green eyes and drove a 1966 sky-blue Ford Mustang, refusing to wear a seat belt. A devoted Baptist, she cooked blueberry pies for church coffee hours and delivered banana bread to sick friends and parishioners in local hospitals. She sewed her own clothes and stitched quilts as gifts. She played bridge. Loved bargain shopping. Growing up during the Depression, she hadn't attended college right out of high school but instead had immediately joined the workforce as a stenographer. She was my first travel idol, bringing home presents from trips she paid for on her secretary salary and my grandfather's electrician income: wooden clogs from Amsterdam, a plastic camel from Egypt, a kilt from Scotland. During my high school years, Mommom enrolled in community college courses, studying religion and philosophy, eventually earning a college degree around the same time I graduated from UVA. I admired her bookworm intellect and her passion for learning. Likewise, she encouraged mine. She loved hearing about my good grades, my spelling bee and National French Contest victories, and other academic awards.

Throughout my childhood and teenage years, my family spent every Sunday after church at Mommom and Poppop's house. Mommom cooked butter beans and pork roast while the rest of us watched football. She whipped up batches of whiskey sours and sangria for the adults, sneaking my brother and me our first tastes of alcohol.

My relationship with Mommom remained steadfast, so long as I didn't express any budding perspectives about religion or politics that differed from the family dogma. At ten years old, I'd made the mistake of repeating something a teacher had said about then-presidential-candidate Ronald Reagan: "He's going to start a nuclear war." Thinking nuclear war sounded pretty bad, I announced at Sunday dinner that, if I were old enough to vote, I'd cast my ballot for incumbent President Jimmy Carter, the Democrat peanut farmer. All four adults quickly admonished me, "Young lady, do not even think about turning into one of those rebellious teenagers who goes against your family's beliefs." I blushed, felt ashamed, but didn't understand what I'd done wrong. Mommom withheld her usual hug goodbye that night.

In high school, when I started learning about controversial social issues like abortion and the death penalty, any attempt to explore a nascent viewpoint that strayed from my family's creed likewise met with withdrawal of connection and affection. Stern looks. Scolding. Withholding of eye contact. Silent treatment.

Having opinions became scary.

My relationship with Mommom changed further when boys began offering opportunities—albeit innocent—to learn stuff my family couldn't teach me. The summer before I left for college, I stayed at Mommom and Poppop's house while my parents were off doing a Bible beach mission somewhere. A friend—a bookish guy I'd known in high school—invited me to a gala at the Smithsonian Museum (where he'd been interning) honoring Christopher Reeve, the actor who'd played the original Superman in the 1970s and 1980s films. I loved the event—my first exposure to the wonder of art museums, capped off with a hug from, and a photo with, the world-famous actor (eight years before his tragic horseback riding accident left him paralyzed). My school buddy drove me home. We must have been late. Mommom stormed out of the house and dragged me from the car without a word.

Once I started dating Trey, he and Mommom bickered over the dumbest things, like whether Michael Jordan was or was not the greatest basketball player of all time. If Mommom said the sky was blue, Trey deemed it purple. It rankled her how much I loved being around his tight-knit family, his horde of cousins, his parents who exerted a huge effort to make me feel special. Each time Trey and I ran off on a fun road trip with his siblings, or enjoyed one of his mother's epic gourmet dinner parties, I paid for it with silent treatment from Mom and Mommom. When they finally spoke to me again, they rebuked me for "choosing Trey's family over my own."

When my marriage splintered and I fled from Virginia to New York, I spent less face-to-face time with my grandparents. Two years later, when Forrest entered my life, the familial competition began all over again. After any voyage someplace experiential—the New Forest in England, the French and Dutch sides of St. Maarten, the Pacific Northwest—to spend time with Forrest's globally diverse and affluent parents and siblings, a supplemental guilt trip inevitably followed.

Though I sat next to Mommom's hospital bed when she died of old age at ninety-two, we never fully resolved the tension between us.

She appears often in my dreams. And my travels. Maybe she's telling me we're okay.

☺   ☺   ☺

I woke up in Skwachàys's Water Suite, surprised to discover I'd slept through the night, a rarity. I dressed and skipped down an inner stairwell in search of food. A fire snapped and popped in a hearth in the hotel's dining area. Two resident artists, Indigenous women in their late twenties, sat at one end of a community table, exchanging ideas for promoting their paintings on social media. I poured coffee into a clay mug and selected a tureen of yogurt topped with homemade raspberry jam. I noticed a basket of fried dough. A handwritten sign said, "Try these Indigenous *bannock.*" *Bannock* are unleavened, flat, and oval, made from flour, water, and lard, then baked or fried. The word derives from the Gaelic *bannach*, meaning *morsel*. Reportedly, Scottish fur traders introduced the word to (and were among colonists that forced new foods upon) Indigenous people of Canada. I placed two bannock on a plate, adding dollops of orange marmalade from ceramic thimbles.

I left the hotel in search of an exercise path through Stanley Park, a thicket of maple, fir, and cedar trees bordering a body of water called Burrard Inlet. I reached a leafy grove surrounding a famous collection of totem poles, sculpted wooden columns decorated with faces of birds—stern green eyes, yellow beaks, black-and-white wings. Totem poles, also called "monumental" poles, memorialize community heritage. Carvings of animals, people, or supernatural beings represent family crests, legacy, and historical events. I pondered how different my individual identity is from my family's. My parents have church and each other. My brother has his wife, his kids, his carpentry. I have travel, writing, boxing, and U2. We lack a common core.

I showered at the hotel, using eucalyptus soap mixed and molded by up-and-coming artisans, then reread an email confirming the sweat lodge appointment details. In the temazcal in muggy Mexico, I'd worn a bikini. In Vancouver, the temperature hovered in the mid-fifties. I dialed the front desk and inquired about recommended attire.

A soft-spoken woman advised, "Just something comfortable. No metal. It gets hot in there."

At 2:20, I rode the elevator to Skwachàys's rooftop. A circle of benches constructed from chopped logs sat in an atrium. A pair of antlers rested on one pew. I stepped onto an outdoor patio, recognizing a halved tennis ball structure. This one sat in a red base—a large saucer—on travertine slabs. Brown, orange, yellow, green, and purple wool blankets covered the dome. A pinned-open entryway flap revealed a soil bed inside.

I turned toward the bench circle and noticed two men, one in his sixties, the other late forties, arriving. The elder one nodded hello and introduced himself.

"I'm Old Hands." *Best name ever.* "This is my friend and helper, Robert." Robert, thin and tall, wore a turquoise-and-bone necklace and one feathered earring. "Have you ever done a sweat before?"

"Once. In Mexico about ten years ago. I was scared," I confessed.

"Ah, well, we won't let anything happen to you, don't worry." Old Hands winked.

"Am I the only one?" I looked around for other hotel guests.

"Looks that way," Old Hands said.

He lit a match and held it to the edge of a bundle of silvery sage.

Robert pulled a folded hotel bathrobe from a cupboard. "Go ahead into this little room and change out of your clothes into this robe. You're going to be close to the soil—representing Earth. You want any synthetic, human-made barrier to be as minimal as possible."

I felt slightly awkward about the prospect of being naked under a robe in the presence of two unfamiliar men but, at the same time, amped to experience this sweat lodge one-on-one with the shaman instead of sardined with nine other people like in Mexico. I tucked into the bathroom to change.

Old Hands swirled the bundle of smoking sage around my shoulders, hips, back, and head—"smudging" my energy. He explained the sweat ceremony involved four stages. Robert would help him maneuver hot stones heating up in a kiln on the patio into the lodge.

As I followed Old Hands outside, my heartbeat revved. I recalled the panic I'd felt in the jungle temazcal in Mexico, the thick steam and close body contact tricking me into thinking I couldn't breathe. But I reminded myself, I *did* breathe. *I am in control of my own lungs.*

Old Hands removed his long-sleeved shirt and pants—leaving him in swimming trunks. He stooped to the ground and disappeared into the sweat lodge. Robert passed two flat drums—the size and shape of tambourines—to Old Hands through the opening, then gestured at me to enter. I gathered the folds of my robe, hunched at the entryway, and climbed inside. The dirt felt cool against my shins. As directed, I crawled clockwise and sat cross-legged on a flat pillow. Old Hands slipped me a small satchel. He listed various herbs it contained, including white sage and a few I didn't recognize. He handed me a drum. In the light trickling in from the entrance, I noticed the drum had a ram painted on it—Aries, like me.

Old Hands asked Robert to start us off with six stones.

"If you get too hot, just lie down," Old Hands advised.

I liked the cold earth touching my skin. I love being cold.

Robert used fireproof gloves and the antlers I'd seen on the bench to move the first stone from the kiln to a spot at the center of the soil bed between Old Hands and me. The heat generated by the single stone expelled beads of sweat from my pores. Old Hands asked me to reach inside the satchel and sprinkle herb granules onto the stone. The herbs burst like shooting stars.

The sixth stone placed, Robert closed the flap, leaving Old Hands and me in darkness. He asked me to slap the drum. I felt dumb, at first. Clumsy. Performative. But I complied. He beat his drum and began chanting a call-and-response. Robert's deep voice thundered in refrain outside the dome. I patted my drum with an open palm. Sweat poured down my cheeks. I focused on the coolness of the ground melding to the bare skin of my glutes, hamstrings, calves, ankles.

Phase One.

Old Hands prompted me to state my name and yell, "All my relations!" *Loudly*. I smirked at the likelihood that all my

Episcopalian and *Baptist* relations would likely be aghast if they knew what I was doing. At that thought, I gripped the rim of the drum with my left hand and hit the goat skin membrane *hard* with my right hand. The percussion, the impact, the collision, felt good. Active, not passive. Old Hands and Robert echoed one another, hollering a word that sounded like "Hopa" or "Oopa."

Old Hands explained, next, he'd place three herbs on the six rocks: more white sage, copal (good for removing negative energy and blockages), and juniper. He asked Robert for more stones. I dusted herbs on them. Particles crackled into starburst.

Phase Two.

Old Hands urged me to beat my drum harder. I hammered it with a clenched fist. Sweat streamed down my spine. My feet stuck to opposite shins.

Old Hands yelled, "All my relations!"

I countered, "All my relations!"

He encouraged, "State what you need. Not what you want. *Why* are you here?"

I hesitated. I inhaled the herbal vapor. Sweat dripped into dirt beneath me. I struggled to articulate necessities and pound the drum at the same time.

I said, "I think . . . I need . . . to let go . . . of fear . . . anger . . . guilt . . . shame . . . anxiety. I need help understanding why conflict . . . with family . . . or with guys . . . freaks me out . . . scares me . . . numbs me. I need to stop feeling afraid of someone not loving me or wanting me. Actually, I need to love me, the real me. Oh, and I need to stir the confidence to write . . . about messy stuff."

Old Hands asked Robert for more stones. I flecked more herbs on them. Sparks combusted.

Phase Three.

Old Hands announced a healing phase. He called me "sweetie" and "little girl." Urged me to do a body survey.

"Where do you hurt?"

Ugh, definitely a moderately dented heart. My ridiculous head-aches. Constant stomach confusion. Blotchy skin. Perpetual blush.

Lungs, bones, and muscles feel okay right now though.

Old Hands explained the ritual of passing the peace pipe. He grinned, declaring the tobacco hallucinogenic-free. "Liability disclaimer," he chuckled.

He held a match to a bowl at the end of a long cylinder, took several puffs from a mouthpiece, and handed the pipe to me. I placed my lips around the stem and sucked.

Nothing happened.

Old Hands chuckled again. "You obviously don't smoke. That's a good thing. Inhale really, really deeply."

I tried. Somehow, I *extinguished* the peace pipe. *My fucking energy snuffed out a peace pipe.* Which reminded me of the time I decided to feng shui (the Chinese practice of arranging one's living or working space to foster positive flow of energy) my first New York apartment and realized a pile of boxing gloves occupied my "love corner."

Old Hands called Robert to relight the pipe. We tried again. To my extreme relief, I generated embers.

More stones. More herbs. More *snap-crackle-pop*.

Phase Four.

Thanking our relations.

I squeezed the drum between my kneecaps and battered it with both palms. Old Hands chanted. We inhaled herby mist. Cold ground pressed into my skin. My sweat—my extract—merged with earth.

At first, I resisted thanking my relations. In my hardest times, throughout all the stuff with Trey and Forrest, most of my relations made things worse, not better. Made me feel damaged. At fault. Told me all the bad stuff happened because I "refuse to give my life to God," because I resist going to church. "If you would choose a Christian man, this wouldn't be happening to you," they'd said. "You need to be brought to your knees," they'd said.

Not helpful. Debilitating rather.

Old Hands wouldn't let me off the hook. "Thank our relations!" he yelled.

I tried. I concentrated on Mommom. I appreciated that she inspired my love of books, my desire to explore the world, my thirst for learning new things. I wish we had talked through our drift. I think she would adore the life I've created for myself now.

I thought of my brother Chris, how different we are but how we've always loved each other unconditionally, listened to one another, and supported our mutual independent streaks— in our respective professional lives, and in needing to break free of parental expectations.

I considered the reality that I know my parents are technically proud of me, my academic accomplishments, how I look on paper. They tell me that all the time. How they brag to their church friends. I just wish they *liked* me.

Wait. Why on Earth does it matter anymore if they like me? I've built a wildly full and rich life—my hilarious friends, my boxing training, my Italian studies, my students, my teaching, my writing, my trips, my adventures, my spiritual connection to U2 music.

Old Hands and Robert chanted. I banged the drum. I felt strong. Proud. Bold. Real. Not anxious or afraid.

Old Hands took the drum from my hand.

The ceremony complete, Old Hands and Robert guided me clockwise out of the hut, back to the indoor bench circle, and handed me a glass bottle of ice-cold water. We chatted a bit, more like bar patrons than humans emerging from a shamanic ritual. Old Hands explained that he and his wife do "a sweat" once a week. They host group ceremonies on private land outside Vancouver.

He handed me a business card: *Old Hands. Reconciliation Consulting. Traditional Healing.* I thanked him and Robert and tendered the "elder fee" the hotel suggested. I grabbed my bundle of clothes and shoes and descended the stairwell to my room, still in the drenched robe.

After a long shower, rubbing peppermint bath oil into my skin, I redressed and set off to find an enoteca called Salt my best friend Clay recommended. (I'd met Clay five years earlier through a mutual Manhattan friend; he and I had bonded immediately over our introversion, obsession with the short-lived yet riotously funny television show *Happy Endings*, and shared love of books, music, fitness . . . and wine.) I chose a seat on a window banquette ideal for people watching. A waiter pushed a low table constructed of bundled twigs and branches, ends sawed flat and lacquered, toward my knees. I ordered a tasting trio of wines with allegorical names: Sage Hills's "Rhymes with Orange," Anarchist Mountain's "The Philosopher," and Echo Bay's "Synoptic." I ate bites of duck prosciutto and thin slices of kielbasa sausage—savory juxtaposed with sweet globs of creamy ricotta cheese and dabs of honey spooned from handcrafted ramekins.

Sipping orange wine, staring out the plate glass window at strangers holding hands, I reflected on the rooftop sweat lodge experience, its remarkable difference from the Mexico temazcal. This time, I felt daring, adventurous, open to the experience. Instead of catastrophizing about suffocating in the jungle, I whacked the drum and yelled. Last time, trauma kept me timid. This time, sweat culled trauma and diffused it into cool earth.

On my flight home, I wrote in my journal: *I do miss affection. I long for the spark, the jolt, the supercharge of feeling attracted to someone new. I don't miss my heart hurting though, the inability to breathe under a blanket of fear . . . of rejection, deprivation, withholding, abandonment. I don't miss contorting myself, suppressing my own fire, to fit someone else's caricature they've drawn of me. I wonder if I will trust enough again to let someone in. I hope so. For now, I'm happy I have the freedom to pick a spot on a map and say, "I'm going there. I'm trying that."*

And nothing and no one can stop me.

4

peru

I woke up, nostrils flaring like a racehorse's, straining for air. My tongue tasted gritty. My throat, pasty. I tried inhaling through my mouth, forming an *O* with desiccated lips. My heart thumped. My chest felt caged, straitjacketed. It took me a solid minute to remember where I was. I fumbled for a lamp switch. No button. No pull chain. My fingers grazed a small disk. I twisted clockwise. Counterclockwise. Finally, light. I rubbed my nose with the back of my hand, trying to manually kick-start oxygen flow. A red streak painted my knuckles. I licked my upper lip. Copper. Wet. Hot.

I bolted from bed, tripping over a suitcase, aggravating an ache in the arch of my left foot. I kicked a hiking shoe out of the way. Noticed a pair of leggings, two layers of sweat-wicking tops, windbreaker, and merino socks laid out on the floor. Like a chalk drawing of a dead body.

Peru. Oh yeah, I'm in Peru. Breathe.

My lungs seemed packed with quicksand.

Breathe. This is normal. You're in Peru. Cusco, remember. You haven't adjusted to the altitude yet. Slow down. Breathe. In. Out.

I lurched to the bathroom. Turned on the shower. Water splashed against stone tiles. The letters on the faucet knobs confused me. I saw a *C.* But no *H. Which direction is hot? What the fuck does* F *stand for? Calm down. Think.* In Italian, *F* is *freddo,* cold. Oh yeah, *frío. Frío* in Spanish. *C* is hot. *Caldo* in Italian. *Caliente* in Spanish. I cranked the valve as *C* as it would go. Steam hovered above the tub basin. I snatched plush towels from a wall rack. Slumped to the floor. Craned my neck over the tub's edge and sucked hot mist. Counted to five before exhaling. Dunked a towel into the hot water and held it against my face, hoping moisture would soothe dried-out nasal membranes. Pink blood stained the towel, dribbling my hands and wrists.

In: 1, 2, 3, 4, 5. *Out*: 1, 2, 3, 4, 5. *You're okay. It's the altitude. This is normal. Breathe.*

I realized I was crying. Nosebleeds always trip a wire.

$$\wedge \quad \wedge \quad \wedge$$

When I was ten, my family moved into a historical yet dilapidating home in Northern Virginia that the church—my dad's employer—rented from the city of Fairfax for a dollar. My brother and I were convinced the house was cursed. Weird things happened the year we lived there. A dump truck ran a red light and crashed through the front porch into my mom's piano room, luckily empty at the time. A vagrant broke into the house when we were away, slept in my parents' bed, and used my dad's razor, leaving gray whiskers in the sink. I got an inexplicable never-ending nosebleed and missed a week of school. I tried napping away boredom at home alone, but creepy footsteps in the attic kept my nerves on high alert.

Later, in high school, one afternoon it snowed. The popular girls—the field hockey stars, the lacrosse players, the cheerleaders—staged a snowball fight. One hurled a cold orb at one of her friends. Missed her target. Whacked me in the face. My nose bled for hours.

Ten years later, a few weeks after my wedding and law school graduation, I was studying bar exam flash cards at one of Trey's fast-pitch softball games. A foul ball flew into the bleachers, slamming into my nose, lips, and chin. Epic nosebleed. Trey took me home, put me to bed with an ice pack and Kleenex, then disappeared. An hour later, I realized he'd left me. Gone back to finish his game.

Stop. None of that is happening right now. Peru. Vacation. Hiking adventure. Relax. Take another altitude pill. Chill.

I rifled through my day pack for a plastic baggie of white pills my friend Justine gave me. A fellow intense migraine sufferer, she'd implored me to pack a few Diamox for Peru.

"At least take a half a pill on the flight to Lima, another before you fly to Cusco, and definitely one the first morning and evening before you start the hiking trip," she urged. "You'll feel worlds better, I promise."

I grabbed a bottle of water from the nightstand and downed a half-moon pill. I noticed a mug resting on a book near the lamp. Very unlike me to risk defacing an author's book cover with a water stain. I grabbed the cup and wiped the gloss of the paperback. I smelled the mug's contents. Coca tea. Its scent—a heavier, bitter-er, green tea. Like fresh grass clippings with a dash of parsley.

When I'd checked into the hotel—a converted monastery— the concierge, the bellhops, the front desk personnel, the cleaning staff, the wide-eyed guests who'd arrived before me, even the roaming hotel dogs . . . all seemed to nod reverently toward a table pressed against a wall in a bookshelf-lined living room. A fire crackled in a stone hearth radiating the fragrance of what I'd erroneously assumed was eucalyptus. The aroma: palo santo wood, revered by Peruvian shamans for its sacred properties. A silver hot-water urn like the one my grandmothers had polished to a sparkle for church coffee hours, a runner woven by artisan hands, and round wooden bowls containing de-stemmed sprigs resembling bay leaves sat on the altar-like table. A tray held painted cups and saucers—expectantly. *Drink me.*

"Place a leaf or two in a mug, steep it in hot water for a few minutes, sip the tea, and the headaches, dizziness, and nausea from the high altitude should stay away," nearly everyone I'd encountered in the last forty-eight hours had counseled.

"So . . . is coca leaf what makes cocaine?" I'd asked the front desk clerk. I've still never even smoked weed. Red wine is my vice.

He smiled and said, "Madam, you would have to drink vats and vats and vats of coca tea to feel even one tiny sensation similar to consuming cocaine. Coca tea is legal and medicinal. Indeed, the leaves of the coca plant contain the same alkaloids as pure cocaine. However, the quantity of the alkaloid in raw leaves is minuscule. Drink the tea."

My mind flashed to Forrest and his California ad agency buddies snorting thick lines of blow off the glass base of the Crate & Barrel cake pedestal Trey and I had received as a wedding gift twelve years earlier. The domed pedestal had only housed an actual cake twice. But I had swaddled in Bubble Wrap, packed, and gingerly moved the two-part dish eight times, dwelling to dwelling to dwelling, since my divorce. A lone chip betrayed its innocence and experience.

The memory of Forrest's louche use of my glassware stirred another montage.

I'd flown home from my Mexico temazcal trip. Entered our rental house in Laguna Beach. Stepped into our living room, our dog Rowan running happy circles around me. I noticed green stains in the white Berber carpet. I crouched down. Touched damp blots. Dialed Forrest's mobile phone.

"Hey honey-bunny," he said. "Um . . . ohhhh, must be the ink from one of my PowerPoint decks. Yeah . . . yeah, I remember . . . I spilled water on it."

As I listened to Forrest's voice link syllables into a straight-up lie, his seductive accent skillful at camouflaging misdeeds, I rotated my head to the left. Noticed plastic containers the size of 35-millimeter film canisters staring at me. From my grandfather's antique side table. Next to my favorite photo of Forrest and me. Tan, grinning. Us against the world.

I saw small tubs of body paint I'd bought in a pathetic attempt to persuade Forrest to touch me, after he'd brought the *Sports Illustrated* body paint swimsuit edition home from work. I thought he'd be into it. The paint had gathered dust in a shoebox beneath our bed, unused.

Until apparently now.

The carpet stains inked the deal. I finally left.

I sipped tepid coca tea in my monastery hotel room, beginning to feel less manic.

I climbed into the mahogany bed, draping a warm wet wash-cloth over my nose and mouth, breathing dampness. I fell back asleep.

My friend Polina, knowing I like travel and self-discovery, had suggested the idea of a trip to Peru. We'd started off as teaching colleagues collaborating on assignments for our students at a Southern California law school, then forged a deeper friendship outside of work. She'd confided curiosity about the tradition of ayahuasca—a medicinal spiritual ceremony said to broaden one's consciousness through consumption of a psychoactive tea designed to purge mental and physical toxins and potentially launch a psychedelic journey toward the true self. Polina's husband wasn't interested, but she thought I might be. Not quite ready for the ayahuasca extreme, I roped her into a six-day hiking tour from Cusco to Machu Picchu led by an adventure travel company. Quelling Polina's initial nervousness about the strenuousness of the daily treks, the company's website promised multiple fitness options per day, ranging from easy to ambitious.

I located Polina at a breakfast table with fellow hikers. Our trip guides—a tall handsome Mexican named Manuel and an earthy, bohemian Portlander named Josh—led introductions while we ate. Our group included a kind, bookish pair of thera-pists in their fifties; a grandfather named Wade and his teenage grandsons; a Manhattanite in her seventies; a wealthy family from Silicon Valley, the Darcys; plus Polina and me. The Darcys—father, mother, daughter, and son, all blond-haired, blue-eyed, and athletic—announced they'd already hiked Machu Picchu on a prior family trip but were "superstoked" to be doing it again.

Manuel and Josh explained that each morning we'd convene at breakfast at an appointed time to hear the "route rundown," a summary of the day's hiking options and corresponding safety protocols. Polina planned to choose the low-key itinerary each day; she wanted to get a reasonable degree of exercise, but her priority in visiting Peru was to relax and absorb the cultural experiences, cuisine, and crafts. I wanted to push myself cardiowise and see if I could handle the moderate, if not advanced, hiking circuits. Polina and I made a pact to meet up at all meals and sightseeing events, but not feel obligated to hike together.

Manuel, Josh, and a Peruvian historian named Hector led our crew on an introductory walk through the town of Cusco, the former capital of the Inca Empire (reigning between the thirteenth and sixteenth centuries), pointing out archaeological discoveries, Spanish colonial architecture, city squares, and Incan ruins. Mr. Darcy—an investment banker—clung to Hector's flank, energetically interjecting his foundational knowledge of Cusco's and Peru's history.

As our troupe approached each set of Cusco's steep steps, the Darcys challenged one another in a footrace. I overheard Manuel and Josh quietly surveying the stamina of the rest of us, anticipating how we'd fare on the upcoming hikes and deciding how they'd allocate their chaperoning responsibilities.

The sun seared. I shed layers of clothing, recalling the weather advisory in the trip brochure: "Peru can offer four seasons in the same day. Snow. Heat. Rain. Fog. Dress accordingly." The tops of my ears burned. I realized the "Virginia is for Lovers" baseball hat I'd brought was not going to cut it in Peruvian sunshine. I kept an eye out for a store or vendor stall where I could buy a hat with a brim circling my entire head.

After a lunch of avocado salad, grilled yucca, and fire-roasted chicken on an outdoor patio, Manuel distributed coca candy (the consistency of caramel chews) to ward off lingering altitude issues. We strolled back toward the hotel, past clusters of

Peruvian women heaped in colorful wool layers embellished with tassels and pom-poms despite the scorching afternoon heat. Noticing a few restaurant signs advertising *cuy* (roasted guinea pig, a local delicacy), Polina and I grimaced. We passed graffiti stating, "No más robos. No más alcohol ni drogas en nuestro barrio." *No more robberies. No more alcohol or drugs in our neighborhood.*

Taking advantage of an unprogrammed afternoon, Polina and I peeled away from the squad to explore the town unsupervised. We poked into artisan shops, smelling palo santo candles and essential oils in mystical flavors. We touched textile blankets and llama-wool sweaters. One shopkeeper—ocean-blue eyes, thick twisty blonde-brown locs piled atop her head, her accent code-switching between American Southern drawl and Peruvian—tried to entice us to consider an ayahuasca tour. Four days in the jungle—literal and psychological. Polina paused to listen. I wandered away toward shelves offering palo santo wood stick bundles bound with twine, handmade soaps, lip balms, skin salves.

Why am I nervous about the idea of ayahuasca? Because you already have dark dreams. Guilt. Shame. Trey. Forrest. Family. Who knows what else is lurking in that abyss. Yeah, but wouldn't it be great to get it all out? Yeah, but who would make sure I didn't do something horrible in the middle of it all?

The ayahuasca lady exuded sexy, strong, femininity vibes. Layers of earth-toned material wrapped around her torso, accenting toned shoulders, abs, waist. Exquisite caramel skin. Lines of woven bracelets coiling both arms. Feet bare except for a thin chain circling one ankle, a silver strand running across her foot, looping one toe. Long dark eyelashes. Effortless moss-green eyeliner. Perfect white teeth.

I glanced at my clunky low-rise hiking boots and the bulky windbreaker tied around my waist. I caught myself making comparisons.

Stop doing that. You're sexy too.

We thanked the lady and left the shop armed with ayahuasca leaflets. Weary from jet lag, spotty sleep, the morning hike-walk, and the relentless heat, we sought refuge in a nearby pisco bar (*pisco* = a grape-distilled Peruvian spirit), squeezing into two open slots at a counter. A smiling bartender placed a bowl of roasted corn kernels between us. Triangle-shaped and brownish, they resembled fried insects.

"I hope these aren't bugs," I said to Polina, popping a crunchy nub into my mouth.

She laughed and handed me a drink menu. I realized I already really liked traveling with Polina. She's easygoing and positive.

"I hate that I barely speak a word of Spanish," I admitted. I never like being the American traveler asking the residents to explain everything in English.

"I took Spanish in high school. I'll see what I can do," Polina offered.

She ordered cocktails on our behalf. Fresh juices mixed with small-batch elixirs crafted from fermented grapes, purple corn, and sugarcane. We chatted about our hiking tour guides and group members, sizing up the different personalities and how our own fit into the mix. We mused about how easy it is to make snap judgments, possible misjudgments, of people. I pulled my hiking shoe from my left foot and rubbed my arch. I'd strained it running on a treadmill before flying from New York to Lima. Not the best timing before forty to fifty miles of hiking in six days.

After a dinner of big salads and Spanish wine at a bustling tavern, and a nightcap of coca tea, watching cinders flare and fizzle in the monastery's fireplace, Polina and I retreated to our rooms to get ready for our first day of hiking. I slept—uninterrupted by nosebleeds.

Fueled further by breakfast—an egg-white omelet topped with smoked salmon, bacon so crispy it disintegrated in my mouth, yogurt, and two cups of Peruvian coffee with creamy milk—I felt primed for the morning's adventures.

Route rundown delivered, Manuel and Josh piled us into an awaiting van. On the drive to our first trailhead, Manuel further elaborated on the day's two hiking options: a three-mile gradual incline, or a five-and-a-half-mile trek involving a sharp initial ascent, followed by rolling hills, capped off with a steep stair-step decline. He explained we'd reconvene for lunch together in a valley near a river, where locals would cook a Peruvian meal and we'd be visited by musicians and a shaman. Josh distributed walking sticks and said, "Even if you don't usually use poles when you hike, they're a great boost for balance and leverage when you need to go up or down a tricky path."

Polina, the therapists, and Wade chose the three-mile option. The Darcys, the Manhattanite, Wade's grandsons, and I selected the longer route. Manuel led my posse toward a stone staircase hidden in vines and shrubs. He hustled up the stairs. The Darcys charged the steps two-by-two behind him. The grandsons scurried after them. The Manhattanite—Blythe—looked at me, then at the botanical portal we were willingly about to enter, not knowing what awaited us once we passed through it.

"We can do this." I clacked my walking stick against hers. We trudged forward.

Sun pierced the tree canopy. Gnats buzzed at my face. When I swatted at them, they stuck to perspiration on my cheeks. I stopped to wrestle a headband from my day pack. In the forty seconds it took to facilitate that maneuver, I lost sight of Manuel, the Darcys, and the grandsons. Ahead of me, Blythe attacked the dirt and rock path with her walking sticks. I jogged a bit to catch up with her and immediately realized the deceptive slope of the hill. Each heartbeat felt like fascia colliding with bone. My lungs labored more than I expected them to at this early stage of the hike. *Relax. It's the altitude. You don't need to be the fastest, or even fast. Manuel is not going to let you get lost.*

I couldn't see Manuel at all, but there seemed to be only one path. Up. I placed one boot in front of the other and inhaled, trying to pull air deep into my belly. The trail orbited a small mountain. Thick foliage and twisted vines provided shade most of the time. I reached a small plateau and saw Blythe stopping to sip water. I joined her. Through a clearing in the brush—like a green porthole—we gazed at the tiered terrain. In the far vista, we noticed blue tents and spiraling smoke.

"Maybe that's the beginnings of lunch," Blythe surmised. "Where do you live in New York?" she asked.

We walked side by side, our sticks click-clacking against pebbles, fallen logs, stones.

"Way downtown," I responded, wondering whether I'd be able to simultaneously maintain a conversation and take in enough air to tackle the incline.

"Upper East Side for me." She exhaled.

We settled into comfortable silence, the only sounds our footfalls and poles tapping topsoil. As we navigated another serpentine twist in the path, we saw Manuel's big smile.

"Bravo! Bravo! Bravo!" he clapped, urging us on.

I smiled, relieved to see him. He high-fived me.

"I may be a little slow at first but I'll get there," I said.

"You're doing great. Go at your pace. Lunch awaits you at the bottom. I'm going to trot on ahead to make sure the others take the correct turn at an upcoming Y-fork in the road. I'll position a local guide at the juncture for you and Blythe. Turn right, not left, at the *Y*," Manuel instructed. "It will lead you the proper route down the mountain to a series of ancient stone steps. Use your walking sticks as you descend."

The adventure company contracted with resident guides to assist with shepherding duties, to ensure no clients vanished into the wilderness, never to be found. Dashing ahead, Manuel disappeared into the thicket. Blythe stabbed the ground with her walking sticks and heaved herself forward. I did the same. We carried on wordlessly, occasionally stopping for water breaks. I noticed an oval stone, red with white streaks, nestled in the earth. I love rocks. I thought of a beach I'd walked in Troncones, Mexico, years earlier where every time a wave curled onto the dull brown sand, a starburst of color erupted, the water transforming bland beach stones into vivid reds, yellows, greens. I'd taken off my T-shirt and collected as many rocks as I could carry. I toted a handful home. I varnished small ones with clear nail polish, mimicking the effect of the ocean's wetness, making their iridescence permanent. I caged each one in wire and hung them from thin leather strips, making rudimentary necklaces I shipped to some of my girlfriends with a note saying, "You rock."

I reached down and picked up the Peruvian stone. Dusting off dirt, I tucked the rock into my day pack, thinking I'd use it as a paperweight each time I printed manuscript pages of my next book project, a tactile ritual that keeps me motivated.

Hitting her groove, Blythe sped up. I stuck to my cadence. For half an hour, I didn't see or hear another human. I briefly fretted whether I would recognize the Y-fork when I reached it, but trusted Manuel's local guide would be waiting. I stopped to sip water. A thin reddish-brown dog appeared at my knee. He hopped around me, his brown eyes peering into mine.

"Hola," I said. *Hop, hop, hop.* Tail wagging with each hop.

I walked farther along the trail. The dog raced ahead, bounded back to me, then sprinted onward again. Pushing a low-hanging branch away from my forehead, I encountered an obvious Y-fork in the path. No guide waiting. No Manuel. No Blythe. No one.

Just the dog. Hopping. Toward the right tine of the fork.

The dog scampered down the path's offshoot, bolted back to me, then scooted down the leafy corridor again. I followed him. He repeated his dance, darting ahead, backtracking to me. He led me to a stone archway—an entrance to a staircase constructed of timeworn boulders, logs, and smaller stones. The dog hopped down a few steps, then hopped back up, as if playing granite piano keys with his paws. Hop, hop, hop, down. Hop, hop, hop, up. I placed a walking stick on the first step. It looked rickety, like any sudden move could precipitate a landslide. Hop, hop, hop, the dog insisted.

"All right, fine, I'm coming."

The red-brown dog escorted me down at least a hundred of those steps, maybe two hundred. I lost count. Vines and branches, some with flowers, others with thorns, scraped my elbows, slapped at my face. As we descended, I noticed a stream with a campsite on its far bank.

The dog and I reached the last step of the staircase, arriving at the brook. I wanted to hurl both hiking shoes off and slide my aching left arch into the clear water. The dog raced across a wood-plank bridge, then dashed back to me, egging me onward toward our goalpost.

I heard clapping. Beyond the bridge, I saw the rest of the gang sitting around picnic tables heaped with platters of food, cheering my arrival—the last one standing. Caps popped from beer bottles. I lumbered the last twenty feet through muddy grass.

Polina greeted me, relieving me of my walking sticks and day pack. Manuel gestured at an empty chair at the end of one table. He placed a Dixie cup of red wine on the tablecloth before me. I removed my sunglasses and wiped my face. I sat in the chair and wrapped dusty fingers around the plastic cup. The red-brown dog leaped into my lap. He licked salty sweat from my cheeks and lapped at my forearm.

Blythe handed me a plate of roasted chicken, corn on the cob, asparagus the color of fresh-cut lawn, sweet potatoes. I kicked my left hiking shoe to the ground below my chair and rubbed my arch. The dog loitered at my side, alternating between my lap and the soil near my knee, bartering cuteness for table scraps, reminiscent of the two beagles I'd shared with Trey for a decade. I slipped pieces of chicken into my hand and let the dog gobble them up. His ribs protruded through his fur. I ached to take him home. His sparkly eyes met mine as he awaited each treat. I realized my flawed assumption his life would be better in New York with me; he spent his days chasing butterflies around Peruvian mountains and picnicking with tourists.

After the meal, Manuel and Josh herded us toward a set of blankets arranged in a meadow beneath an arbor of trees. I hobbled on one shoe and one sock, carrying my left hiking boot in my hand. Polina and I chose a blanket and sat on it together, dry pine needles poking our undersides. Manuel introduced a shaman dressed in layers of Peruvian wool, a riot of colors and textures. A hat with earflaps and pom-pom tassels covered black-silver hair, accentuating an angular nose and cheekbones.

The shaman and his assistant—a woman dressed in equally vibrant garb—sat lotus style on a quilt in front of our group. The woman arranged seashells, yellow and pink carnations, individual flower petals, a bowl of coca leaves, and rocks around the shaman. Four musicians emerged from a grove. They beat drums and blew into wooden flutes. The shaman and his assistant closed their eyes. I shut mine as well. I focused on the rhythmic *thump-thump*. Noticed the pine needles pricking my hamstrings and glutes, not painful, just there. I smelled spice, a scent resonant of a wildflower that grew along a fire trail where Forrest, Rowan, and I had taken walks in California.

I felt someone's hands touch mine. I opened my eyes. The shaman's assistant pressed three coca leaves into my palm.

The shaman instructed us to think of three prayers, one for each coca leaf, perhaps a person, a situation, a dilemma. I realized I wasn't struggling with anything major or traumatic in my life at the moment. I wasn't anxious or depressed. My family dynamic oscillated with tension—American politics and parental displeasure over my avoidance of church in traditional form—but that was nothing new. I considered who in my life was going through rough stuff. My college friend was grappling with logistic efforts to adopt a child as a single mom. I decided my three prayers would be (1) a smooth adoption approval process for my pal; (2) a détente with my family so we could hang out without playing emotional Whack-a-Mole; and (3) a cool, sweet, kind boyfriend.

The shaman chanted. I fingered my three coca leaves and thought about what type of guy would be good for me, good *to* me. I craved interesting, exciting, provocative, unconventional— my definition of "edgy"—but also caring, romantic, and affectionate. Into fitness but not obsessive about perfection. Would work out with me. Has a job he loves—I don't care what it is. Likes to travel. Curious. Is nice to other people. Passionate. Unafraid to express emotion, get vulnerable with me, or apologize if he made a mistake or hurt my feelings. Willing to accept an apology. Has been through relationship rifts. Wouldn't care that I'd been married and didn't have or want kids of my own. Would share his interests and friends with me and would be supportive of my emotional investment in mine. A positive and consistent communicator. *Does this guy exist? Well, I exist and I'm those things.*

The assistant collected our coca leaves in a half shell. The shaman lit a palo santo stick and waved woodsy smoke over the leaves.

As the ceremony concluded, the hikers stood up and headed to the picnic tables for dessert. Polina lingered on our blanket with her eyes closed. I rubbed my aching foot. Gathering their talismans and materials, the shaman and his assistant noticed me. The shaman gestured toward my foot. I nodded.

He moved toward me, sat on the grass, knees inches from mine, and removed my sock. His assistant passed him a fistful of coca leaves. He rubbed them vigorously between his palms. He closed his eyes for a few seconds, then opened them and placed the coca leaves on the arch of my foot, cupping my skin with his warm hands. Manuel arrived with a compression wrap. He and the shaman bound the coca leaves to my arch with the bandage and slid my sock over the binding. The shaman clasped his hands in a prayer gesture and bowed toward me. I scrunched my nose so I wouldn't cry.

On the drive back to the monastery, Polina immersed in a book about ayahuasca. I pressed my forehead to the van's filmy window and stared at blurring landscape. The Darcys occupied the front row, the daughter listening to music through headphones while her parents and brother chatted about his upcoming football camp. I felt a confusing spell of annoyance at the family's interface. Mr. Darcy seemed like a grown-up version of the preppy boys who'd attended the boarding school where I grew up as a faculty kid. Good-looking, clean-cut, sporty, confident. His constant barrage of questions toward Manuel and Josh demonstrated a genuine interest in Peruvian history and culture. He was obviously smart and intellectually curious. He never steamrolled his wife in conversation. She kept apace right next to him, in every dialogue. He showered attention on her and the kids. Though obviously wealthy and accustomed to privilege, they treated the guides, waiters, cooks, van driver, and everyone else kindly and with appreciation. There was nothing not to like about them. Why did they irk me?

Ah.

Their tight-knittedness rankled me. An impenetrable family unit. A foursome protected by a love force field. They enjoyed each other's company. They valued each other's diverse needs and interests.

I was *jealous*.

After showers, a change of clothes, and a Peruvian cocktail in the hotel bar, Polina and I chose a secluded two-top table in the monastery dining room, needing a break from group interaction. We dined on grilled plantains, baked fish, and vegetables in delicate but spicy sauces. The Darcys laughed with the therapists and Blythe at a faraway table. Wade's grandsons snuck sips of wine from goblets waiters kept refilling. Muscles aching from the day's exertion, Polina and I waved *buenas noches* to the group and headed to our rooms.

Sliding into bed, I realized the arch of my foot had stopped hurting.

I dreamed of the shaman and the red-brown dog.

The breakfast bell rang before sunrise. I dressed in extra layers, heeding Manuel's and Josh's warnings that snowfall might accompany our morning hike. In the dining hall, I loaded my plate with buckwheat pancakes and berry jam.

The van dropped us at a park entrance. Manuel pointed toward a rocky trail edged with spiny shrubs. The Darcys galloped ahead. The rest of us fanned out, the grandsons trailing the Darcys, the therapists trekking a good pace with walking sticks, Blythe in step with Wade, Polina and me forming the caboose. Josh walked next to us, pointing out cactus flowers, nodding *buenos días* to shepherds sporting Nike sweatshirts, the swoosh logo an odd juxtaposition against Incan ruins and free-range livestock. The shepherds called out in Spanish to small dogs corralling herds of goats. We passed female shepherds dressed in wool sweaters and plaid skirts layered over checkered pantaloons. One had a baby goat strapped to her back in a sarong, its rear legs dangling free. We passed a donkey, an enormous hog napping in a ditch, and two Rottweilers lazing in the sun on the porch of a bodega advertising Coca-Cola products.

The morning hike was easy—three miles, relatively flat. We arrived at a llama farm where guides handed us stalks of wild grass to feed the woolly creatures. We lunched on avocado sandwiches and couscous salad with cucumber and feta, then loaded into the van for transport to a nearby village.

Manuel and Josh walked us through a cluster of dwellings linked by clotheslines draped with handwoven rugs, scarves, belts, bracelets, and satchels. Women and children peered at us from cottage doorways. The moms smiled but remained on their doorsteps. The kids raced to greet us with giant brown eyes, dusty dark hair, little bodies wrapped in Technicolor wool—sweaters, pants, hats—and feet in scuffed rubber clogs. One little boy sat beneath a clothesline licking a red lollipop as big as his head.

Manuel encouraged us to browse the textiles. He explained, to sustain their community, the women weave wares to sell to tourists while their husbands work as sherpas on the iconic Inca Trail—a path carving through the Andes Mountains, offering an inside look at Incan ruins and varied ecosystems like cloud forests. The men carry heavy bottles of water and other supplies for hikers who obtain official permits from the Peruvian government. Polina and I had booked our trip too late to secure two of the limited number of Inca Trail passes issued by the Peruvian authorities each year. The Darcys and the therapists had the proper documentation.

Polina shopped for belts and coin pouches for her two daughters. I ran my hands through woven bracelets, each strand approximately twenty inches long, tiny white beads sewn into the trim of wool filaments in pinks, maroons, blues. As a lady took my hand and wrapped a cord multiple times around my wrist, knotting its ends, Manuel whispered, "According to ancestral lore, the traditional bracelets invoke protective spirits."

I bought two, plus a belt and a cross-body bag. I wrapped a scarf in shades of blues, oranges, and whites—my University of Virginia colors—around my neck. The wool scratched my skin. I bought it anyway. We waved goodbye to the women and children and followed Manuel and Josh down a hill toward an elementary school.

As we arrived by foot, our van pulled into the schoolhouse driveway. Josh propped the vehicle's rear doors open with bulging bags of rice. As part of its philanthropic ethos, the adventure company hand delivers food or supplies to underresourced communities. Josh began unloading cartons of bananas and oranges, directing us to distribute them to the students.

Fifty or sixty neighborhood children emerged from classrooms, scurrying to find spots to sit on a mulchy hill. We doled out fruit. Some of the children—sun rashes dotting their cheeks—immediately peeled the bananas and devoured the yellow-white pulp. Others shoved theirs into pockets, grinning, giggling, pretending they hadn't received one yet. I stood there in my bougie hiking pants feeling massively spoiled.

Cartons emptied, we reconvened in the van, the children singing and waving goodbye.

"Next stop! The salt mines!" Manuel announced.

I'd read about the salt mines in the trip catalog. The prospect of a sunset hike along a grid of crystalline white flats intrigued me even more than Machu Picchu. When we arrived though, Josh nudged us toward a gift shop displaying sacks of pink and white salt for purchase, suggesting we spend a half hour shopping before we'd head back to the monastery for dinner. I saw the Darcys and Manuel trot off toward a mill.

"Where are they going?" I asked Josh.

"They're doing the salt flat hike. We'll meet them back at the hotel."

"Actually, some of us want to do the salt flat hike too," I said.

Blythe and the therapists nodded.

"Oh, Manuel and I assumed you all were done for the day," Josh said. He looked at the sky. "Sun will be setting soon. Probably best for this group to just shop for salt."

"We really want to hike the salt flats," I repeated.

My insides twisted; thirty minutes earlier at the schoolhouse, I'd felt embarrassed by my cushy American life, yet here I was pouting about being excluded from a hike.

Blythe chimed in, emphasizing, "It's an experience many of us might never have the opportunity to try again, and why some of us came all the way to Peru."

"Okay, well you'll need to hurry to finish before it gets dark," Josh urged.

He called Manuel's mobile phone, relaying that a few of us were going to do the salt flat hike as well. Gesturing toward the trail entrance, Josh instructed, "Follow that footpath. Try to keep a good pace if you can. Manuel will meet you at the end and guide you back to the van."

Blythe, the therapists, and I raced toward the pathway, clutching our day packs and walking sticks. We scampered past shopping stalls vending miniature bags of salt in shades of whites and pinks. No time for retail. A dirt walkway opened into a dazzling panorama, a patchwork quilt of glistening white squares the size of coffee tables, small cisterns holding water, salt crystals clinging to rims of each quadrangle, nearly blinding white against a backdrop of green hills. Gold-orange flecks of sunrays foreshadowed rapidly approaching dusk.

Blythe and the therapists stutter-stepped along the narrow route, barely the width of an outstretched arm. I endeavored to stay within ten feet of them, a bit hesitant with my gait at first, speculating how deep the salt pools on either side of the slim conduit were and what would happen if a hiking boot slipped off a ridge into one. Were the reservoirs deep? Did they have a floor? Was the liquid watery? Or thick like mud? Could I pull myself out if I fell in? *Yes. Yes you can. Keep going.*

I concentrated on the ground, the earth, a few paces ahead of my toes, willing myself to appreciate the scene's natural beauty instead of mentally leapfrogging to potential worst-case scenarios: Tripping into a bottomless pool to the right or left of me. Tumbling pool-by-pool-by-pool down the tiered topography. Plummeting into salty oblivion.

The sun set swiftly as Josh had warned. We hoofed along the precarious passageway, the horizon towing us along, the white of the salt turning silver, gray, pewter, steel, as light dwindled. Ahead, I saw a tall figure waving at us, pumping a fist in the air. Manuel. He clapped and cheered as we crested the last knoll, left the salt flats behind, and ran across boggy grass depositing us into a residential cul-de-sac.

"The van is up ahead! Dinner awaits!" Manuel called out.

I felt happy we'd pushed to see our salt.

⋀ ⋀ ⋀

Over dessert, Manuel announced an itinerary change. Because of a rumored transportation strike across Peru, we needed to catch the Inca Rail train to Machu Picchu a day earlier than planned, which meant an early morning wake-up call, luggage packed, ready to depart the monastery for good.

Archaeologists report that Machu Picchu—a composition of stone structures perched on mossy mountain peaks, often shrouded in eerie, hovering clouds—was originally constructed as an estate for Incan emperor Pachacuti in the fifteenth century. While Pachacuti's given name was Cusi Yupanqui, his chosen name meant "reformer of the world." Admirers called him "the earth shaker." Hiram Bingham III, an American explorer and academic, publicized the existence of Machu Picchu in the early 1900s when—guided by Indigenous farmers—he "discovered" its location.

The Inca Rail station looked like the set of an Indiana Jones movie: tourists dressed in khaki hiking gear, guides sporting suede fedoras. The throng squinted down the railroad tracks, willing a train to arrive to transport us to Machu Picchu before the transit strike hit. A horn sounded. The crowd cheered.

We boarded the Inca Rail, a vastly different aesthetic from the many grungy American trains I've ridden in my life. Glossy wooden floorboards, tables, and wall paneling. Plush leather seats. Spotless windows yielding unobstructed views of the Andes Mountains on the ride toward one of the Seven Wonders of the World. (Apparently, Greek historians and scholars were the first to list seven wonders of the *ancient* world, such as the Pyramids of Giza. The number seven represented "perfection and plenty" and the planetary system known at the time: five planets, plus the sun and the moon. Modern-day lists itemize seven natural wonders, seven engineering wonders, seven underwater wonders, and more.)

Nearing the end of the scheduled three-and-a-half-hour ride—which approximated four hours due to frequent stops in the middle of nowhere for no apparent reason—the train chugged into a station inside a water mill. We disembarked, stepping onto a rickety landing constructed of bolted logs. Manuel and Josh led us past a tumbling waterfall through an archway of rocks, trees, and flowers toward our next inn, a jumble of cabins surrounded by lush greenery, stone fountains, and ponds. We entered the hotel's atrium. A library annex occupied one wall; rows of novels, memoirs, and multilingual dictionaries balanced on slats of plywood hanging from Tarzan-style ropes reinforced with vines and tree branches.

I ran my fingers along the jute cords. *Bookshelf goals.*

I found my room—a cozy studio. A puffy duvet covered a four-poster bed. Bars of Peruvian chocolate rested on plump pillows. Bathrobes hung from knobs of a rustic armoire. A basket of shea butter soaps, organic shampoos, and lotions sat on the bathroom sink's edge. I unpacked and regrouped with Polina for a walk into town.

Along a labyrinth of pathways, signs identified each genus and species of jungle flora. The air smelled sweet yet spicy. Moisture dripped from leaves above us. Four waterfalls later, we emerged from thick vegetation into open air. Clouds hung *below* emerald mountain peaks.

"Wow, they weren't kidding about the altitude here," Polina noted. "The mountaintops are higher than the clouds."

We crisscrossed streets, weaving into town in search of nontouristy boutiques and cafés. We entered a crystal shop, interior air thick with the aroma of incense, a man resembling our Cusco shaman reading a book in the corner.

Polina had transported a small sack of crystals to Peru, having read that "charging" stones at Machu Picchu reinvigorated their power. Still mostly a crystal novice, I noticed a bowl of smoky pink rose quartz resting on a shelf next to a small sign: "Good for attracting fresh love, intimacy." I bought one.

Polina and I browsed an open-air market, vendors selling Machu Picchu trinkets and souvenirs. One table displayed a collection of small figurines, brass, burnished to a golden brown.

I picked one up; it had the heft of a paperweight. On one side, two hands clasped a paunch above a protruding penis. On the other side, hands hugged a belly below two flattened breasts. A three-tiered hat topped a dual-sided head. Identical genderless faces on both sides.

"I think that's a variation of a Pachamama statue, the Earth Mother," Polina explained. "I'm not sure who the dude on her back is. Pachapapa, perhaps?"

I exchanged Peruvian *soles* for the statuette. It fit snug in my hand, somehow cold yet warm at the same time.

We found a health food café called the Greenhouse, ate tuna tartare and feta couscous, and sipped pisco sour cocktails until we felt tired enough to sleep.

The next morning, I located both Manuel *and* Josh in the breakfast area and informed them I definitely wanted to do the day's advanced hike. A peak called Montaña offered the most rigorous climb in our Peru itinerary. I wanted the exercise but also the mental, and possibly emotional, challenge of ascending it. Only the Darcys so far had signed up for Montaña. Both Manuel and Josh assured me I could handle the hike—logistically and physically—and that it didn't matter what my pace was; we had no time limit, and one of them would make sure I finished (and didn't accidentally drop off a precipice).

Reaching Machu Picchu involved a terrifying shuttle ride up a steep mountain face. Mid-series of angular switchbacks, I made the mistake of glancing out the window. My brain immediately summoned imaginary newspaper headlines: *Machu Picchu Tour Bus Flies off Cliff.*

At the entrance to the Incan ruins, Manuel and Josh gave us a moment to regain our equilibrium, suggested we obtain Machu Picchu stamps in our passports from a nearby booth, then steered us into the archaeological wonder.

The guides divided us into two troupes—the Montaña squad and the Machu Picchu historical walking tour gang—and

distributed brown paper bags with packed lunches for the day.
Josh repeated the route rundown, advising the Darcys and me
to take our time ascending and descending the stairs on Montaña's steeper inclines and hug the stone walls as we maneuvered
around some of the more daunting turns.

"The mist from the low clouds makes the stones slippery.
You won't see a lot of guardrails on this mountain," Josh cautioned. "Also, absolutely no taking photos on Montaña unless
you stop at a designated rest area. Every year, Machu Picchu
loses at least one tourist who falls off the mountain snapping a
selfie. I'm not trying to be alarmist, but safety on this hike is no
joke. It's a rainy and foggy day, and the trail will be wet. Okay,
ready, climbers?"

"Yup." I waved at Polina. "See you guys this afternoon."

Already familiar with the layout of Montaña from their last
Machu Picchu trip, the Darcys beelined toward the trailhead.
Josh and I strode side-by-side. I realized I hadn't yet spent much
time talking to him. I asked how long he'd been a hiking guide,
how they crafted the trip itineraries, what he does for fun during
his time off. He spoke of his love for snowboarding and surfing in
his offseason. We arrived at the entry to Montaña's hiking path. I
stared upward. Saw the Darcys jogging the initial gradient.

"I'm gonna start a little slow, so if you want to catch up with
them, I'll be okay. I just want to take it at my pace until I feel
comfortable," I said.

"I'm hanging with you. We have literally all day. No time
pressure at all. It's slippery today, so slow is good. Somebody—I
can't remember who—once said, slow is fast and fast is slow,"
said Josh. "My dad told me that phrase comes from the Latin,
festina lente, which means something like 'make haste slowly.'
But I don't know exactly what that means either."

I laughed, forcing a much-needed exhale.

The trail mouth tapered quickly to a width incapable of fit-
ting two bodies. Josh gestured for me to pass ahead of him as we
approached our first set of stone stairs, wet with raindrops and

mist from morning fog. Trees bordering the steps hid Machu Picchu. I advanced; Josh followed. Our conversation segued to quietude.

My boots pressed into damp leaves and botanical debris papering railroad ties bolted to stone. Josh gave me space yet shadowed me. As we surmounted a sharp rise in the terrain, the tree line opened, revealing jade mountain peaks, fog floating between them like cotton candy. Eerie. Stunning. Quiet.

"Want me to take your picture?" Josh offered at a lookout point.

I handed him my phone and tried to relax, though my gaping eyes betrayed recurring jolts of adrenaline surging through my nervous system. As bands of hikers of various nationalities passed on our left, I hugged the rock face on my right. Each additional body seemed to render the trail thinner, more perilous. Passing trekkers offered friendly shouts of *Merci! Grazie! Merhaba! Ciao! Cheers!* We moved upward, Josh in my wake. Physically, I felt mostly fine, breathing okay, joints functioning, leg muscles firing appropriately. Mentally, I wrestled. With each step, the world seemed to magnify exponentially. The valleys deepened. The drop-offs sharpened. In America, three layers of guardrails and warning signs in multiple shouty languages would have clanged alarm bells of potential hazards. Here, nothing. Except nature.

Turns tightened. Altitude heightened. As we curved craggy walls, the lack of any barrier between us and the plunge to the valley floor started to freak me out. New crews of hikers appeared around each bend, greeting us with abrupt exuberance, two-stepping around me as I froze, trying to clench a flat rock facade. Nothing tangible to grasp.

Keep going. It will be worth it at the top. Will it though? What more is there to see?

I kept going. At that point, down seemed worse than up.

Josh patiently encouraged, "Not too much further! We're almost to the summit!"

He was right. Fifteen minutes later, the trail burst open onto a stone landing. Hikers relaxed on benches in a wooden pergola, eating bananas and granola bars. Mossy peaks for miles, including Machu Picchu—geometric stone structures arranged like rust-gray slices of cake on tiers of green. Identifying the switchbacks I'd just tackled, I felt a ripple of vertigo.

Don't look down. Look up. Look over. Look around.

Josh hopscotched across a narrow stone connector between the open-air gazebo and another ledge where the Darcys sat like Incan conquerors, munching on apples, eight legs dangling sheer rock. I approached the crossing. The stones seemed disconnected, as if hanging in midair—like a magic trick. The Darcys and Josh waved me over.

I looked forward, not down. I stepped on one rock. Crossed a chasm to step onto another one. Another gap. Another rock. And so on. Heart hurtling against my rib cage.

Josh high-fived me and handed me a fresh bottle of water and a Peruvian chocolate bar. I sat on a boulder near the Darcys.

Mr. Darcy ventured, "Hey, great climb, huh! So it's really cool you do this stuff by yourself. Incredibly brave. So, what type of law do you practice? I hear you're a superfancy New York lawyer." He smiled.

I smiled back. I tore foil from the chocolate and offered him a square. "Ha, I don't know about superfancy. I used to practice construction litigation—like sports stadiums, power plants, hospitals. Now I teach."

He handed me an avocado-and-cucumber sandwich from his pack. He asked about my classes, what I teach, whether I like it better than lawyering, where else I've traveled. He listened, seemed genuinely curious. Interested in me as a human. I ate the sandwich. We talked about other active travel trips that sounded intriguing: a multisport exploration of Morocco; a bike tour through India; a Patagonia hiking adventure. I glanced at his wife, her arms around both children. The daughter snapped a selfie of the three of them.

"You have a really good family," I said to Mr. Darcy.

"Yep, they give me a great life, that's for sure."

He smiled at them, then at me.

In that moment, I wanted to be a Darcy. I wanted a dad confident enough in the steadfastness of his family's love that he could engage in benevolent dialogue with a female stranger while his wife shared a quiet minute hugging her kids. I wanted a mom that would embrace me after we just conquered a physical, mental, and emotional challenge together. I wanted a mother that would even undertake such a challenge with me, or at least cheer me onward toward one. I wanted a mom that would insist on taking a selfie with me. I wanted parents that loved me as much as they loved each other. I also wanted a dad who recognized I was on the verge of an anxiety attack and distracted me with genuine conversation and active listening, getting me talking about work and travel and books and things I love, so I could be calm enough to enjoy an astonishing view and our individual and collective accomplishment.

"Thank you," I said to Mr. Darcy.

"For what?" He winked.

"I realize what you did just now, and I appreciate it."

"Hey, you're an honorary Darcy making this hike with us today!" He reached out to shake my hand and looked me in the eye. "For what it's worth, you seem like a force of nature. A quiet hurricane. Underestimated, perhaps."

I finished a last bite of avocado. Consumed a peanut butter granola bar. Ate an overripe banana I didn't want but figured would sustain me through another hour of exertion. The Darcys gamboled across the stepping stones back to the pergola. Josh extended a hand and pulled me to my feet.

"Ready to explore Machu Picchu?" he asked. "C'mon. Let's do it."

He followed me as I recrossed the stone bridge. I let a few hikers pass in front of me to enter the trail, then began the descent. The straightaways felt easy, a gentle slope. But as soon as we approached the first turn, the exposure to the plunging abyss seemed much more extreme than before, the stones wetter, the curve dicier without a guardrail. I froze. I turned around to look at Josh.

"I got ya." He positioned himself at my right flank. "Ready?" He stood millimeters from the precipice.

"You might fall!"

"I won't fall, Heidi. And there's no way I'm letting you fall. Trust me and trust yourself. You've got this."

I flattened my left hand against the mountain wall and took a step. Josh took a step. I took another step. He took another step. We took the first turn like that . . . together. And the next turn like that. And the next one.

I didn't fall. He didn't let me fall. He also didn't pressure me, or make fun of me, or make me feel like a wimp, or act like I'd been out of my league or a burden to him or anyone else in attempting this climb. He acknowledged the legitimacy of first-time-Montaña-hiker nerves, and guided me through them. He helped me realize I'm not *too much*, as I've been told more than once. I'm *me*. I don't want to skip out on hard challenges, but I also need to figure them out my own way.

The trail leveled out. We saw the Darcys taking family photos at a turnout. They waited for us, then asked a stranger to take a picture of our "Montaña squad." Mrs. Darcy put her arm around my shoulder. "Team!!" she cheered.

The six of us descended the rest of the trail together, stopping for water and snapshots at rest areas, while Mr. Darcy inundated Josh with historical questions about Peru. As we emerged into the clearing, Manuel pointed at us, whistling and applauding. Polina sprang to her feet, ran to me, and gave me a hug. "How was it?"

"Awesome, actually."

Dazed, I don't remember much of the guided tour of Machu Picchu's ruins that afternoon, except two small reflecting pools, circles inside triangles capturing rainwater mirroring the clouds and sky above us. While the others listened to a historian explain the structure's architectural significance, I thought of New York's Twin Towers, the massive commemorative pools at the World Trade Center Memorial site, the names of 9/11 victims etched into dark granite. I contemplated how the Tower card in tarot portends change, welcome or unwelcome. I knelt and dipped my fingers into Peruvian rainwater. I murmured *thank you* to the Incan gods and goddesses, for my life. For Josh, getting me up and down Montaña alive. For the Darcys. Polina. The other hikers. My brother. My friends. For the countless times I've been pushed to the precipice by conflict with my parents, by the collapse of my relationships with Trey, with Forrest. I've never fallen over the edge though. I've been able to hang on. Often with help. Just as often alone.

As I left Peru and flew home to New York, I pondered Pachamama—the Earth Mother goddess, a sculptor of mountains, a provocateur of earthquakes. I promised myself I'd continue striving to understand that, like Pachamama, I am the sorcerer of my own power—to create my art, my life's story, my future.

5

dublin

As a teenager in the mid-1980s, MTV introduced me to a world of music beyond Sunday school songs about the "joy, joy, joy, joy down in my heart." Madonna, Prince, David Bowie, Billy Idol, The Police, Cyndi Lauper, Boy George, and Tears for Fears offered my first peep into culture, fashion, styles, accents . . . and provocative ideas and opinions that differed from those of my parents and grandparents.

The popular girls in my high school drifted through the hallways wearing expertly distressed U2 and R.E.M. concert tees. I envied them from the fringe. My first and only concert in high school was Norwegian synth-pop band A-ha, best known for their hit "Take on Me" and accompanying MTV video—a charcoal pencil sketch springing to life. A sixteen-year-old boy I liked invited me to a Depeche Mode show; my parents nixed that offer as I was only fourteen.

After high school, I ran off to the University of Virginia. Jumping up and down with my roommates in our basketball arena as the band 10,000 Maniacs opened for R.E.M., I closed my eyes and floated, free, nobody telling me how to act, what to wear, when to smile. Each week, I'd write term papers about Baudelaire, Stendhal, and Shakespeare, then bounce off to INXS, Ziggy Marley, and UB40 shows in college auditoriums. My friends and I slipped crumpled dollar bills to bouncers guarding the entrances of dive bars where we watched Dave Matthews sing and Boyd Tinsley fiddle before they became superfamous. We traded another dollar or two for bottles of Rolling Rock beer, waking up the next morning with glow-in-the-dark "21 and over" stamps on our hands, though we had a few birthdays to go before we could legally drink. I kept neon venue wristbands wrapped around my forearms for days, savoring the feel of paper against skin, my first totems of independence.

Though U2's *Joshua Tree* album hit record stores the year I graduated from high school—1987—the band's role in my life soundtrack started in soft volume. I chose their song "Unforgettable Fire" as the last entry on the DJ playlist I curated for my wedding to Trey a month before I graduated from law school. I didn't really understand the lyrics, but its dramatic crescendo entranced me.

When our marriage detonated in an unforgettable fiery mess six years later, I moved to New York, sublet a fifth-floor walk-up in the West Village that reeked of syrupy candle wax, and played Dido's *No Angel* album nonstop. New York's chaos pummeled me at first. I flinched every time a taxi driver honked at me or an ambulance siren screamed. I sat on my apartment floor painting really awful art. I wrote—a lot. I scribbled words into notebooks, sipping troughs of red wine to fall asleep and temporarily dull my guilt, grief, and shame.

A year and a half into my new life in Manhattan, four months after the Twin Towers fell, U2 played the Super Bowl halftime show. At the end of the song "Where the Streets Have No Name," Bono yanked open his leather jacket, revealing a silk American flag lining his coat. A curtain behind the band rippled the names of the 9/11 victims. Bono's voice radiated defiance . . . love. The band's intense facial expressions—Larry Mullen Jr. on drums, The Edge (the nickname of David Howell Evans) on electric guitar, Adam Clayton on bass—gripped me.

When you're ready . . . and you ain't ready yet . . . we'll be here, they seemed to intone.

Life slowly got better. I switched law firms for the second time, wrote my first book (a how-to manual for junior litigation attorneys), and met Forrest on our blind date. A few years later, Forrest and I packed our stuff and road-tripped to California with our dog Rowan, embarking on our "great West Coast experiment." California sunshine exposed relationship dysfunction we'd ignored in New York, where I'd pretended every red flag was a shiny balloon. His physical rejection fueled my insecurity; he claimed my insecurity spurred his rejection.

One afternoon, a male work colleague invited me to lunch. Biting into shawarma wraps from a kebab stand we liked, we traded relationship updates.

"Britney Spears's 'Oops! . . . I Did It Again' should be my theme song," I joked. "I can't believe I'm about to crater another long-term relationship."

My coworker, a music aficionado, laughed at the Britney reference. "Who's your favorite band right now?" he asked.

"U2."

I'd been repeatedly blasting tracks from the *Joshua Tree* and *Achtung Baby* albums, weaving my little convertible along the Pacific Coast Highway, Rowan in the passenger seat, her velvet ears flapping in the breeze.

"How many times have you seen them in concert?"

"Um, none, actually," I admitted.

"What?! No, no, no . . . we're fixing that immediately."

A couple weeks later, my friend (whose nickname, poetically, is J.T. like *Joshua Tree*) took me to U2's *360°* show at the Rose Bowl in Los Angeles. While J.T. swayed back and forth to each song, hands in pockets, calm and composed, my insides spontaneously combusted. I could barely function. I ached to be closer—to the lyrics, to the vibe, to the art, to Bono, Larry, Adam, and Edge.

As we left the Rose Bowl, my bones vibrating, I turned to J.T. and asked, "How can a concert make you want to be a better person?"

He smiled. "U2 will never be just a band to you again."

Thereafter, U2 dominated the soundscape of my split from Forrest. I listened to U2 the night Rowan died of old age in my arms. I blasted U2 through headphones as I boarded a one-way flight from LAX Airport to JFK Airport, holding keys to nothing—no vehicle, no home, no office—having snagged a new law professor job in New York, sold my car, donated most of my furniture, and yanked the plug on the great West Coast experiment.

I played U2 when I ran on the treadmill most mornings in Manhattan. When I sipped wine at night. When I rode trains and didn't want to talk to anyone. I started following a local U2 tribute band, Unforgettable Fire, around New York City. If I squinted my eyes enough, Fake Bono looked like the real one, and Fake Larry resembled actual Larry. I jumped up and down at the edge of their stage, eyes closed, yelling lyrics until I was hoarse.

In 2014, when U2 released the *Songs of Innocence* album, I played and replayed every track. I analyzed each stanza. I wanted to burrow into the band's heads, learn what they care about, what bothers them, how they make their art, how they communicate with each other, what it feels like when they know they have a good new idea.

In 2015, I attended three shows on the iNNOCENCE + eXPERIENCE tour: one in Los Angeles and two in New York. Each time, I arrived at the arena early. I watched a badass female stage manager—walkie-talkie dangling from a pocket of her camouflaged cargo pants—check in with Larry's drum technician as he tested equipment configurations and sound levels. The Edge's guitar technician pressed amp pedals and tossed guitar picks to happy fans lining the stage rail in the General Admission mosh pit. A seatmate told me the guitar tech's name: Dallas Schoo.

Watching the shows from different stage angles, I began noticing nuances. The intentional choreography of the musicians' movement around the stage. The band grinning at each other between sets. Bono making subtle hand movements to communicate with sound crew about microphone or earbud volume. Dallas popping up from below the stage when the lights softened between songs, handing The Edge a different guitar. A guy standing in the shadows near Larry holding extra drumsticks in case he accidentally dropped one.

Mid-October, my parents began texting me about holiday planning: "Are you coming to your brother's place in North Carolina for Thanksgiving? Have you bought a ticket to Florida for December?"

Exhausted and rattled by 2015 prepresidential-election drama (Trump era . . . Round One), I yearned to skip Thanksgiving and inevitable familial political friction. Curious, I checked U2's tour schedule. From social media, I learned the band had left the United States and was midway through the European leg of the iNNOCENCE + eXPERIENCE tour. I ran my finger down the list of remaining tour stops. Barcelona. Antwerp. Cologne. Then London, Glasgow, Paris, Belfast. Finally, *Dublin*. The tour would end in Dublin . . . during Thanksgiving week. Their hometown.

I've never been to Ireland!

I scoured the internet and found a ticket to one of four sold-out Dublin shows through a UK-based concert ticket resale website. I booked a flight. I'd heard that Bono and The Edge owned shares in a Dublin hotel called The Clarence, but of course, it had no vacancies during tour week. Even if lodging there had been available, I didn't love the aesthetic of the website photos—1980s Holiday Inn-esque. I searched for "boutique Dublin hotels" that seemed more my style. One called The Morgan in the neighborhood of Temple Bar—a hub of pubs, restaurants, galleries, and shops along the River Liffey—was only a short tram ride from the concert venue, 3Arena. I reserved a room.

Two weeks before my departure, on my way into my apartment building after an exercise class, my doorman handed me an international express mail envelope. I opened it. My concert ticket! I ran a finger over its silver hologram, perforation, and two barcodes, exhaled in relief that it looked legit, ran upstairs, and tucked the treasure into my passport.

Twelve days before my Dublin trip, terrorists attacked Paris. On November 13, suicide bombers executed deadly blasts outside the Stade de France, a packed sports stadium, during a soccer match. Shootings and additional explosions tore through cafés and restaurants. Violent extremists seized hostages at a concert of the band Eagles of Death Metal at a theater called Le Bataclan.

U2 was originally scheduled to play in Paris on November 14—the day after the tragedy. When the shots fired and bombs discharged, Bono and the guys were mid-rehearsal at the Accor Arena, two miles from Bataclan. Their security team evacuated them. French officials canceled U2's remaining Paris shows (they'd already played two gigs there earlier in the week). The band vowed to return to Paris to complete the tour. Bono called the attack "a direct hit on music," expressing concern for Eagles of Death Metal band members and fans. Bono, Edge, Adam, Larry, and their spouses attended vigils, contributing bouquets of white roses and lilies to candlelit memorials blanketing Parisian sidewalks. The guys flew to Belfast to press on with their tour.

I never considered canceling my trip in the wake of the terrorist attack. Quite the opposite: I felt compelled to show up.

On the six-hour overnight flight from New York to Dublin, I couldn't sleep. Every half hour, I touched the inside pocket of my handbag, checking for the concert ticket.

My first Ireland stamp secured at passport control, I asked a ruddy-faced information desk attendant how to find a city bus. I boarded a double-decker transport to town and hopped out on Fleet Street a few blocks from The Morgan.

The hotel lobby pulsed with cheerful funk. Oversized Alice in Wonderland chairs. Mirrored pink chandeliers. A naked Mona Lisa painted on elevator doors.

A hip concierge—bright eyes framed in heavy black liner, chunky red-auburn bangs tucked aside by barrettes—offered to store my suitcase until my room was ready. I borrowed a hotel umbrella and slipped outside into light rain.

Even at breakfast time, Temple Bar's streets buzzed with energy. Hungover—or perhaps still inebriated—college-aged boys trundled along cobblestones, arm in arm, singing. Couples in peacoats surveyed restaurant menus advertising shepherd's pie and Irish soups. One pub declared: "Today's stew: whiskey."

I began searching for The Fumbally—an eclectic breakfast spot touted on several Dublin travel blogs. I walked the south bank of the River Liffey, finally grasping the geography of the north-south city divide. At U2 shows, Bono often introduces the band as if they're playing their first public event ever, "We're an Irish band . . . from the Northside of Dublin."

I wandered the grounds of Christ Church Cathedral and St. Patrick's Cathedral—shamrock-green gardens dotted with stone benches—until I found The Fumbally. I joined a short line of patrons and ordered a large coffee with milk and a Fumbally breakfast platter. The dining area bustled with families in thick argyle sweaters, hipsters typing on laptops, groups of girlfriends balancing toddlers on laps. I spotted an empty two-top table and sat down. A cute waiter with facial scruff wearing a faded Brooklyn Beer Garden T-shirt greeted me with a sexy Irish lilt. I commented on his shirt.

"I worked in New York for three months! What brings you to Dublin?" He pronounced it Doo-blin.

"U2 concert on Friday!" I sort of shouted.

"Ah, yeah, I heard the lads gave a great show the other evening. Two more in Dubs this week, right? At the 3Arena?"

"Yes!"

I felt hyper. Wired. Excited the band had *two* shows left in Dublin, not just one. I had a ticket for Friday; I needed to figure out how to land one for Saturday's gig too.

The waiter delivered a ceramic bowl of steamy coffee, a matching flask of warm milk, and a plate of thick brown bread, sunshine-yellow scrambled eggs, chunks of pink ham, and charred bites of fire-roasted tomato. The pork, salty and tender. The eggs, buttery. The bread, hearty and sweetened with traces of tomato juice. I wrapped both hands around the coffee mug and sipped.

I retraced my steps to the hotel, collected my luggage, took the naked Mona Lisa elevator to my room, and stepped into fifty shades of white: white bedcovers draped with faux-polar-bear-fur blankets, white lacquered desk holding a single green apple, Lucite desk chair, groovy frosted lampshade. I locked my concert ticket and laptop in the room safe and took a quick shower. I had to fight an urge to nap; my U2-themed bike tour started in an hour, and I didn't want to be late.

I located the bike shop burrowed among high-end boutiques on Fade Street near a trendy restaurant called Fade Street Social where paparazzi had recently spotted The Edge and his wife. I opened the bike shop door, jangling a bell. Flyers advertising yoga classes and vegan cafés rested on a shelf. Bikes of diverse sizes hung from ceiling hooks—like a cyclist's meat locker. A brawny man in a crocheted Rasta tam appeared from a back room.

"Hi," I said. "I'm here for the U2 bike tour?"

"Ah, Julian will be here in two seconds."

I loved hearing a guy wearing a Bob Marley caftan speak with an Irish accent.

A middle-aged man, gray-blond wisps of hair darting around windburned cheeks, entered the bike shop.

"You must be Heidi." Julian pumped my hand. "Here to see the lads, are ya? Which night do you have a ticket for? Tomorrow or Saturday?"

"Just Friday. Still hoping to get one for Saturday."

"Well, let's see if we can bring you some Irish luck." He winked.

I looked at my watch. Seven minutes after the appointed start time for the excursion. No other guests in sight. Like my sweat lodge experience on the Vancouver hotel roof, I wondered, *Am I the only subscriber?*

After a quick physical size-up and a couple questions about my bike-riding experience, Julian lifted a hybrid road bike off a hook and set it on the floor, popping a kickstand. He handed me a yellow vest with reflective yield signs and a Styrofoam helmet, which smelled of sweat and tobacco. I hoped the rain and cool air would wash away or mask the pungency.

"Ready?" Julian asked. "It's a beautiful day," he joked, echoing a U2 song.

He held the shop door open. We waved goodbye to the store owner and wheeled two bikes onto the sidewalk, slick with rain. I thought about a verse I like from the band Garbage about being happier in rain than sunshine . . . preferring complicated to easy. It's true; textured weather makes me feel alive.

Julian mounted his bike and pedaled down Fade Street, hooking a right turn at Fade Street Social. I hopped on mine, hand brakes squeaking as I tested their force. I hoped the bike wouldn't slip out from under me on wet pavement, and that Irish bus drivers look out for jet-lagged cyclists accustomed to riding on the opposite side of the road. I pumped pedals to catch up to Julian. He grinned and yelled, "First stop, Dublin Wall of Fame!"

We wheeled along city streets, squeezing between Guinness beer trucks hauling kegs. I alternated between pressing the ear-splitting brakes and pedaling frantically to keep pace with Julian. We entered a pedestrian zone. Julian hopped off his bike. He pointed toward a photo wall of famous Irish musicians, including a large poster of U2—the guys in their twenties sporting puffy 1980s hairdos, Bono before his trademark sunglasses, preglaucoma-diagnosis.

Around a bend, a sign bolted to a wall above a rusty brown guitar announced "Rory Gallagher Corner," referring to an Irish guitarist, singer, songwriter, and producer sometimes called "the greatest guitarist you've never heard of," an homage to his extreme talent and influence on the development of numerous musicians. We pushed onward to St. Patrick's Cathedral Grammar School. Reportedly, Bono—a rebellious kid—was "encouraged to leave the school." We cycled past Guinness Brewery to Christ Church Cathedral, a brass sculpture of a barefoot unhoused person asleep under a blanket on a bench in the church lawn.

We rode to Windmill Lane, U2's early recording studio, now demolished and replaced with new construction. We pedaled to Hanover Quay in the south docklands, a more recent recording locale. Julian snapped a photo of me signing my name in graffiti on the recording studio's front door. I had to fake my signature; my stubborn pen refused to lay ink on the textured layers of paint.

We journeyed onward to Merrion Square, a lovely park featuring a statue of Irish poet and playwright Oscar Wilde reclining on a large boulder, grasping the lapel of a green and red jacket, one leg outstretched, his other knee jauntily raised in the opposite direction—perhaps the original "manspreading." Steps away, a sculpture of his naked pregnant wife, Constance, topped a granite pillar. An armless torso of Dionysus—god of winemaking, among other things—rested on a neighboring column. Julian showed me handwritten Oscar Wilde quotes scrawled by famous playwrights, artists, poets, and politicians in white-gray ink on both pedestals.

"This one is in Bono's handwriting." Julian traced his finger along cursive words: "Man is least himself when he talks in his own person. Give him a mask and he will tell you the truth."

I read the scribbles and thought of masks Bono dons, or characters he embodies, on stage: Mirrorball Man, a television evangelist in shiny disco clothes . . . and paradoxically, MacPhisto, a devil in a gold lamé suit and horns. Perhaps even his simple accessory of sunglasses serves as toggle between man and megaphone of truth.

On our way back to the bike shop, Julian paused in front of a hearing aid store called Bonavox, the original inspiration for Bono's nickname (birthname: Paul David Hewson) bestowed by his childhood friend Guggi. *Bonavox*: Latin for *good voice*.

Rain soaked yet famished again, I surrendered my bike to Julian and meandered back to Temple Bar, searching for another restaurant I'd read about in Dublin travel blogs: Gallagher's Boxty House. A boxty is a traditional Irish potato pancake. Another whiskered waiter welcomed me, guiding me to a wooden table near a window in the mostly empty restaurant, lunch rush come and gone, too early for the happy hour crowd. Not much of a beer fan but not ready for wine, I wanted to try a light Irish lager. I ordered a Guinness Blonde. I picked up a package of boxty mix serving as a paperweight on a set of napkins. The label read: "Boxty on the griddle, boxty in the pan. If you don't eat boxty, you'll never get a man."

Well then.

I ordered a beef boxty—a thick crepe folded around Irish steak and sautéed mushrooms, drizzled with peppery white sauce. Its taste, beef-stroganoff-esque. Garnishes of fresh spinach and pickled beets added splashes of color to the plate.

I returned to The Morgan, peeled off wet clothing and damp shoes, set an alarm for 6:30 p.m., and fell into bed for a nap.

When the alarm jangled, I resisted hurling the phone across the room and sleeping until morning. I reminded myself the whole point of the three-day whirlwind trip was to soak up as much Dublin and U2 as possible. I'd committed to an evening historical Dublin/U2 walking tour that would start and end at a club called The Church, a former house of worship on the Northside of Dublin, across the River Liffey from Temple Bar. A U2 tribute band called the Joshua Tree would play there later. I felt a flash of self-consciousness thrusting myself into a group activity I probably couldn't escape once I showed up. But I knew

I needed to start meeting people if I had any shot at landing a ticket to Saturday's sold-out show. I took a hot shower, dressed, and set off for The Church.

As a minister's daughter, I've seen the inside of a *lot* of churches in my life. Elaborate chapels gilded with bloody crucifixes. Evangelical megachurches bedazzled with electric guitars and high-tech light shows. Strip mall basements comparatively bare other than plastic folding chairs, stainless steel coffee urns, and damp vanilla wafers sticking to Styrofoam plates. Many other iterations in between.

I walked into The Church and smiled, immediately comfortable.

An oval brasserie-style bar dominated the ground floor of a cavernous two-story space. A stage anchored one end of the expansive room, already arranged with a drum kit, microphone stands, and necks of sparkly electric guitars leaning against a keyboard. I looked skyward toward a choir loft and noticed an immense organ, copper pipes reaching to an arched cathedral-style ceiling. I looped the main floor, climbed a flight of stairs, and circled the balcony. A placard resting on the organ's crumbling ivory keys noted: "The Renatus Harris Organ: George Frederick Handel, of *Messiah* fame, lived on nearby Abbey Street and was a regular visitor to St. Mary's to make use of the organ."

I snapped a picture of the placard and texted it to my parents; they'd met in music college singing in a traveling choir. My father is an exceptional organist, and my mom—a piano and voice teacher—wrote a book about Handel's oratorio, *Messiah*. I've often tried to explain to Mom and Dad how U2 concerts can feel like a church service, Bono devoting every ounce of his creative marrow toward rousing a sense of community, family, connection to a greater purpose, and spirituality in the souls of eighty thousand strangers in a football stadium. I've made other attempts to use band facts to chart common ground with my parents: When I learned Bono's father loved opera, I shared that tidbit with my opera-aficionado parents. Mom retorted, "Well, he should have taught Bono to sing." I never have a decent in-the-moment comeback to those types of gratuitous slams. They just sting.

Following instructions posted on social media for the walking tour, I descended a staircase to the basement of The Church to find a U2-themed bar. U2 songs blared from speakers. Posters and photographs of Bono, Edge, Larry, and Adam spackled columns and walls. Music videos played on TVs hanging from ceiling rafters. I slid onto an empty barstool and grabbed a laminated menu offering specialty drinks with U2-inspired names: Mary Bloody Mary, Bonavox, The Unforgettable Fire. I flipped the menu over to check out the wine list, not expecting much. Irish bars in America are notorious for undrinkable wine. To my surprise, The Church offered an assortment of Italian, French, and Spanish wines by the glass. I ordered Spanish Rioja, my favorite, feeling supremely validated after years of New York friends ribbing me for ordering wine instead of beer in Irish American pubs.

I took a sip and surveyed the sparse crowd. A woman in her twenties sat at a table staring into her phone, fingers coolly tapping a pack of French cigarettes. Two tall women—one brunette, one blonde—both with thick flowing hair, laughed and toasted one another. A man wearing wire-rimmed eyeglasses and a military-style overcoat joined them, clinking his beer stein against their champagne flutes. My favorite upbeat U2 song, "Where the Streets Have No Name," started playing. I closed my eyes. I like to listen for the sound of The Edge's fingers sliding along guitar strings in that song.

The dark-haired woman approached me. In an American accent, she asked, "Hey, are you by yourself? Come join us!" She began dragging my barstool—with me in it—closer to her blonde friend.

"Are you here for the walking tour?" the blonde asked. "I'm Michele and this is Renee."

I introduced myself. They invited the woman with the phone, a French girl named Sophie, into our fold. The man in the military jacket introduced himself as John, our tour guide.

Michele and Renee explained they'd been college roommates in Louisiana two and a half decades ago, had fallen in love with U2 back then (though Renee started off as an INXS fan), and while they now lived in Los Angeles and Atlanta respectively, they'd met up to attend nearly every U2 tour together in various cities around the world. They'd visited Dublin countless times for shows.

"We do the whole GA experience," Renee noted.

I didn't know exactly what "the whole GA experience" meant, but I nodded and said, "That's so cool!"

"Do you have tickets for this weekend?" John asked.

"I have one for Friday but not Saturday."

"Are you traveling alone?" Renee asked. "That's so brave of you!"

Sophie, quiet up to this point, intervened. "If you need a ticket for Saturday, I can post your request on the fan page." In a soft French accent, she described a "members only" group on a social media platform in which true U2 fans—vouched for by other diehards before they are allowed to access the virtual meeting place—exchange or sell tickets at face value.

Within minutes, Sophie posted my request for a single Saturday ticket on the electronic bulletin board, submitted my name to the group's host, vouched for me, and secured an offer for a face-value ticket from a fan named Brendan. Brendan immediately messaged me, offering to meet up at a pub on Saturday and do the swap—my euros for his extra ticket. I nearly cried. My four new friends smiled and said, "Welcome to the U2 family."

John distributed laminated "All-Access Passes" that said "U2 *Walk On* Pub Crawl." ("Walk On" = a U2 song title.) Michele explained that John played the drums in a Dublin-based U2 tribute band; they'd met him years earlier on their first trip to Ireland and become close friends.

I touched John's shoulder and said, "So you're basically Larry Mullen Jr.!"

He laughed and put his arm around me as we headed outside into nippy evening air.

The walking tour hit many of the same spots as Julian's bike tour, but Michele, Renee, and John added narrative. They shared snippets of U2 history, highlighting pubs where the band played as underage teenagers after Larry Mullen Jr.—at fourteen years old—posted a sign on a school bulletin board indicating he wanted to start a band. The four guys met in Larry's kitchen in 1976, establishing U2 first under the name of The Larry Mullen Band, then Feedback, then The Hype. Part of why I admire the band so much, and why I sometimes envy their foresight, is the fact they discovered they had something truly unique and special as *teenagers* and transformed an adolescent bond into a professional and personal commitment enduring nearly five decades. Bono and Larry also met their life partners at the same time the band formed, and have sustained those romantic relationships as well, notwithstanding megastar status and decades of life on the road.

John infused chronicles of Dublin's knotty politics into the tour, showing us the exact location where one of three Irish car bombs killed thirty-three people on May 17, 1974, during The Troubles—ethnonationalist conflicts between Protestant and Catholic sects over issues such as whether to stay or leave the United Kingdom.

"You know the lyric, 'Registration 1, 3, 8, 5, double-you, zaid?'" John asked, referring to a line from U2's song "Raised by Wolves." "It's the license plate of a blue mink Ford, one of the cars in the 1974 bombings."

It struck me that terrorism had only closely touched me personally since 9/11 in 2001, yet the Irish and citizens all over the world have dealt with sectarian violence for lifetimes. I pondered the role of religion in conflict; it's certainly served as the chief driver of my familial strife. My parents don't understand why I won't adopt the same dogma they do, and to the same degree. Likewise, I struggle to comprehend why they look down upon individualized spirituality.

The rain picking up, our group getting antsy for beverages, we returned to The Church, snagging five seats around the curve of the main floor's oval bar. Scrolling their phones, Renee and Michele showed me the many close-up photos of Bono they've captured over the years as devoted veterans of the GA (General Admission) experience. They explained GA: For each concert date, they join a fan-managed GA line a day or two before the show. First, they obtain numbers inked in Sharpie on their hands by volunteer "line managers." The line managers mark ticket holders' names next to chronological numbers in a spiral notebook, mandating three or four subsequent early-morning and early-evening check-ins to keep coveted sequential ranks in the GA line. The day of the show, arena security coordinates with the line managers and lets ticket holders with Sharpie numbers on their hands into the performance space in numerical order. Fans walk briskly (no running allowed) to their favorite vantage points directly on or close to the stage rail—front, side, center— then wait two or three hours for the show to start. Die-hard fans with desired rail spots experience the show with literally nothing between them and the band members except a small moat patrolled by security guards and the band's road crew.

The tribute band took the stage at The Church. Renee and Michele lingered at the bar; I weaved my way to the front of the dance floor. Fake Bono didn't look nearly as close to the real thing as my Fake Bono back in New York, but his stage gyrations, facial expressions, hand movements, and engagement with the crowd were spot-on. I belted lyrics and danced with strangers.

The band played until midnight. After the last encore, everyone in The Church—patrons, bartenders, bouncers—joined arms and chanted the refrain of a song called "40" (inspired by Psalm 40 in the Bible). I rejoined Renee and Michele. Walking across Ha'penny Bridge—a famous crossing connecting the

Northside and Southside of Dublin, built in 1816 and named for the half-penny toll pedestrians once paid to traverse it—we planned to meet up the next afternoon to catch a different tribute act before heading to 3Arena for the real show.

"We know Fake Bono and Fake Edge in tomorrow's tribute band, Vertigo. It will be fun and the perfect way to get us revved up for the real thing! The pub is really close to the 3Arena tram," they explained.

After pausing to watch moonlight shimmer on the Liffey, I entered my hotel, placed a Do Not Disturb sign on my door, and slept, dreams linking lyrics to my life.

Rain tap-tapping the window woke me up. I lifted the room's blackout shades, revealing gray and overcast skies. I checked my phone: 10:18 a.m. I'd missed the hotel breakfast. I climbed back into bed, pulling sheets to my chin. It felt weird—and refreshing—not to have a writing project to edit, work pressures to attend to, a New York gym class or brunch to race toward. Anticipating a long day . . . evening . . . night—meeting the girls for the preshow tribute band gathering, the actual concert, another after-show meetup at The Church—I loafed in bed until noon, reading a travel memoir called *Turn Right at Machu Picchu* by Mark Adams, invoking memories of my adventures in Peru.

Eventually restless and hungry, I headed out to find a third restaurant on my research list: The Woollen Mills Eating House, where author James Joyce supposedly once worked.

I crossed Ha'penny Bridge to the Northside of the Liffey, looked the wrong way for oncoming traffic, nearly got flattened by a double-decker bus, hurried across the street, and entered The Woollen Mills.

The aroma of bacon, coffee, and fresh bread permeated the room. An open-plan kitchen buzzed with chefs and sous-chefs. A green-eyed Irish guy and a dark-haired girl with even greener eyes manned the host stand.

The girl asked, "How many? There's a wee bit of a wait for lunch if you have a crowd."

"What's the wait for one person?"

"One?" They peered behind me, searching . . . for someone. Anyone.

"One."

"Oh! We can seat you right now."

Score one for Team Solo.

The girl led me to a nook in a window ideal for one human and returned with a menu and a jam jar of cold water. I ordered a large coffee and fresh-squeezed juice and scanned the menu. I always confuse schnitzel with spaetzle, but starving and not caring which one I ended up with, I ordered turkey schnitzel. An American guy at a table next to me explained stock market analysis to a gentleman who seemed to be interviewing him. Two British ladies on my other side sipped tea and spread marmalade on biscuits. I thought of Forrest's Saturday morning ritual: pressing the doughy side of halved New York bagels into a bowl of melted Kerrygold Irish butter, then slathering Keiller's Dundee orange marmalade on each bite. Peaceful moments amid our relationship storm.

My schnitzel arrived: crunchy breadcrumb-coated, flattened turkey breast on a bed of roasted scallions, brussels sprouts, and Irish potatoes, laced with a deep-red raspberry sauce.

I ate every speck of food. I guzzled another cup of coffee. I paid the check and headed through a downpour toward the Dublin Writers Museum. I spent an hour in an eighteenth-century mansion immersing in Dublin's literary history. I often romanticize the lifestyle of writers working on their craft in foreign lands—Hemingway, Gertrude Stein, F. Scott Fitzgerald— daydreaming that if I could do my life over, I wish I'd moved to New York or Paris or Rome at the age of twenty-one instead of going to law school, and tried to be a "real writer."

I caught myself. *Actually, you are a real writer.*

Drenched head to toe, I ducked into the foyer of the Hard Rock Café to catch a reprieve from the rain. A colorful Trabant, a boxy car, hung upside down from ceiling beams, its license plate

reading "Zoo TV." Trabants were cheap vehicles built in social-
ist East Germany with a habit of disintegrating after moderate
wear and tear. In 1989, East Berliners drove Trabants across various geographical borders and left them roadside when they fell
apart. U2 learned about these cars while recording their *Achtung
Baby* album in Berlin in 1990. In 1992 and 1993, they incorpo-
rated brightly painted Trabants as political and artistic statements
into their *Zoo TV* tour.

Back at the hotel, I took a hot bath to warm up. I pulled my
concert ticket from the hotel safe, checked its date for the ump-
teenth time, and listened to a U2 playlist while ironing wrinkles from a vintage T-shirt I bought at a secondhand shop in
New York's SoHo neighborhood—a silk-screened image of the
haunting eyes of a shirtless young Irish boy, Peter Rowen, who
appeared on U2's *Boy* (1980) and *War* (1983) album covers. His
visage appears in black, the word U2 in green, on my shirt. One
of my friends declared my shirt a fake; that concert T-shirt style
never existed. I don't care. I love it.

Running late to meet Michele and Renee, I forgot my umbrella. I held my jacket over my head to deflect raindrops, crossed
the Liffey, and found the gals at a pub called Lagoona Bar halfway
between The Church and 3Arena. They waved me toward a high-
top table, frosty beer steins bumping against a platter of fried potato wedges. I ordered a half-pint of Guinness Blonde. Fake Bono
appeared at our table: Leather jacket with many zippers. Huge
dark sunglasses. Microphone in one hand. Hair slicked into a
mullet. He hugged Michele and Renee. Turned to me and said in
an Irish accent, "I'm Mark. Fake Bono. I love your T-shirt."

Fake Edge—part of the duo forming the tribute band Vertigo—strummed the first few bars of "I Will Follow." The crowd
began hopping.

We drank beer, dipped fries in spicy ketchup, sang every chorus loudly, laughed as we screwed up words. Fake Bono
frequented our table, once placing his sunglasses on my face,

hugging me as he sang "All I Want Is You." Throngs of fans filled the bar. A group of guys circled our table with a U2 *War* flag, Peter Rowen's penetrating eyes mirroring those on my T-shirt. I checked my pocket for my ticket every twenty minutes. My watch clicked to 6:30 p.m., the moment the 3Arena doors opened. Michele and Renee planned to head to the venue closer to 8 p.m. show time; they had seated tickets instead of GA this time. I wanted to experience some of the preshow hype and make sure my ticket was legit.

On a break between sets, Fake Bono showed me where to buy a token for the tram ride to the arena. I hugged everyone goodbye as if we would never see each other again, though we planned to meet up four hours later at The Church.

"Is this your first live show?" Fake Bono asked.

"I'm so nervous, you would think so," I laughed.

I waved goodbye for the fourth time and raced outside to catch the tram.

My ticket worked, of course. Once inside 3Arena, I found my seat at the end of the B-stage—a circular platform connecting to a catwalk extending from a larger main stage. Fans called the small circle the "Experience" stage, reflecting half the name of the tour: iNNOCENCE + eXPERIENCE.

I jittered in my seat during the playlist leading up to the show's start, watching stage crew—characters like The Edge's guitar tech, Dallas, his shaggy blond hair now recognizable to me—make final equipment adjustments to guitar amplifiers and Larry's drum set configuration. My seatmates—older Irish couples—were friendly. Hearing the first few bars of Patti Smith's song, "People Have the Power," we exchanged giddy glances, knowing this was the last track we'd hear before Bono's voice emerged from the bowels of the arena. Minutes later, the lights dimmed.

In the glimmer of a single spotlight, there he stood. One arm raised. Fist clenched around a microphone.

I realized I'd lifted both my arms into the air as well, as had many fellow fans around me.

Bono climbed a set of stairs and strutted the catwalk from the round Experience platform to the main stage—the Innocence one—where Edge, Adam, and Larry appeared like holograms. Adam and Edge strummed the first three notes of a song called "The Miracle (of Joey Ramone)." *Dun-nnn-nnn.*

The crowd erupted.

I bopped up and down with my seatmates for two hours straight. I snapped pictures of Edge bathed in floodlight, far away on the Innocence stage. I captured intense moments of him playing the piano closer to me on the Experience stage while Bono sang a slowed-down version of "Every Breaking Wave," his voice quivering with emotion on long notes. I relate to the lyrics of that song, especially words about "shipwrecked souls" understanding the anguish of an existence without intimacy. My life with Forrest.

I tucked my phone into the back pocket of my jeans. I wanted to try to take it all in, let the real-life images imprint my memory through my eyes and ears and the goose bumps on my skin, not through a camera lens.

Between songs, Bono spoke about the Paris terrorist attacks, the plight of Syrian refugees, efforts to provide medication to stem HIV/AIDS in Africa. Not preachy but just enough to underscore the privilege we collectively possessed, being able to spend two hours bonding through rock 'n' roll instead of fighting for our lives.

The band played twenty-six songs, ending with "One." Linked arm-in-arm, the foursome took bows, turning toward all sides of the stage, acknowledging every section of the arena.

Like flotsam, I folded into a tide of humanity leaving 3Arena, watching herds press into overpacked tram cars. Wanting concert nirvana feelings to saturate instead of evaporate, I decided to walk to The Church. Passing empty warehouses, I mulled whether the area along the docks was safe at night. Listening to fans behind me crooning the refrain from "40," I figured I'd be fine.

Reaching The Church, I joined a fan horde congregating at the door. I found Michele and Renee at our same bar spot. We recapped the show, noting slight adjustments to the set list from prior gigs on the tour. The tribute band took the stage. We stashed our coats in an empty guitar case and danced until 1 a.m.

I awakened to a jostling of the hotel room doorknob. Rain pelted the window. I heaved myself out of bed, asked the cleaning lady to please come back in one hour, and checked the clock: 10:23 a.m. My phone pinged a message from Brendan, the fan holding my second concert ticket. He asked if we could meet at 2 p.m. at Sackville Pub.

I'd missed the hotel breakfast again. Another comforting Woollen Mills meal beckoned. Forcing myself to turn left instead of my usual right out of the hotel, exploring a different route to the Liffey, I crossed O'Connell Bridge (named for an Irish politician who championed social reform) and turned left toward Woollen Mills. The same hostess seated me in my window nook. Feeling compelled to taste something new, I ordered a bowl of broth with leeks, potatoes, chunks of ham, and slices of blood sausage the thickness and circumference of poker chips. And coffee. The soup was my only Dublin food misstep, the blood sausage too gamy. I asked the waitress if I could box it to go and instead ordered butternut squash bhaji—a flat fried fritter layered with spinach and poached egg, topped with mango coulis and yogurt sauce. Mashup of sweet and savory. Walking back to Temple Bar, I handed the blood sausage soup carton to a guy panhandling in the rain on Ha'penny Bridge. He set the box next to his belongings.

I strolled to a jewelry shop I'd passed on the U2 bike tour: ThunderSolas Leather Designs on Cow's Lane in Temple Bar.

Windows displayed handcrafted leather bracelets, cuffs, necklaces, and belts. A sign advertised the option of personalizing
messages on stainless steel or brass tags tacked to leather strips.
Celtic crosses, hearts, and peace signs hung from rainbows of
leather bands exhibited in cases. I entered the store, tucking my
umbrella behind a tin bucket overflowing with shoppers' wet
rain gear. I touched a heavy black leather cuff embellished with
metal loops and tried fastening it to my left wrist. Very punk
rock. I heard familiar laughter and turned around.

"Look who's here!" Michele and Renee embraced me, our
sopping wet hair intertwining. "We've been coming here for
years!"

They yanked up shirtsleeves to reveal leather strips coiling
their wrists, a variety of colors and metal designs reflecting their
two distinct personalities.

"I was thinking of having the designer personalize one of
these thinner bands with a U2 lyric translated into Gaelic," I
said, tinkering with a tray of leather cords bearing metal message
tags.

Michele and Renee pulled out their phones. We typed dif-
ferent lyrics into a translation app, converting words from En-
glish to Gaelic, then back again to double-check the translation.
We howled at the discovery that a favorite word from the song
"Bad"—*surrender*—seemed to translate to *give up* in Gaelic.
Not exactly the zen message we desired.

I opted for "love the higher law," from "One." I wasn't sure
if the syntax meant love as a noun *is* the higher law, or the words
were a directive *to* love (in verb form) the higher law (God? The
universe?), or that love and law are linked in a different way.
For years, I'd felt the law was the wrong profession for me until
I finally found a love for teaching and writing about it. I liked
the ambiguity of U2's unpunctuated four words. The translation
app gave me the Gaelic: "Is breá an dlí níos airde." An artisan
behind the counter helped me select a width of white leather
that could accommodate the phrase. I chose stainless steel for the

metal plate. We wrote out and confirmed the Gaelic translation, complete with funky accents (a right-slanting line over certain vowels called a "síneadh fada"), on a pad of paper. The shop-keeper said I could pick up the wristlet in a few hours. I also pur-chased a thin brown leather band that wrapped around my wrist twice, its tag embossed with one Gaelic word: *áthas. Joy*. I bought one more that looped my wrist three or four times and fastened by weaving a loose strand through two lobes of a four-leaf stain-less steel Celtic knot—a quaternary knot said to represent four seasons or elements (fire, earth, air, water).

I promised to meet Michele and Renee for happy hour at Lagoona Bar to hang out with the Vertigo tribute band again before I attended the real show alone. They didn't have tickets. Michele felt a bad cold coming on, and they had to catch an early-morning flight back to the United States.

I looked up the address of Sackville Pub, actually called Sack-ville Lounge—a misnomer that sent me into a temporary tailspin when I couldn't find the bar on a map, worried it didn't exist, and freaked out I wouldn't have a ticket to the final Dublin show af-ter all. I located the establishment on the Northside of the Liffey and squeezed through a trio of large Irishmen smoking cigarettes in front of the entrance. One opened the door for me. I crossed the vestibule and hesitated. Husky men occupied every barstool, cheering at a soccer match blaring from a lone television. A tall fellow ventured toward me.

"Are ya Heidi? I have your ticket!" He hugged me, pulling me toward the bar. "I'm Brendan. Fancy a pint?"

Not desiring a midafternoon beer but excited and nervous about the ticket transaction, I said yes. Brendan ordered a half-pint of a craft lager for me. He hustled me toward a group sitting on stools by a window, three women wearing flannel shirts over U2 tees, two men in well-worn *Joshua Tree* baseball hats and sweatshirts. Brendan pulled the concert ticket from his pocket. It looked just like the other one: hologram, barcodes, perfo-ration. The correct date. He pointed to the face value price. I counted euros and handed him the bills. He insisted I take off my coat, drink my beer with them, debrief last night's show. The guys pressed me with questions like "Didya think Edge missed a note on the piano during 'Every Breaking Wave?' . . . What song on the I+E album do you love the most? . . . What's your number one track overall?"

The group ordered another round of beers. When I declined a second one, Brendan offered me a shot of Jameson whiskey. I bowed out, turning to the women to suggest they all come to Lagoona Bar for the Vertigo tribute band bash before the real show. Brendan gave me a bear hug. "Here's to a great night!"

I loved that these strangers were so nice to me, that we connected over an admiration for four guys who'd met as teenagers in a Dublin kitchen thirty-nine years earlier, began messing around with instruments, and pieced syllables into songs.

I stepped outside into a haze of smoke. Feeling reflective, having a few hours before I needed to be anywhere, I walked to Merrion Square—the garden park with the Oscar Wilde statue. I reread the quotes scrawled by famous people on the nearby pillars and tried to choose a favorite. None of them resonated with me. I looked up Oscar Wilde quotes on the internet and selected one I liked better: "Every woman is a rebel."

Still an hour too early for the preshow festivities at Lagoona Bar, I drifted into an enoteca. Dusty books lined mahogany shelves. Labeled spigots invited guests to sample wines by the glass. I sat at a low table lit by candles twisted into necks of empty Bordeaux bottles, red wax dribbling onto white table linens. I thought of an old Chianti bottle encased in straw Trey and I had used as a candleholder for a decade of romantic dinners throughout my twenties. Some of my favorite moments together. No anxiety. No insecurity. Just love blindness.

A waiter brought a goblet shaped like a tulip. I watched an older couple kiss on a nearby couch. Young lovers snapped selfies in dusky candlelight.

At Lagoona Bar, I found Michele and Renee surrounded by reveling fans sporting various vintages of concert T-shirts. After an hour, I reluctantly said goodbye, unsure when I'd see my new friends again. We made a pact to "see you on the road!" A few guys standing near us asked if I wanted to ride the tram with them to the arena. I declined; I felt like walking.

I ambled north along the Liffey. I began to *wist*—actively, on purpose, in verb form—noting the physicality of my usual rise and fall, my natural undulation, of travel emotions. Rocket high. A drifting down. A little twist of melancholy.

This trip has been a well-earned high. You've put yourself out there and connected with beautiful strangers from unfamiliar lands. You're allowed to feel a little sad this adventure is wrapping up. But remember, you're not losing anything that can't be felt again another time. Let it go for now. Surrender. Detach, in a good way. No desperate clinging.

As 3Arena came into view, I heard music pumping. A tram jammed with concertgoers whizzed by, faces animated in laughter, giddiness, joy. I approached the pavilion, took out my ticket, and joined a security line. I watched a man try to squish between barricades unnoticed and get summarily ejected by two female security guards who barked at him to "get the feck out." I prayed my ticket would work. Of course, it did.

As I entered the concert hall, my skin tingled from the buzz of the crowd mingling near beer stands, merchandise tables, stand-up bars. I snapped a picture of the sound equipment and texted the image to my brother, a drummer in his younger days. He's not a U2 fan, but he appreciates the artistry of live music. In my twenties, married to Trey, I liked going to my brother's band performances, witnessing his free-form artist's life compared to my buttoned-up existence as a lawyer . . . as a wife.

My ticket offered a much better view than the previous night: the left side of the stage (which fans call "Edge's side"), twenty rows back from the GA mosh pit, three seats in from the aisle. An Irish couple sat to my right; a French couple who'd had tickets to the canceled Paris show sat to my left. The French woman confided her nervousness about being in a packed public meetinghouse, admitting she didn't really want to be there. Her husband left and returned with two giant beers. They chugged their drinks and chatted in vivacious French.

As the last stanza of Patti Smith's "People Have the Power" blasted through the speakers, the lights flickered. The crowd roared. I scanned the arena floor to see where Bono would pop up, fist raised, strutting in leather pants toward the small staircase at the end of the circular Experience stage.

A spotlight caught the glint of his shades, the sheen of his hair. I looked toward the main stage. Saw the fringe of Edge's leather jacket sway as he swung a guitar strap over his torso. He smiled at Adam. Larry looked serious as always. Bono reached the main stage. Edge and Adam strummed the first three notes of "The Miracle (of Joey Ramone)." *Duh-nnn-nnn.*

Here we go.

As I fell asleep near midnight, music reverberating in my ears, my brain replayed memorable show vignettes . . . Edge's cool choreographed stutter step as he glided along the catwalk between the two stages . . . Bono's sweet grin and beautiful rendition of the French song "Ne Me Quitte Pas" in honor of the Paris victims, sending my French seatmates into a sob fest and prompting a few tears of my own . . . Edge breaking a guitar string . . . my Irish seatmates explaining (so I wouldn't feel left out) that the drag queen dancing with Bono on stage to the song "Mysterious Ways" was named Panti Bliss . . . the crowd once again chanting the lyrics of "40" in the parking lot, along the pathway of the tram and the banks of the Liffey, echoing deep into the Dublin night.

The next day, snug in my window seat on my flight home to New York, fingering my new bracelets with their Gaelic inscriptions, I imagined what Bono, Edge, Adam, and Larry might be doing in that moment—as flesh-and-blood humans waking up after a great show, maybe still sleeping, alone or with their spouses, how they would spend their day off. I already missed my new friends—Michele, Renee, John the tour guide, the Fake Bonos, the Fake Edges, the Fake Larrys, the Fake Adams, fans I'd met. I thought of the lyrics from the last stanza of "One," how we have the privilege of lifting one another up, and being lifted up by others. I made a pact with myself: *Let this music and these people carry you sometimes. You don't have to do everything alone. This can be a different family for you. Where you can be your weird wild self.*

6
australia

When Melbourne Law School announced its plan to host the Global Legal Skills conference, I immediately submitted a proposal. In advance of the spring launch of my new book—*Untangling Fear in Lawyering*, the upcoming sequel to my first well-being book, *The Introverted Lawyer*, and my sixth book overall—I wanted to test-drive a rebellious talk about how much I dislike and resist our society's obsession with bravado toward fear. Slogans like "Just conquer your fears!" and "Fake it till you make it!" and "Feel the fear and do it anyway!" and "Do something every day that scares you!" make me stabby.

I've *always* faced my fears. They just laugh in my face.

The conference accepted my application. I bought a plane ticket and began visualizing the twenty-five-hour journey from my New York apartment to Los Angeles to Melbourne.

A few nights after I booked the flight, I met my friend Jenna for dinner in Manhattan. On a hiking trip in Patagonia, Argentina, sliding into the back row of a transport van, Jenna and I had introduced ourselves and within five minutes of conversation realized we'd both graduated from the University of Virginia five years apart and lived ten minutes away from each other in New York City.

Between bites of penne, crabmeat, and peas, I mentioned Australia.

"Hey," she said, touching her wine glass to mine. "No pressure. But what if we meet up in Hamilton Island?" Hamilton is part of the Whitsunday Islands—a collection of seventy-four isles off the coast of Queensland, Australia, at the edge of the Great Barrier Reef. Captain James Cook, a British explorer, apparently sailed through the islands on Whitsunday—the seventh Sunday after Easter, in 1770 . . . almost exactly two hundred years before my birthday.

"We could snorkel the reef," Jenna suggested. "Who knows how much longer it will be there."

As Jenna mused about paddling among delightful sea life in the middle of the Coral Sea, I pictured the shark who'd eat my face.

We crafted a plan to convene in Hamilton Island after my Melbourne conference, rent a condo there for four days, then head to Sydney. Jenna would fly home right before Christmas Eve to see her family. I'd stay a little longer and return home on Christmas Day, my favorite calendar date to be on a quiet plane far away from piles of shiny presents and that Mariah Carey holiday jingle that makes me want to act out and smash ornaments. My adolescent and early adulthood Christmas memories invoke two dioramas, neither nostalgic. The first: lots of church services. The second: Mommom distributing black plastic garbage bags of presents with stapled name tags because "gift-wrapping is a waste of money." My trash bag usually contained thrift shop shoes a half size too big for my feet, lacy camisoles (mortifying to open in front of my father, brother, and grandfather), religious figurines, and dog-eared used books including Judy Blume's young adult novel about puberty, *Are You There God? It's Me, Margaret.* I love winter, kind of hate Christmas, and am a weirdo about gifts. My love language is words of affirmation. Gift receiving makes me uneasy.

Jenna *excels* at trip planning. Instantly realizing our travel compatibility in Patagonia—hiking, eating, drinking, laughing, and shopping together—we'd met for dinners countless times in

New York to devise other adventures. Most recently, she'd flown to Rome to pull me out of book writing hibernation. My brain a useless pile of mush from thirty straight days of working on *Untangling Fear*'s manuscript, Jenna orchestrated a getaway to the island of Ischia in the Tyrrhenian Sea. Unlike neighboring Capri, Ischia lingered mostly under the radar of American tourists. Jenna researched trains, ferries, condos, restaurants, beaches, and natural spas with hot and cold springs. She savvily dangles adventure to entice me out of my introvert cave.

Jenna and I already had breathed the air of three continents together: South America, North America, Europe.

Next stop: Down Under.

~ ~ ~

Venturing to Melbourne involves a six-hour hop from New York to Los Angeles, a two-hour layover, then a fourteen-hour long haul over the Pacific Ocean. The JFK-LAX trip already feels lengthy (a daytime journey—wide awake—compared to over-night flights to Europe which offer at least the ruse of whiling away a few hours asleep), but I had to adjust my mindset. I burrowed into my window seat and read a memoir about solo travel called *Alone Time* by Stephanie Rosenbloom. Since 9/11, I've had trouble finishing novels. But true stories by unfamous humans conquering real challenges sustain my attention.

Landing at LAX, I hustled off the jet bridge, boarded a shuttle bus, and walked into an international terminal with all the swank of a turnpike rest stop.

Jenna had recommended buying compression socks for the transpacific flight, to help with circulation and prevent "deep vein thrombosis." I debated whether to pull the tight socks up to my knees or leave them bunched around my ankles until I boarded the plane bound for Melbourne. The instant the aircraft's wheels lifted from the Los Angeles tarmac and tucked into the fuselage, I tugged the compression socks to my knees—then stressed out for forty-five minutes about whether they were *too* tight, cutting off my circulation.

The plane touched down in Melbourne. I taxied to a boutique hotel recommended by two Australian friends in New York, an artsy place called the Larwill.

A cheerful concierge—attuned to traveler weariness after long journeys from faraway lands—recommended I grab a coffee from the lobby bar before heading to my room. I walked through a chic atrium. Curvy contemporary seating. Aboriginal art in bright colors. Light-wood bookcases. A series of orange hardbacks, including a title by Hunter S. Thompson: *Kingdom of Fear*. A reinforcement of my trip's theme: untangling fear. Simply *facing* my fears never worked for me; I prefer *untangling* them, dissecting them, separating the bad bits from the potentially instructive.

I poured a caffè americano from a self-serve machine, added almond milk, hauled my suitcase to my room, and noted another sign from the universe I was in the right place . . . I love the cover of my first well-being book, *The Introverted Lawyer*. Six white (extroverted) light bulbs hang from short electrical cords, like soldiers in formation. A seventh bulb (the independent introverted one) veers to one side, shining bright yellow. Since that book launched, I'd been noticing quirky light bulbs throughout my travels, which I interpret as cosmic encouragement. In my Melbourne hotel room, an Edison bulb (a reproduction of a vintage filament bulb) beamed from a lemon-yellow lacquer birdcage dangling from periwinkle-blue wire twisted around a black bracket. A pillow with the words *Put Your Heart in It* centered the bed's headboard. Postcards showcasing the art of David Larwill (the hotel's namesake) trimmed a bulletin board, along with handwritten messages like "Stay Inspired!" Larwill, who died of cancer at the age of fifty-four, cofounded an artists' collective called Roar Studios, an effort to cultivate an antidote to art-world bias against marginalized groups. I peered out the window. Two floors down, in a courtyard, two blue boxing bags hung from white metal frames against a brick wall painted silver. Like my light bulbs, boxing motifs often follow me in my adventures.

Knowing I needed to stay awake to begin adjusting to Melbourne's time zone (a sixteen-hour difference from New York in December), I showered, changed, and ventured downstairs to the hotel café.

"Hi! I'd like to try a local coffee," I said to a waiter, pointing at menu options, "but, quite honestly, I don't know what any of these words mean." *Flat white. Long black.*

He laughed and asked, "How about turmeric? Do you like it? Helps with the jet lag."

A person with an Australian accent could be saying the most outlandish thing imaginable, yet I'd murmur reverently, "That sounds lovely; please tell me more."

A mustard-colored turmeric latte arrived in a clear glass, a sprinkle of cinnamon speckling a layer of foam. I ordered avocado toast—thick hunks of bread spread with smushed avocado, a layer of pea shoots, and two perfectly poached eggs.

The bill seemed astronomical, but then I remembered one Australian dollar approximated sixty-six American cents.

I set a simple goal for Day One: Stay awake until at least 8 p.m. This level of travel exhaustion was beyond anything I'd ever experienced. A regular overnight flight to Europe was jet lag kindergarten by comparison.

I exited the hotel into a thicket of humidity, Australia's summer season just beginning, which felt strange in December. I aimed toward Melbourne's Central Business District (nicknamed CBD) to find Hosier Lane—a corridor renowned for ever-changing layers of street art. A mecca for graffiti lovers like me.

Vibrant murals coated the alley's walls. Tourists snapped selfies. Artists worked on new projects. Spray paint cans loitered on curbs—metallics, glosses, mattes. Droplets clung to white nozzles.

A male artist stood on a step stool, his beret, cargo pants, T-shirt, and high-top sneakers miraculously spotless—not a single splotch of paint. His index fingers pressed dueling nozzles of aerosol cans, splashing black and white acrylic on a wall. An image of a grim reaper emerged.

A female artist—in ripped black jeans, cutoff T-shirt baring a taut midriff, one lock of a hip haircut tucked behind a face mask shielding her from paint fumes—thickened a black border around a pudgy pink pig.

The pedestrian crowd grew. Feeling dizzy and claustrophobic, I escaped to a side street. Every inch of surface—industrial trash bins, staircases, doors, ladders, metal bars on windows—screamed color, patterns, phrases. One image depicted a young girl in a headband holding an open book, its pages itemizing a list: "Things to Do: Marriage Equality; Women's Rights; Fix Homeless Problem, Racism, Wage Gaps; Find Love; Find Peace; Be Kind to Everyone; Stop Domestic Violence." *Different location, same societal issues.*

I moved onward to the National Gallery of Victoria. (Victoria = a state in Southeastern Australia.) Ambling aisles of artwork, I activated my gallery ritual, mentally logging all the paintings that stir me, and if I were either a royal or an art thief, I'd cart home with me, hang on the wall across from my bed, and stare at every morning. I chose a portfolio of three. One by Picasso: a portrait of a woman with a green face and pink lips, a nun lurking in the background (thematic of my religious upbringing always looking over my shoulder). Two abstract pieces by Aboriginal artists. The first: side-by-side canvases—black backdrops parceled by thick vertical gray, orange, pink, and white stripes. The second: swaths of orange, red, yellow, and blue with brush lines lingering in the texture, like property boundaries on a map. An impressionistic version of the cartography stamped in my memory from the Gallery of Maps in Rome's Vatican Museums.

Segueing to the Royal Botanic Gardens, I traced pathways along marshes, cactus beds, and ponds dotted with lily pads, then sat on a bench to watch black swans with red and white beaks swim figure eights around floating fronds. I stopped in the garden's Vietnamese restaurant, Jardin Tan, another recommendation from my Aussie friends. I ordered a ginger beer. I decided to try the Bánh Xèo, described as "a signature dish of sizzling mung bean, turmeric, rice flour, and coconut pancake, cooked crispy and traditionally filled with pork and prawn." A platter arrived with lettuce and mint leaves. I wrapped greens around morsels of textures and flavors, dipping bites into spicy sauces. I sipped cold ginger beer through a wilted paper straw.

I walked back to the hotel, leftovers in hand, drew the blackout shades, and crashed.

I awoke at 4:30 a.m., disoriented, unsure which meridian lines slicing the globe contained me. I tried to doze again. Unsuccessful, I flicked the switch of the Edison bulb, dragged exercise clothes onto my body, and trudged to the hotel's empty gym, darkness shrouding the boxing bags outside. Workout complete, I exited in search of coffee just as a team of muscular Australian fitness trainers entered the facility.

I dressed for the Global Legal Skills conference and walked in morning heat to Melbourne University, drenched in dewy sweat by the time I arrived. For two days, I attended workshops and lectures, meeting acquaintances from American and Australian law schools for happy hours and meals. The day of my *Untangling Fear* presentation, my confused body clock overrode most of my usual performance anxiety. I didn't have the energy to care about looking unintelligent compared to my peers. Plus, the symposium's attendees fizzed with warmth and openness to new ideas—not always the norm with law faculty.

The conference planners had scheduled me last in a lineup of three panelists. The first two speakers—both male—exceeded their allotted time, ignoring the (female) moderator flashing time cards and a stop sign. I watched agitation permeate other female faces in the room. When the guys finally stopped talking, I stood up, smiled, and gripped the edges of the podium. I delivered a feisty outline of certain outdated practices and traditions in legal training that I believe propagate unhealthy fear in law students: survival-of-the-fittest culture, extrovert bias in classroom dialogue, ranking systems, scarcity mentality, misplaced one-size-fits-all advice like "fake it till you make it." I highlighted lessons we could glean from other professions (medicine, engineering, sports) and shared techniques that have helped me untangle my own fears: journaling, boxing lessons, solo travel . . .

The audience applauded our three talks. My copanelists cornered me at the lectern, insisting, "But you can easily conquer performance fear by just practicing and preparing."

That's what people who've never experienced debilitating fear always say.

When I first started giving speeches and book talks, I thought I had to reach *everyone* in the room or my mission had failed. Recalibrating my stakes helped a lot. Now if I reach *one* person, if I help *one* individual feel less afraid, I feel I've done my job. And the one person can even be *me*. I knew these guys weren't my audience; I didn't need to convince them of my approach toward fear. I extracted myself and skipped the closing dinner of the conference, already overstimulated by human interaction. I wanted to walk Hosier Lane again, see if any new graffiti had popped up overnight, and grab a quiet meal before repacking to fly to Hamilton Island.

At dusk, Hosier Lane bustled with tourists. The colors, textures, and themes of the walls had morphed again, like a nonstop slideshow rather than stationary concrete. Near the end of the alley, I slipped into a wine bar called MoVida and settled onto a black leather barstool at the corner of a dark-wood countertop.

A bartender greeted me. "How ya going?"

I liked the Aussie phrasing. *Going*, not *doing*.

He placed a wedge of fresh bread on a wooden cutting board in front of me, charred crust flaking like tree bark. He poured olive oil into a divot in the board, then sprinkled salt crystals around the circumference of the small pool. I tore a hunk of bread, dipped a corner in the oil, lightly touched an edge to the salt, and put the bite in my mouth.

Grammarians like to tell me *impactful* is not a word. I disagree. That bread, *impactful*. Spongy yet chewy. Tang of oil. Bang of saltiness. I closed my eyes, opened them again, and surveyed my surroundings—a ritual when I'm walloped by a travel moment. Engrave every nuance of the memory into my brain so it won't flee.

The bartender replaced the cutting board with a saucer holding an amuse-bouche (I love the French word and concept for *delight the mouth*): a pastry shell filled with yellow custard, peas, prosciutto, and black pepper. As I dug into a plate of grilled asparagus on a bed of ricotta speckled with hazelnut pesto, the bartender conversed with two men sampling artisanal beers, their Australian accents a hypnotic soundtrack.

When a server delivered my check, he said, "Enjoy Melbourne!" He pronounced it *MEL-bin*.

≈   ≈   ≈

On the three-hour flight from Melbourne to Hamilton Island, I scanned the seascape, wondering if dark shadows in the translucent water represented innocent coral ecosystems or something more predatory.

The news warned of a typhoon. Curious, I looked up the word and learned a typhoon is the same weather event as a hurricane, just different geography. Both typhoons and hurricanes are tropical cyclones, from the Greek *kyklon* for *moving in a circle*. Typhoons—stemming from the Greek word *typhon*, meaning giant, father of the winds, or smoke—occur in the Indian or Western Pacific Oceans, while hurricanes roil the Atlantic and Eastern

Pacific Oceans. The word *hurricane* derives from either a Spanish/ Caribbean term for "god of evil" or Huracan, the Mayan god of wind and storms.

I love bad weather—all of it. Wind, rain, snow, sleet, light-ning, thunder. A reminder we're not in control of everything. An excuse to hunker down, burrow in, read, write . . . I just hoped Jenna's connecting flight through Los Angeles wouldn't be disrupted, and obviously that the storm wouldn't wreak car-nage—human or material.

At Hamilton Island Airport's outdoor baggage claim carou-sel, a woman in a baseball hat approached me, tapping a pen against a clipboard.

"Are you Heidi? How ya going? Here are the keys to your golf cart and condo." She dangled a lanyard. "Richie here will show you how to work the cart and will get ya into your place."

A porter—evidently Richie—grabbed my bag and rolled it toward a lineup of red golf buggies.

I'd not driven any vehicle, let alone a golf cart, in a long while. I reminded myself Australians drive on the left side of the road. Richie explained the machine's basic maneuvers. Key in-sertion. Brakes. Forward. Accelerate. Reverse. Island rules: No driving late at night or under the influence. He tossed me the key lanyard and gestured for me to slide behind the wheel. He hopped into a neighboring cart. I turned the key in the ignition and pressed the brake pedal hard to release it. The cart lurched.

To keep up with Richie, I gunned the accelerator, but the electric buggy—at maximum speed—moved about as fast as a motorized wheelchair. I looped a traffic circle, eyes trained on carts in front of me to ensure I stayed on the correct side of the avenue. Ascending a hill, I smelled floral bouquets, heard squawks from birds swooping overhead, noted magenta bougain-villea cascading iron gates. Richie hung a left into a condo com-munity. I jammed my foot on the brake to avoid colliding with a bus. Richie pointed at a parking spot. I shifted into reverse and backed into the space. He lifted the trunk of the vehicle and showed me how to plug an electrical charger into an outlet hidden in a planter.

The two-bedroom condo opened onto a patio overlooking a landscape of three descending tiers: bright-green lawn; jumble of plants, trees, and flowers; a bay. I opened a sliding glass door and stepped onto a tiled lanai. A mini kangaroo hopped by. Then another. And another. Wallabies!

I reclined on a chaise and watched wallabies spring around the lawn. Screeching birds the size of French bulldogs landed on the patio. Bright-white feathers. Sunshine-yellow plumes on their heads. Curved black beaks. Googly eyes. One strode right toward me with a look like "Who exactly do you think you are, and what exactly are you doing on my patio?"

Sulphur-crested cockatoos. Badass birds.

I napped, occasionally opening one eye at the sound of rain-drops pelting parquet flooring. The wallabies and cockatoos ignored the weather, playing tag around the grassy knoll.

A few hours later, I unplugged the golf cart from its charger, looked both ways at least eight times before inching the vehicle onto the main street, and pumped the brakes down the hill toward the airport.

Jenna and I hugged in the baggage claim area, thrilled that her *three* flights from New York, Los Angeles, and Sydney ran smoothly. Happily relinquishing the buggy's key to her, I leaped into the passenger seat and gave turn-by-turn directions to the closest grocery store. We stocked up on happy hour wine and regional cheeses, laughing at Aussie packaging descriptions like "strong & bitey."

We caught up on our veranda over glasses of Australian wine, entertained by parading wildlife. Rain squalls came and went.

Hungry, we walked to a marina, strolling docks of bobbing yachts and motorboats, browsing restaurant menus. We passed ominous signs relaying messages like "Irukandji—a small and transparent jellyfish—can be present in the waters of the Whitsunday Islands. Symptoms of an Irukandji sting include severe pain, muscle constriction, and breathing difficulties, and require immediate medical attention." Another gem: "Dangerous sharks inhabit Cid Harbour—do not swim."

Over plates of linguini and shrimp at an Italian restaurant on a wooden pier, we planned our week.

"Okay," Jenna asserted. "We are definitely snorkeling the Great Barrier Reef. I researched a charter company, and they have open time slots for tomorrow!"

Snorkeling. In the open ocean. On purpose. With toxic jellyfish. And savage sharks.

Okay. Time to untangle this fear.

I love staring pensively at, and listening to, the ocean.

I'm still a wimp about getting into it.

In my mid-twenties, Trey and I booked a Caribbean cruise with his brother and our sister-in-law. The three of them wanted to snorkel. I wanted to not get eaten by barracuda. I felt fat. Sunburned. Seams of a neon bikini I bought on sale at T.J. Maxx pinched my blotchy freckled skin. We boarded a tour boat with strangers. Passengers jumped off platforms into crystalline Caribbean water, laughing, splashing. Trey dove. His brother cannonballed. Our sister-in-law jackknifed. I clutched the plexiglass edge of the boat, staring into the fathoms, scanning for anything two feet long with teeth. I was petrified. Trey and the others swam away.

A kind member of the crew helped me down a ladder into the sea. I pulled a rubber snorkel mask over my nose and bit down on its mouthpiece. I dipped my face into the water, testing air flow. My inhales and exhales sounded like a hospital ventilator. I wriggled neoprene flippers strapped to my feet. I wanted to move but didn't want to be noticed by any marine life. I paddled in small circles. I *did* see barracuda; they kept a watchful distance.

I don't remember marveling at the aquatic realm that day. I don't remember awe. I don't remember wonder. I don't remember beauty. I remember terror. And feeling alone.

≈   ≈   ≈

Jenna raised her wine glass. I clutched mine, condensation mingling with perspiration. "To adventure."

Purple sky shifted to fiery orange as the sun set. We climbed our hill in twilight, looked up, and exclaimed in unison, "Look at all the bats!"

Webbed wings fluttered against ginger sky. Shuddering, we hustled to the condo.

Lying in bed, I tried reframing my feelings about the Great Barrier Reef boat excursion. I knew I had to snorkel the coral. I'd traveled twenty-five hours to Australia. Who knew when I might ever return. This was a once-in-a-lifetime opportunity to see a natural wonder with a friend who cared about my well-being, safety, *and* thirst for self-growth. Yes, I was scared to swim in the open ocean. I can't remember the precise pivot point in my adolescence when I began to fear water other than swimming pools. Men I loved had teased me about my hesitations, or blew past me to flex their innate daredevilishness. Periodically though, strangers, not lovers, took time to help me.

≈   ≈   ≈

At thirty-one years old, I tried waterskiing for the first time. A year after my marriage shattered, I sat on a motorboat in Mecox Bay in Long Island, New York, next to a guy I'd met at work who was trying to woo me (way before I was emotionally ready to share my airspace with anyone). He coaxed me to don a life jacket and try getting up on skis. Still steeped in divorce depression and somewhat numbed to my usual dossier of fears (I believed I'd already ruined my life, so I figured I deserved to get bitten by an eel or hit in the skull with a water ski or shredded by a speedboat motor), I said yes to slipping into the murky water. My date coached, "Bend your knees. Angle the skis upward and parallel. Keep your arms straight."

His buddy, a lanky real estate agent serving as boat captain, hit the gas. The speedboat rocketed forward. The rope flew from my hands. I face-planted. The skis detached from my feet. I swallowed briny water. My bikini wedged between my glutes.

I hated it.

My date pushed me to try again, repeating his technical directions. I tried. And tried. And tried. Tears mixed with salt water, but I didn't care if the guys saw me cry. I felt I deserved to be punished for leaving my marriage. The guilt and shame hurt so much I wanted to die, but I was too paralyzed to do anything about it.

After the sixth or seventh try, the real estate guy stopped the boat. He jumped into the water and swam behind me. No lecturing or judging or chiding. No impatience or exasperation. He simply said, "I've got you." He grabbed the sides of my life vest, his fingers grazing my shoulders. He pulled my torso backward a few inches into the water toward his body, causing my legs and skis to bob on the surface at a better angle. He yelled to my date to gun the motor. As the boat shot forward, the guy held his grip on my life jacket just long enough till the precise instant the slack in the rope disappeared, then released me. I popped up, out of the turbidity. My skis caught the waves, shooting me forward in a controlled pull by the taut rope. I bent my knees, kept my arms straight. I leaned back and watched the skis on my feet cut through the boat's wake like sabers.

I'm doing it!

The boat curved. My skis rode curls and swells. I didn't fall. For the first time in months, I relaxed. I tested body positions, clenching and flexing quad muscles, bending then extending my knees ever so slightly, noticing how incremental tweaks improved my balance. Eventually, the boat slowed. I sunk into bobbing waves—gently. I jettisoned the rope, floated on my back, and stared into the sky.

Trust yourself. Things are going to get better.

Jenna and I packed day bags with swimsuits, sunscreen, and books. We found a coffee shop in the harbor and ordered lattes. As the cashier handed us a placard with a table number, Jenna said, "I'll be right back. I'll go see what time the charter leaves and book two tickets, as long as you're okay with that!"

My brain screamed *no.* My head nodded *yes, of course; I'm totally into this.*

We boarded a charter boat with twenty-five people, a wide range of ages. Families with children, older couples, us. Crew members relayed safety instructions about life preservers and on-board behavior. Jenna and I secured two spots on a deck near the bow. We sunbathed as the boat left the harbor. The charter hugged the shoreline at first, passing beaches and coves along neighboring Whitsunday Islands. Soon, we turned toward the open ocean, aiming for the reef, leaving dry land behind. We kept going.

After a half hour motoring out to sea, the crew called us inside the vessel for a briefing about the snorkeling part of the journey. One crew member, holding a laminated chart display-ing varieties of sea life, described different fish we would see.

"If we're lucky, we'll spot a shark!" he said in an upbeat Aus-tralian accent. "These are harmless reef sharks. They hang out near the sandy floor."

Harmless never sounds credible as an adjective accompany-ing *shark.*

As he explained types of coral and marine creatures we'd encounter, I regretted not updating my life insurance benefi-ciaries.

A peppy female crew member distributed thin wet suits she called "stinger suits." She explained we were not quite yet in Irukandji jellyfish season but, "Better safe than sorry!"

Jenna and I pulled damp neoprene bodysuits—complete with mittens and hoods—over our feet, legs, torsos, arms, hands, necks, and hair, leaving our faces exposed. The logo blaring from our chests read: "Adrenalin Extra Heavy Duty Shield."

Adrenalin is right.

I didn't understand the logic of wearing a protective suit that left chins, cheeks, foreheads, and lips exposed. What if we swam face-first into Irukandji tentacles? I hoped the snorkel mask was the size of a dinner plate.

Having massive misgivings about saying yes to this certain disaster but not wanting to disappoint Jenna, I crawled on hands and knees in my stinger suit to the railing of the charter's bow and peered into the sea. I saw clear water, then blurry shadows of reef, just as the crew had depicted. The boat slowed, then eased to a stop, dropping anchor. A crew member hopped into a skiff. Two more crew climbed onto surfboards, paddled out to sea, and formed a triangle with the skiff. Passengers squeezed feet into rubber flippers, grabbed foam swimming noodles, and lined up at the stern's ladders. One by one, they jumped into the ocean. Jenna leaped into the sea and began propelling toward the surfboards. When the last little kid scooted off the aft edge with a giggle and a splash, I remained the lone passenger on the deck. Fish shaped like vertical Frisbees flapped at the surface of the water a few feet away.

"They're your welcome committee," a crew member urged, smiling and offering a hand to ease me into the abyss.

I released the handle of the ladder and lurched into the ocean. Gravity tugged me below the surface. I popped up again. The cool water felt invigorating. My heart began its usual slam dance. *Deep breaths. You're okay.* I suctioned the snorkel mask to my face and practiced breathing through my mouth, listening to my own inhales and exhales. *Breathe in. Breathe out. Kick your feet.*

Initially, my heart banged wildly, like a drunk drummer. I lifted my head and scanned the water to find the closest crew member straddling a surfboard. He was twenty feet away. I kicked my flippers and aimed toward him. I figured I could stay mostly calm if I knew I could reach that surfboard in a few fierce swimming strokes. Using Jenna's blonde locks (some of which had escaped her stinger suit) and the surfboard as visual buoys, I dipped my face into the water, straightened my body, which had tightened into a ball, and flexed my feet. For the first time, I peeked at the reef.

Schools of clown fish—a pageant of orange and black stripes—played in front of my nose. The Frisbee fish loitered nearby, shimmying in purples, pinks, and greens. Coral came into focus, its texture resembling a soft sponge. Deceptive. We'd been instructed not to touch it—to preserve the environment but also to avoid getting cut by jagged calcium carbonate exoskeletons. I estimated the depth to the reef floor, maybe twenty feet from surface to sand.

I watched braver snorkelers dive to the sandy bottom and shoot back to the surface for air. I floated face down, occasionally bobbing my head above water to check my markers—Jenna's hair and the surfboard. One crew member slid off his board, plunged to the seabed, and lifted an object the size of an eggplant. He ascended, climbed back on his board, and beckoned for us to look at the sea cucumber he held in his palms. He encouraged me to touch its bumpy skin. An orifice at one end opened and closed.

We snorkeled for forty-five minutes. I swam one more loop within my safety triangle, then separated from the group, feet and flippers powering me back to the boat. Along the way, I peered at the coral layers, noticing colors and textures. I gazed once more at the sandy floor of the reef.

And there I saw him.

A reef shark. Hovering a foot above the seabed. Just hanging out. Maybe four or five feet long.

I stopped and stared. *I'm literally out in the middle of the ocean swimming with a shark. And I'm actually not freaking out.*

I reached the boat. A crew member extended a hand, helping me climb the ladder. I removed the flippers and snorkel, suction marks imprinting my forehead and cheeks. My heartbeat decelerated. Jenna joined me at our sunbathing spot on the bow. She offered a fresh towel. Passengers ate bologna sandwiches and chips, then slipped into the water for a second round of snorkeling. Uneager to tempt fate, I stayed onboard. I sipped cold beer, sea salt crystallizing on my skin. Jenna swallowed a seasickness pill and napped.

I stared into the Coral Sea and thought of my shark.

At sunset, Jenna and I rode our golf cart up a hill lined with foliage to hear live music. A tiki bar called One Tree Hill offered cocktails, but we'd brought our own: a bottle of wine and plastic wine glasses secured in our golf cart's drink holders. (One Tree Hill is a volcanic peak in Auckland, New Zealand. It's also the name of a U2 song dedicated to one of the band's road crew, Greg Carroll, a Maori New Zealander, who died in a motorcycle accident in Dublin in 1986 at the age of twenty-six.)

Listening to reggae, we debriefed our reef experience and contemplated additional outings. The typhoon still far enough away, we decided to book another half-day boat excursion. Jenna had always wanted to see Whitehaven Beach, famous for swirling sand formations that shift and transform with wind gusts and tides.

In the morning, we joined a new set of passengers at the dock. This boat ride—mostly a sightseeing tour—brought no sea life anxiety, though the crew still recommended stinger suits for swimming breaks in island coves. The charter slipped in and out of crescent inlets, sunshine refracting off wispy white sand.

Our boat eased into the curl of a bay. The crew ferried us to shore in a rowboat, four passengers at a time. A guide suggested

we drop our beach gear near a grove of low palm trees and follow a wooden path to an upper viewing deck to photograph
the white sand swirls. I kicked off rubber sandals and left them
near a shrub, soon regretting that decision. Following fellow
passengers along a path of wooden slats through thorny shrub-
bery, an onslaught of pebbles, twigs, and prickers jabbed the
arches and pads of my feet. I stopped trying to keep up with the
pack. I slowed down, placing each foot in spots on planks free of
barbs and plant debris. A flash of yellow pulled my attention. A
polka-dotted lizard several feet long lazed on a rock. If I'd have
been hurrying, I'd have missed him.

I reached the observation deck.

In law school, my roommate had referred to guys with clas-
sic good looks but who gave us no romantic jolts as "empirically
good-looking." The prismatic water and unblemished sand of the
Whitsunday Islands indeed were empirically beautiful. Immacu-
late postcard images. But like flawless Laguna Beach, California,
where I'd lived with Forrest, the prim Hamptons in New York,
or camera-ready Capri in Italy, pristine beaches rarely inspire
me. I crave grit and edge, not perfection. Ideal "sunny and 72"
weather also bores me. I prefer unpredictable, messy, textured.
Maybe that's why graffiti and tattoos intrigue me. An interrup-
tion of the expected. Paint or ink placed on canvases that aren't
"supposed" to have anything sketched or written there. Precur-
sors to a growing yearning to draw my own life map. A rejection
of, or rebellion against, lines and shapes dictated by others.

I snapped pictures of the seascape anyway. Mostly unmoved
by the view, I returned to the beach, soft sand a respite for my
torn-up arches and heels. Jenna joined me. We donned soggy
stinger suits and swam in the shallow bay.

As the outer bands of the typhoon began drumming the coastline of Hamilton Island, Jenna and I spent two rainy days vis-

iting an eco zoo, staring at cute koalas napping in eucalyptus trees. According to the zookeeper, koalas sleep up to eighteen to twenty hours a day. Occasionally, one would wake up and notice us through drowsy eyes, its scruffy wet fur reminding me of my dog Rowan after a bath—an experience she deplored.

Our last night in Hamilton, Jenna and I treated ourselves to a meal at a resort called Qualia—a philosophy word meaning *subjective, individual experiences or qualities of perception . . .* i.e., how each of us processes tastes, sounds, colors, temperatures, emotions such as pain, joy, and awe differently.

The typhoon stranding most of the hotel's expected guests on the mainland, we had the restaurant all to ourselves. Rain drove divots into sand beyond the terrace railing. I wore the long tie-dye dress in gradations of blue I'd bought in Akumal, Mexico, a reminder of my temazcal sweat lodge experience and Puglia, where I'd worn it last. After a meal of shrimp salad with grapefruit and arugula, and triangles of dark chocolate torte for dessert, Jenna snapped a photo of me standing under a trellis, infinity pool behind me, tempestuous typhoon sky behind it.

When I travel, I rarely take pictures of myself. I love photographing street art, farmers' markets, urban architectural textures, cool fonts in restaurant placards. I'm a horrible selfie taker; I'm always looking at the wrong part of the camera, or my smile looks too forced or smug. I seldom ask strangers to take photos of me. Often, returning home from a trip, I realize I have no visual mementos of me subsumed in the scenery. I like the image Jenna caught of me at Qualia. Vivid green of palm fronds. Breeze lifting strands of hair. Serenity of the infinity pool. Typhoon brewing on the horizon. One hand around a column. Body leaning away from the structure. Bicep flexed. Happy. Carefree. Blue dress invoking memories of other transformative trips. I'd evolved since then. More fears untangled.

In the morning, Jenna and I wedged our luggage in the back seat of the golf cart, returned the vehicle to the airport parking lot, boarded a two-and-a-half-hour flight to Sydney, and found our apartment in Bondi Beach.

Turquoise and white tones—wallpaper, kilim rugs, throw pillows, ceramic vases—gave our condo a beachy vibe. We walked a few blocks toward the ocean to a restaurant called *bills* (I loved the proprietors' insistence on a lowercase *b*), sat outside, ate poached eggs with spinach and red pepper cream, sampled different coffee styles, and people watched. Bondi Beach seemed overrun by fitness models. Men in tank tops and gym shorts, bulging muscles, tattoos, faux-hawk haircuts. Women in booty shorts and bandeau tops showcasing bounty of genetics or plastic surgery.

Cloud cover dampening our plan for a day of sunning and swimming, we wandered Bondi's shoreline. We doffed shoes and shuffled barefoot in the sand of Bondi's main beach, watching surfers catch waves. We climbed sets of cement stairs on the right-hand side of the cove. I paused at a sign describing the origin of the word *bondi* (pronounced *bond-eye*). The Aboriginal word allegedly means *noise made by sea waves breaking on the beach* or *noise of water breaking over rocks*.

On a pathway tracing the coastline, we encountered Icebergs, an Instagram-famous fifty-meter swimming pool situated *in* the ocean. Waves crash over the sides of a concrete enclosure, mixing salt water with chlorine water, pummeling the heads and bodies of lap swimmers in marked lanes. On a landing overlooking the pool, people exercise—lifting weights, twisting bodies into yoga poses, competing in sit-up and push-up challenges.

On our walk back to the condo, as Jenna purchased a Turkish cotton beach blanket from a bodega, I noticed a storefront sign: Bondi Ink. I'd spied the tattoo shop on a map when scoping the town's topography for restaurants to try. For a while, I'd been pondering getting a tattoo—my first. The word *bondi* lodged in my mind as an option. I liked that the word has five letters and ends with an *i*, like my name. Its Aboriginal definition reminded me of U2's song, "Every Breaking Wave," the one with the lyric about shipwrecked souls subsisting without intimacy.

I've always been squeamish about needles and blood. I mused about whether I could tolerate the pain of five little letters.

For our second day in Bondi, the weather still lousy, we purchased tickets to a wine tasting adventure—an organized sampling tour of various vineyards and barrel rooms. Early morning, a van picked us up at the condo. The driver—doubling as the tour guide—collected four couples from hotels around town and drove us two hours up the coast and inland to Hunter Valley, past rows of grapevines and clusters of grazing cows.

As I stepped off the van at the first stop on our itinerary, the fragrance of fermenting grapes transported me back to wine tasting adventures in my twenties with Trey.

In 1773, an Italian viticulturist named Filippo Mazzei embarked on a journey to the American colonies with European grapevines in tow. During his trip, he visited Thomas Jefferson at his home in Virginia: Monticello, meaning *little mountain*. Jefferson persuaded Mazzei to plant European vines on a plot of land nearby. Thereafter, Mazzei formed a Virginia wine company with thirty-eight shareholders, producing their first barrels of wine from homegrown grapes. Wine making didn't really blossom into an industry in the southern state, however, until two centuries later in the 1970s. By the 1990s, while Virginia vineyards still didn't have anywhere near the same name recognition as California or other states like Oregon or even New York, fifty wineries operated in hills and valleys within driving distance of the University of Virginia. Now, the state boasts over three hundred wineries, offering a robust lineup of wine festivals and wine education events.

In the 1990s, wine tasting offered a form of inexpensive and fun entertainment for UVA students on limited funds. Trey and I spent many a Saturday tasting local reds and whites at vineyards scattered around Charlottesville's undulant hills, learning about harvesting processes and differences between wines aged in oak barrels versus stainless steel. I remember naively declaring—at twenty-one years old—"Red wine tastes like dirt." Now I can't get enough of that dirt—*le terroir* (a concept encompassing microclimates, topography, and cultivation methods—in addition to the soil) or *la terre* in French . . . *la terra* in Italian. Earthy, spicy, volcanic, mineral flavors.

Wine tasting will always remind me of falling, and being, in love with Trey.

～ ～ ～

Our Australian driver/sommelier encouraged us to hold each sip of wine in our mouths much longer than we normally would, noticing how tastes and textures change and evolve even over the span of a few extra seconds tarrying on one's tongue and palate. He demonstrated how to place a small pour into a tasting goblet, lay the glass on its side on a tabletop without spilling its contents, and observe the wine's colors, shades, and character.

At the third winery, we paired even more wine with shrimp and mango salad, massive steaks, fried potato wedges, and roasted tomatoes. On the ride back to Bondi, everyone snored except the driver.

Over the next few days, Jenna and I walked a coastal path from Bondi to Bronte Beach, watching the color of the water in the Icebergs pool transmute. The original clear, freshly chlorinated pool water shifted to aqua blue, then turquoise, then teal, then jade, then emerald, and finally moss green, before the pool managers drained the concrete reservoir and started again with fresh water not yet commingled with ocean waves. Each time we passed the sign defining the word *bondi*, I touched my ribs and pondered a future tattoo. Lying in bed at night, I skimmed online customer reviews of Bondi Ink. I chickened out.

The night before Jenna flew back to New York to celebrate Christmas with her family, we found an open-air bar on the corner of Hall Street—Bondi's primary shopping promenade—and Campbell Parade, the main oceanfront avenue. We ordered cocktails and listened to a guitarist croon Bob Dylan songs.

I noticed a guy leaning against a countertop, his dark hair cut into Bondi's popular faux-hawk style—shaved close on the sides, thick and wild on top. I loved his look: tan, tattoos, biceps, grit, edge. His eyes met mine. We both looked away. A girl materialized next to him, caressing his elbow while chatting with her girlfriends. She went outside to smoke, reappeared at his hip, then disappeared to the ladies room with her posse of friends. He looked at me again.

The musician took a break. Jenna and I drained final sips from our glasses and paid our check. We weaved through rowdy tables toward the doorway. I felt a hand on my shoulder. I turned. *The guy.* He said, in gorgeous Australian accent, "You know there are a lot of successful, available guys in here who want to know you."

I smiled and, for once in my life, had a decent comeback. "Are you one of them?"

He smiled back. "Yeah, well, not so much available . . . "

"Bummer."

He laughed, touched my back, and drifted away.

Jenna and I walked home in moonlight, Bondi waves crashing against distant rocks.

Sliding into bed, for the first time on the trip, I craved someone's skin next to mine. Someone a bit maverick yet capable of attentiveness. Sexy yet sweet, affectionate. Confident yet open to vulnerability. *I know I need to be more approachable, make myself available, put myself out there, go for what I want. I don't know. I'll work on it.*

In the morning, after Jenna and I said our goodbyes—or more like *see-you-soons*—I lounged on the condo couch, pondering options for my next few solo days. I checked email. Two notable messages in my inbox. First, the copy editor assigned to my *Untangling Fear* book returned the lengthy manuscript with final changes, requesting I proofread three hundred pages within *ten days*. My stomach immediately twisted with deadline anxiety. Second, my publisher sent four photos—the proposed cover art for my book. The first three options underwhelmed me, not tantalizing at all. The fourth I loved . . . shiny white cover with black boxing gloves hanging from tangled red laces. A magical moment—seeing an image embodying days, weeks, months of waking up early, brewing a pot of coffee, lighting a candle beside my bed, and writing.

I love author Steven Pressfield's advice from his book on the creative process, *Do the Work*: "Get the first version of your project done from A to Z as fast as you can. Don't stop. Don't look down. Don't think." When my teaching semester had ended and I'd finished grading, I'd bought a plane ticket to Rome, rented a flat in the Olympic Village near Rome's Stadio Olimpico (the site of my soccer game date five years earlier with Luca), and wrote two hours every morning for thirty days. After my quick detour to Ischia with Jenna, I flew home and wrote every day for thirty more days. Then I started at page one again and edited. A to Z. A to Z. Again and again. My soul lay bare in those pages. I'd exposed all my fears and sought to untangle them.

Seeing the boxing gloves and tangled laces on the cover for the first time, I felt almost ready to let the project go into the world.

But first, final page proofs.

To review three hundred pages in ten days, I needed to start right away and parcel the workload into incremental chunks. *Thirty pages a day for ten days.*

I needed a printing shop.

I dressed in exercise gear and grabbed breakfast at *bills*. Walking Bondi's main street, I scanned storefront awnings and found an electronics store doubling as a copy center. I printed ninety pages—three days of proofreading work. I scurried back to the condo, sipped a turmeric latte, and circled lingering manuscript typos in blue felt tip ink.

For two days, I edited, shopped, and walked the coastal path from Bondi to Bronte, clutching a coffee cup with "AF" scribbled by a barista on the plastic top. *A* for almond milk; *F* for flat white. I decided it meant "Australian as fuck." I watched Bondi waves crash onto a graffitied ledge near Icebergs pool, revealing, then covering, then reexposing letters spelling "One World." I bought a silver tote bag made from recycled paper, sunglasses with blue tortoiseshell frames, and an aquamarine crystal—my birthstone. I laughed at a handwritten card explaining the mineral's properties: "Helps to invoke tolerance of others." Strolling Campbell Parade, passing Bondi Ink, I peeked in the windows at bored tattoo artists, chatting, awaiting clients.

I sat on a barstool at a restaurant called Hardware known for its spicy margaritas. The bartender didn't recognize me, though Jenna and I had talked to him before. He designed an artisanal cocktail for me: smoky mezcal; thin slice of charred lime floating above a lone block of ice; pink, red, and white salt crystals gracing the glass rim. I dipped haloumi cheese and cucumber slivers in olive oil and sesame seeds. I listened to a sultry musician—camouflaged pants, perfect facial scruff—play guitar and sing Lenny Kravitz songs slightly off-key. I looked up the lyrics to U2's song "Bad" and took a screenshot, contemplating whether I could handle eleven words inked into my abs.

My last night in Bondi, suitcase packed and zipped, I fell asleep early but woke up in the middle of the night, sensing movement in my hair. I reached. Felt something. Clenched my fingers around it. Threw it. Flipped on the bedside lamp. A gargantuan insect crawled the seams of the comforter. I leaped and grabbed a shoe. Normally, I don't kill bugs. This intruder needed to go. I chased it along the floor, up a wall, and finally nabbed it, carcass and guts splattering on the paint. Shuddering, I shut the bedroom door behind me, ran to Jenna's empty room, swept back the bedsheets to check for more critters, slipped between the covers, and tried—unsuccessfully—to fall back asleep.

At dawn, I lit a candle, proofed thirty book pages, showered, dressed, and called a taxi. Christmas Day. Time to fly home.

Five months later, in May, U2 issued a surprise announcement: They'd added a new leg to their *Joshua Tree* thirtieth anniversary tour, a retrospective of the band's iconic 1987 album. New Zealand and five cities in Australia in November. Then onward to Asia in December.

I texted my U2 girlfriends, Michele and Renee. The timeline, international travel, and expense didn't seem realistic for any of us. But just in case, I checked the tour website for any show dates that wouldn't conflict with my fall teaching schedule.

Two shows in Sydney . . . the weekend before Thanksgiving.

I had absolutely zero business even thinking about traveling to Australia for the second time in twelve months. I knew I'd be under intense scrutiny at work throughout summer, fall, and winter leading up to my February tenure vote at the law school—a month before my fiftieth birthday. At this point, I'd been teaching for twelve years at three law schools. At the first two institutions, as a legal writing professor, I'd never been eligible for tenure, just renewable two-year contracts. Once I landed the job of *directing* a legal writing program, leading a team of ten professors, tenure finally became possible. My publication record and public speaking persona definitely qualified me for the professional accolade. But the vote wouldn't be a cakewalk. I'd made necessary but controversial changes to the writing program. I'd attracted detractors. Vociferous ones.

My rational brain: *Be responsible. Don't indulge the fantasy of Australia.* My Aries/blossoming-rebel/nomad brain: *Tenure schmenure. You only live once.*

A serendipitous email appeared in my inbox. The coordinator of the Global Legal Skills conference at Melbourne Law School forwarded a call for proposals for another teaching conference. In Sydney. On Thanksgiving Day. The conference theme: *Teaching as a Subversive Activity.*

I grabbed my draft syllabus and monthly planner. The vice dean already had scheduled me to teach Mondays and Wednesdays in the fall. I calculated travel time to Australia. If I departed New York right after my Wednesday class the week before Thanksgiving, I'd land in Sydney on Friday morning. I could hit the U2 show Friday night, a second one Saturday, sleep Sunday, rest for two days, attend the conference Wednesday through Friday, then fly home. I wouldn't miss a single class; I didn't teach during Thanksgiving week anyway. A definite whirlwind—flying twenty thousand miles round-trip for seven days in Australia. And totally *subversive* skipping family Thanksgiving *again* for a rock concert.

As a paying member of the official U2 fan club, I received presale codes for the Down Under leg of the *Joshua Tree* tour. The ticket overlords scheduled the advance sale to launch at 9 a.m. in the time zone of each concert venue. This meant, precisely at 9 a.m. local time, I needed to log into a ticket website account with a password, choose a show date, select a seat (or GA), input the presale code, and pay with a credit card—all while a clock counted down and hundreds, if not thousands, of other fans around the world tried to nab the same ticket. The process requires poise and nimble fingers while adrenaline surges with the force of a fire hose.

Calculating the fourteen-hour time difference between Australia and New York in May (different from the sixteen-hour gap in December), 9 a.m. in Sydney meant 7 p.m. a day earlier on the East Coast in America. One glitch: The precise time of the Sydney ticket presale, I was supposed to be (undistractedly) enjoying the band, the National, at Prospect Park in Brooklyn with my friend Clay and four other pals. To multitask, I had to confess my crazy Australia plan.

Just as the opening act for the National strummed their first guitar chord, I raced to the edge of Prospect Park. I found a spot where I could sit on wet grass and facilitate my international transaction. Kids and mosquitos buzzed around me. I frantically clicked tabs on my tiny mobile phone screen, inputting password, show date, presale code, credit card. My hands jittering, I prayed my bank would not reject the foreign operation, presuming transpacific fraud. An hourglass icon whirled on the screen. A timer clock counted down. Six agonizing minutes later . . . a confirmation screen announced, "You're going to see U2 in Sydney!" *OMG.*

Now I just needed to get accepted to the teaching conference, buy a plane ticket, book a hotel, and not get fired.

The conference accepted my proposal: another *Untangling Fear* book talk. My international public speaking persona was gaining momentum.

🌊 🌊 🌊

Summer morphed into fall, and a new academic semester began. Inaugurating an updated and more rigorous curriculum for my law school's writing program, pressure at work amplified. Evaluative scrutiny intensified. Multiple run-ins with one outspoken and hot-tempered colleague kept me up at night, causing me to doubt my intellectual and operational instincts. Her public criticism of me during faculty and committee meetings triggered my *freeze* response; I was so taken aback at such personal attacks happening in an academic forum (compared to the marital, familial, and law firm settings of my past), I didn't assert or defend myself in the moment. My blush fired up, a visual and visceral onset of another shame spiral, my body's knee-jerk acceptance of someone else's assumption I'd erred. Later in the safety and comfort of my apartment though, I was better able to discern what was happening, like a detached bystander instead of a myopic participant. I halted the negativity ripple effect faster. *You haven't done anything wrong. You have nothing to be ashamed of. You are doing your job the best way you know how. Trust your instincts. Trust your process.*

Shame still skulked, but I mostly defused it, journaling and punching my trainer Lou's mitts during weekly one-on-one boxing lessons. I focused on teaching my students, trying to motivate my writing program team, and traveling domestically for book talks. Indianapolis. Albuquerque. San Francisco. Charlotte. Phoenix. Amherst. Philadelphia. Charlottesville.

As each workweek ticked by, I wrestled with whether to cancel Australia. *Self-indulgent? Irresponsible? Reckless?* I finally decided, *No. You're absolutely going. You've aligned everything perfectly.* I'd only miss two actual in-office days, Thursday and Friday before Thanksgiving week, when barely any faculty are on campus anyway. I kept both days clear and unencumbered on my appointment calendar.

At JFK Airport, a Delta agent tagged my suitcase stuffed with copies of my *Untangling Fear* book "heavy," which made me laugh. My baggage—literary, physical, and relational—*is* heavy.

I unabashedly tugged my compression socks to my kneecaps and nuzzled into my window seat. Twenty-four hours later, I landed in Sydney.

The Bondi Beach apartment I'd rented was chic and clean, and reeked of insecticide. I'd emailed the host mentioning my chagrin at waking up with a giant bug in my hair the last time I visited Sydney. She'd responded, "Well, in November and December in Bondi, tropical insects are a given." But judging from the chemical smell permeating the condo, she'd taken my critter aversion seriously.

A faux cowhide chair, a telescope, and a leather couch in the living room brought to life interior design photos I'd scanned a dozen times on the apartment rental app. A staircase led to a loft with a queen bed. Lavender sprigs topped a stack of laundered towels. Bergamot soaps rested on twin sinks in the bathroom.

I couldn't risk lying down to take the long nap I craved. A U2 friend, Ryan, had already texted me, urging me to get to Sydney Cricket Ground no later than 3 p.m. to guarantee a place in the GA early lineup and secure a spot close to the stage for the show. I'd met Ryan in Los Angeles in 2018, when Michele and Renee convinced me to camp out all night in their SUV outside LA's Forum to ensure amazing GA spots on the stage rail for that U2 show—my first time in the front row of any major concert in my life. At dawn, equipment trucks and trailers had arrived from Las Vegas where the band had played the previous night, drivers honking horns in solidarity with crazed fans sleeping in Jeeps and tents near the Los Angeles arena. Ryan and I had stayed in touch. He's a professional stuntman, lives in Nevada, and took forty-five days' leave from work to travel to *all* the shows on the New Zealand–Australia–Asia leg of the *Joshua Tree* anniversary tour. U2 fans commit.

With less than three hours until I needed to be at the stadium, I forced myself to stay awake. I changed into running shorts and a tank top and strolled to Bondi's beach for a quick glimpse of the ocean before breakfast at *bills*. The air smelled of ash, the sky obscured by smoke from Australia's bushfires that had been raging for months.

I sat outside at *bills*, reprising meals I ate there with Jenna: thick slices of ham, poached eggs, coconut bread with creamy butter. I drank a green juice, hoping it would perk me up.

Returning to the beach, I removed my running shoes. I watched my bare feet form potholes quickly filling with water as I plodded in shallow surf toward the steps leading to Icebergs pool. Swimmers stroked the blue-green water, waves crashing on heads and shoulders. I traced the coastline to nearby Bronte Beach, listening to surf pounding crags of rock. Curtains of bougainvillea, flowers of luscious colors and fragrances, burst from patches of soil and moss.

I looped Bronte, pivoted, and returned the way I came. I bought coffee at a juice shop, smiled at the "AF" the barista wrote on my cup, and scooted back to the condo. Dressing in tight jeans, combat boots, and my vintage U2 *Boy* T-shirt, I wrapped a black camouflaged jacket around my waist. According to the weather app on my phone, the forecast looked iffy. Thunderstorms. I texted Ryan to let him know I was on my way and called a taxi.

The driver dropped me at the GA check-in tents at Sydney Cricket Ground. My heart drummed with anticipation as the GA line manager jotted the number 326 in Sharpie ink on my hand. I entered the security checkpoints, praying my ticket was valid, the irrational paranoia I experience at every show. The ticket checker scanned my barcode. After a comforting beep, he waved me through metal detectors to a waiting area. Preshow music boomed from speakers. I texted Ryan: I'M HERE!

He responded: AWESOME! I CAN'T LEAVE MY SPOT. I'M #5 IN LINE! BUT LOOK FOR ME WHEN YOU GET INSIDE. I'LL BE ON THE RAIL AT THE B-STAGE, CLOSE TO THE CENTER POINT.

I stood in a paddock with fans from different countries one-upping each other with U2 anecdotes. I had a doozy of my own to share. But I kept it to myself.

Two and a half years earlier, I awakened to my mobile phone vibrating beneath bedsheets in a Boston hotel room. I answered it. I rarely pick up unscheduled phone calls. (Introvert Rule #1.)

My college and law school friend Todd's voice: "Hey! Where are you? Please tell me you're in New York."

Groggy. "I'm in Boston. I met Michele and Renee here to see U2 play Gillette Stadium in Foxborough last night. Had to ride a bus an hour to the arena. Took forever. Didn't get home till like 1 a.m. I'm wiped out." *Yawn.*

"Get up. Get dressed. Get back to New York ASAP. I got us two tickets to see U2 play a semiprivate show tonight in Times Square. It's an event sponsored by a foundation called MusiCares. Adam Clayton is getting an award for his work with musicians in recovery from alcohol and substance abuse."

"What are you talking about? There's no show in New York tonight. They're in Boston."

"Heidi, get back to New York *now*. I'll meet you at PlayStation Theater in Times Square at five."

I didn't know whether to believe Todd or not. Plans we discuss—travel mostly—don't always come to fruition. But due to his lobbying work, he does have major connections in the music industry. I got out of bed. I flew home, took a shower, made myself look as rockstar as possible—ripped black jeans, low-cut black top, chain-mail-style necklace filled with aquamarine stones, leather jacket—and took the subway to Times Square.

In a 2,100-seat auditorium, Todd and I watched singer Macy Gray, the band the Lumineers, and other artists perform songs in homage to the philanthropic work of U2's bass player, Adam Clayton. Adam appeared from the eaves, approached the microphone, and gave a heartfelt speech about unconditionality—in his humble yet elegant timbre. He thanked musicians like Eric Clapton and Pete Townshend (of the band the Who) who helped him stop drinking in 1993 when, on an alcohol bender, Adam missed a Sydney show on U2's *Zoo TV* tour. Adam expressed love and appreciation for his bandmates, plus his wife who had only known him sober. He confided, "I'm not used to achieving anything on my own. This is very unusual. An award for *not* doing something."

Bono, Larry, and Edge joined Adam on stage. They played three songs: "I Will Follow," "Stuck in a Moment," and "Vertigo."

The event transpired so quickly, the whole thing seemed like a mirage. I had trouble processing zigzagging emotions stirred by such an intimate performance.

Adam's fete complete, Todd and I loitered at the top of an escalator, debating where to go for drinks and dinner downtown. I glanced down the escalator and saw Macy Gray—immediately recognizable by her towering height, her signature cool Afro hairstyle, and a psychedelic coat she'd worn on stage—riding the moving staircase up to the landing where Todd and I stood. She sauntered across the vestibule, passing right by us as she exited the building.

Thirty seconds later. A bolero hat. Wesley Schultz, lead singer of the Lumineers and wearer of said hat, ascended the escalator.

"Um, Todd." I yanked his jacket sleeve and whispered, "Todd . . . I think all the musicians are coming up the escalator. What if . . . "

Elevator doors opened a few feet away from us. Two enormous venue security guards emerged. And Bono.

Todd is frequently around celebrities because of his lobbying work. He took one look at my wide eyes and gaping mouth and murmured, "BE COOL. Act like we belong *right here* so they don't make us move. BE COOL."

Bono strutted by us, out the door, into a crush of paparazzi and fans.

Subtly hyperventilating, I turned back to Todd. I peered down the escalator and saw The Edge floating up it, an entourage of ten people bunched around him. He strode by us, out the door. My eyes bulged. I couldn't breathe.

"Be cool," Todd reiterated.

Thirty seconds later, Adam Clayton rode the escalator with a single handler, a guy barely twenty years old. They stopped in front of Todd and me. The handler asked me to take a photograph of Adam and thrust a mobile phone at me. I eked *congratulations* to Adam, fumbling the phone like a circus juggler. I couldn't make the device, or myself, function. Adam waited patiently for about ten seconds, kindly smirked at me, turned, and departed the building. I nearly burst into tears.

I . . . cannot . . . believe . . . I just blew my one moment with Adam.

Mortified, I whirled toward Todd. I noticed a blond blur jogging up a staircase adjacent to the escalator.

Head down.

No bodyguards. No entourage. No handler.

Alone.

Larry.

Larry Mullen Jr. gazed up the staircase. I looked down the staircase. I mouthed, *Larry?* He stopped . . . at the top of the stairs . . . next to *me*. I babbled about how much I love him and the band, and that I'm grateful for everything they do.

I owe Todd a giant debt of gratitude because, in all his infinite presence, coherence, and wisdom, he asked Larry if it would be okay to snap a picture of us. Larry leaned in, rested his head against mine, placed his hand on my waist, and smiled. Larry's public smiles (and photographs with fans) are somewhat rare. I gushed a few more words of adoration and appreciation. He smiled again, nodded, and departed.

⌇   ⌇   ⌇

In the GA line in Sydney, I touched my phone in my jeans pocket. Its screensaver: the photo of Larry and me. His head touching mine. My hand grabbing his shoulder in a death grip. A couple extra buttons on his shirt unfastened. Both of us dressed in head-to-toe black.

At 5 p.m., security guards opened the stadium gates and corralled GA ticketholders in an orderly fashion—chronological numbers scrawled in Sharpie on our hands, paper wristbands with sequential numerals wrapped around our forearms—through tunnels into the open arena. At number 326, I entered the cricket ground in the fourth swath of a hundred fans. We speed walked toward desired spots around the main stage and the "tree stage," a secondary platform shaped like a Joshua tree connected to the primary one by a catwalk. I spotted Ryan— long hair, lanky frame—waving from the center point of the tree. Front row, on the rail. Fans already congested three standing rows behind him. A buddy saved Ryan's coveted perch as he pressed his way through bodies to greet me. He handed me a Ziploc bag.

"I've been holding on to this to give you for over a year now!" he exclaimed.

I opened the plastic pouch and pulled out a vintage David Bowie T-shirt. When Michele, Renee, and I met Ryan in the wee hours of the night in Los Angeles, camping outside the Forum, we'd played David Bowie songs—too amped to sleep. During the 2018 eXPERIENCE + iNNOCENCE tour, Bono riffed David Bowie's lyrics during the shows while photos of the late singer (he died of liver cancer in 2016) flashed on large screens. The band credits him as one of their artistic influences.

"I love it!" I pulled the shirt on over my U2 tee and hugged Ryan. We turned toward the crowd filling space around the tree stage, now five rows deep in some areas.

"I don't want you to lose your primo spot!"

"I've been traveling with that particular lot of U2 lunatics for three cities now," he said, pointing at a trio of fans with elbows resting on the security rail near center stage. "They'll save my place, don't worry."

We spent a few minutes catching up about his travels to New Zealand and Melbourne and nuances of the gigs in those locales. I started getting antsy about securing my own position for the show. I promised to reconnect with him afterward. He edged his way through the crowd back to the rail.

I wanted to watch the concert from a vantage point around the tree stage away from the center, closer to Larry's drum set. I gently stepped around fans sitting on the ground, amazed no one was stopping me from maneuvering toward my targeted destination. I found a clearing with only two rows of fans standing between me and the barrier behind Larry's drum chair.

Gazing around Sydney Cricket Ground, I exchanged smiles with fans as we accidentally bumped shoulders and elbows, an undercurrent of excitement about what we were about to experience together. Thunder growled overhead. Gold ribbons of lightning painted gloomy skies. Wind carried smoke from the bushfires into the stadium. For an instant, I pondered the idiocy of standing dead center in an open-air arena, surrounded by electronics, in the middle of a brewing storm. I decided it was worth the risk . . . like riding on the back of Luca's motorcycle in Rome . . . like the sweat lodge in Mexico . . . like climbing Montaña in Peru . . . like snorkeling with a reef shark in the Great Barrier Reef . . . it felt better to lean into the world rather than fixating on worst-case scenarios.

A man next to me removed a white denim jacket and placed it over his teenage daughter's bare shoulders to shield her from chilly raindrops beginning to fall. Decades of U2 concert buttons ("badges" to Europeans) decorated the jacket, along with an autograph scribbled on a lapel. I peered more closely at the handwritten letters. *Larry Mullen Jr.*

I closed my eyes and breathed in smoky air, feeling fat dollops of rain smack my cheeks. I opened my eyes and saw a security guard gesturing at me from a platform. He tossed a packaged rain poncho at me, and said, "This is from that guy," pointing at Ryan. I placed my palm on my chest.

U2 doesn't always have an opening act, or "support act" as the Europeans say, but they did on this tour: Noel Gallagher and his band, the High Flying Birds. In the 1990s, I'd loved the British band Oasis, both famous and notorious in part due to Noel's constant feuding with his brother and covocalist Liam. The High Flying Birds took the main stage punctually, exactly at showtime. One of U2's many positive attributes: Their concerts routinely start on time. Noel sang a few throwback

Oasis tracks, plus some new hits, and joked with the crowd. He dropped f-bombs and poked fun at our ponchos. With his trademark jest and sarcasm, he whined about the downpour, asserting, "I bet when fecking Bono takes the stage, the rain'll vanish."

Sure enough, as the preshow soundtrack segued to the Waterboys' "The Whole of the Moon"—the anniversary tour's signal to fans that U2's set was about to start—the rain dwindled, then stopped.

Suddenly, Larry appeared—solo—on the main stage. The crowd cheered and bounced up and down. Larry strode alone down the catwalk to the tree stage, giving his signature low wave to fans. He settled on a stool behind his drum kit, making last-minute adjustments. The distance between us so minimal, I could see the individual filaments of the zippers on his high-top shoes. I watched his feet test the pedals of the bass drum and cymbals. The lights faded. He grabbed drumsticks. The instant his sticks struck drumheads, the speakers exploded with the first bars of "Sunday Bloody Sunday."

Bono, Adam, and Edge came into view, traversed the catwalk in individual styles of swagger, and fanned into choreographed positions around Larry's drums, blasting the music and lyrics of the song memorializing the day British soldiers shot into a crowd of civil rights advocates and bystanders in the town of Derry, Northern Ireland, in 1972.

Bono stoked the audience, imploring into his microphone, "Hold us up . . . Hold Larry up . . . Hold Adam up . . . Hold up The Edge . . . Hold me up . . . " I like how his words suggest we're all in this together; we're all gathered in the same space to cocreate, to witness and participate in something magical. Not hierarchical. Not unilaterally transactional.

The band spent the first half of the show orbiting the tree stage, rotating around Larry's drum set, close enough for me to discern crinkles around their eyes, The Edge's wedding ring, their jovial smirks at one another, their fingers caressing instruments and microphones, their secret communication code through subtle hand gestures and nods.

For the second half of the set list, they transitioned to the main stage. Bono donned a preacher hat as a character called Shadow Man, meant to represent his alter ego or inner voice. In a fierce performance of an eerie song called "Exit," allegedly portraying the mental script of a serial killer, Bono strangled the neck of a stationary microphone stand, circling it in an aggressive high-knee march.

At the lowest point in my divorce grief, as I grappled with depression and confusion about where my life was headed, worried I'd made a colossal irreversible mistake, my mom admonished me, "You need to be brought to your knees by God." She probably meant that deep healing first requires a humbling, but at the time, I needed the exact opposite message. I needed to be lifted from my knees. I needed hope, not regret. I needed unconditional love, not another dump truck delivery of shame. As I watched Bono's preacher character stomp around the microphone stand, I vowed to release myself from ever again trying to subjugate my beliefs, my persona, my soul to any religion, institution, or family perpetuating toxic subordination. I will only surround myself with people who pull one another up from dirt and grime, who tend to one another's scraped and bruised knees.

Nearing the end of the show, Larry hopped off his drum chair to join Bono, Adam, and Edge for a final bow, but then realized they had a song remaining—"One." With a sheepish grin, Larry bounded back to his drum kit. Finally, the band said good night.

Ryan found me in a mass of fans moving toward the arena's exits. "Hey, let's go find the GA line managers *right now* to get a number on our hands and secure a primo spot in line for tomorrow's show!" he urged.

Dead tired, I wanted to escape to my Bondi apartment and sleep, but he promised staking numerical places on the GA list would be worth a few minutes of detour. In the parking lot, we found his tour buddies holding a spiral notebook and Sharpie markers. They jotted our names next to sequential numbers, wrote corresponding digits on our hands, and directed us to return the next morning at 6 a.m. for another check-in or we'd forfeit our positions in line. I grimaced at Ryan, predicting zero chance I'd be awake and back at the stadium that early. I hugged him good night, hopped in a taxi, and went home to crash, not bothering to set an alarm.

My body clock woke me at 7 a.m. My phone flashed a text from Ryan: HEY, IF YOU'RE UP, COME TO THE STADIUM AND GET A NEW NUMBER. THERE AREN'T THAT MANY PEOPLE HERE!

I'm awake. I might as well. I dressed quickly and taxied back to the cricket arena. Ryan hustled me to the line managers who wrote a new number on my hand: 222.

As Ryan had never seen Bondi Beach, we cabbed to the coast, ate breakfast at *bills*, walked Campbell Parade, then agreed to meet at center stage again once we entered the arena.

When I arrived at the venue, security guards scanned my ticket (which worked, *whew*) and directed me into a corral for fans bearing numerals between 200 and 300. Ryan waited in the 1–100 paddock. At 5 p.m., staff opened the gates, again allowing us to speed walk across the cricket pitch. When I approached the tree stage, I saw Ryan signaling to me, again from the front row. Fans around him opened a path for me. He grabbed my shoulders and pushed me right to the rail. He gave me his spot.

"I'll be on the rail for the entire tour. I figured I could let you have this experience tonight," he explained. "I'll stand behind you and get some good pictures."

Gratitude and guilt jockeyed in my head. I thanked him profusely but sensed he liked me in a way that didn't feel reciprocal. *Why don't I ever fall in love with the nice guys?* I'd started reading books about relationship attachment styles—anxious, avoidant, and secure—like Amy Chan's *Breakup Bootcamp*, and Dr. Amir Levine and Rachel Heller's *Attached*. Reflecting on my romantic history, I knew I had an anxious attachment style and tended to be attracted to avoidants, not attentives. Recognizing this and doing something about it though seem to be two different endeavors.

I leaned on the stage rail and watched roadies lift a tarp hiding crawl space beneath the tree stage, protecting instruments and equipment from rain and ash until showtime approached. I caught a peek at Larry's snare drum, cymbals, bass. Eventually, crew members lifted the drums piece by piece onto the stage. Security detail paced the trench between the rail and the edge of the "tree." Fans pointed out a muscular guy with cropped silver hair: Bono's personal bodyguard, Brian Murphy. He smiled. I grinned back. A blond teenager moseyed by, bulky camera hanging from a neck strap. Everyone around me whispered, "It's Larry's son!" A cute older man with spiky hair chatted with a stagehand; the ID hanging from a lanyard around his neck read "Sebastian Clayton." Adam Clayton's brother.

The show started. My physical proximity to the band was almost too much to handle this time. Sensory overload.

At one point, Bono stood face-to-face with me, nothing but air between us, singing right *at me* with a look of such ferocity, his expression seemed to border on disgust. Irrationally, I felt like he was mad at me. My idol, disappointed in me. We locked eyes. Time halted. I studied every wrinkle in his beautiful, craggy face. Watched the bones in his hand choke the microphone tighter. Noticed his free hand tightening and releasing in sync with each syllable he sang. Felt each ripple of raspy texture in his voice as he held a particular note an extra beat.

We blinked. He backed away.

When the show ended, my pensiveness quickly shifted to exhaustion. I craved solitude. Processing time. Ryan sought togetherness.

"You're a really interesting woman, and I'd like to get to know you more," he disclosed as we stood on an empty sidewalk in smoky Sydney air.

"I'm really complicated," I responded.

Actually, I'm not complicated. I'm complex. I should like Ryan. He's kind. Sweet. Interesting. Into my band as much as I am. Well traveled. Loves dogs. Performs risky Hollywood stunts like jumping out of planes for a living. Brave. Adventurous. But I'm not feeling hit by my usual romance truck. Probably a healthier start, but still . . .

I hugged him. "Thank you so much for the Bowie shirt and for giving me your spot on the rail. It was truly epic. I hope you have an awesome next show in Perth and beyond. Let's stay in close touch, okay?"

I felt like a colossal jerk punching buttons on my phone to summon a taxi.

〰️ 〰️ 〰️

For two days, I relaxed. I walked the coastal path from Bondi past Bronte farther to Coogee Beach (named after an Aboriginal word meaning *stinking seaweed* or *the smell of seaweed drying*), silver smoke from the bushfires hovering over the shoreline. I trekked the opposite direction to explore Watsons Bay.

Midweek, I attended the "subversive teaching" conference at the University of New South Wales. At each plenary session, the conference organizers spotlighted me as the attendee who'd traveled the farthest, from New York. I gave my *Untangling Fear* presentation, advocating for inspiring rather than terrifying the spark out of law students. One audience member snapped a photograph of me and posted on social media, "Prof. Heidi K. Brown delivering a talk on fear in legal education. Room full of furious agreement."

I flew home to New York, soul replenished, body a bit worn out, brain gyrating with memories of musical notes, crashing surf, and squawks of high-flying birds.

〰️ 〰️ 〰️

Growing up as a minister's kid, getting a tattoo wasn't exactly an option. The most rebellious thing I did as a teenager was pierce my own ears. I'd swabbed each lobe with cotton balls saturated with rubbing alcohol. Numbed my ear cartilage with ice cubes, water droplets dribbling down my neck. Penetrated the flesh with pointy heart-shaped studs I'd borrowed from a friend and sterilized with a match. My mom discovered my deed when—in the middle of dinner in the dining hall of the boarding school where we lived—a preppy clamshell clip-on fell off my ear and bounced onto the table, landing beside a platter of coagulating veal parmesan.

I touched my first tattoo at thirty-one: an animal skull inked into the shoulder of the first guy I let into my New York walk-up apartment after my divorce. Its backdrop was supposed to be a moon but totally looked like a sombrero.

I kissed an Italian waiter with Sicily's Trinacria (meaning *three-pointed* or *three-legged*) symbol embossed on his bicep: three legs bent at the knee, circling the head of Medusa, her hair writhing with serpents. While he ranted about Italian politics, I nodded, pretending to understand, tracing the tattoo with my fingers.

Whenever bouncers at music venues stamped the inside of my wrist with glow-in-the-dark ink, I liked the way the imprint looked on my skin the next morning. I let those markings linger as long as possible until shower soap washed them away.

When my dog Rowan died, I pondered a tattoo of her name along the interior of my forearm. I played with fonts. I drew letters with ballpoint pen on my inner wrist.

I traveled to San Francisco for work, browsed a bookstore, and bought tattoo artist Ed Hardy's memoir, *Wear Your Dreams: My Life in Tattoos* (coauthored by Joel Selvin). Reading his vivid descriptions of needles penetrating skin, I wondered, *Could I endure the pain?*

I daydreamed about word tattoos. *If I got one word, what would it be? What language? What font? What location on my body?*

I started following tattoo artists on social media. One appeared in my saved screenshots a lot: Jessica Valentine. I liked the way she captured her work and described it: "Medusa for Julia's first tattoo . . . "

Days after my return from my second trip to Australia, Jessica posted Australia-themed "flash" (an artist's stock of tattoo design drawings) on Instagram—koalas, kangaroos, boomerangs—announcing she'd contribute all proceeds from tattoos based on the Down Under theme to Australia bushfire relief efforts. I took the geographical synchronicity as a sign. I booked an appointment for a microtattoo. Made a credit card deposit.

Two gentle yet firm reminders about Jessica's twenty-four-hour cancellation policy landed in my inbox. I didn't cancel. I popped two Advil and headed to Haven Studio in Brooklyn. I followed Jessica's directions: "Go up the creepy staircase to the black door on your left."

Two French bulldogs greeted me at the studio entrance. Jessica introduced herself. Matte purple lipstick. Black eyeliner. Punk rocker boots. Tattoos on her neck, hands, the skin peeking through rips in her jeans. Another striking woman in tights and cutoff jean shorts, dark bra showing through a white T-shirt, moved silently from couch to chair.

Sunshine dappled the one-room workshop. I glanced around. David Bowie candles lined a mantel. Female empowerment messages emanated from picture frames. Cheerful pillows adorned a comfy couch. Two tattoo benches—the shape and size of massage tables—loomed near windows. Shelves displayed bottles of Technicolor ink. Jessica started talking to her fiancée—Cameron—about her art being featured on a series of wine bottles. As I signed consent forms, Jessica's relaxed banter with Cameron, a dog hopping into my lap, the artsy music . . . calmed me.

"So, you want the word *bondi*, right?" Jessica asked. I'd described my tattoo idea in her website intake form.

"Yes. It's my first, so I want a little one to make sure I can handle it. Lowercase letters, in a feminine, girly font."

She showed me different typographies on her computer screen, helping me narrow my preferences to a few. She played around with the curl in the *b*, the loop in the *d*, the dot in the *i*. We made the word slightly bigger, smaller, then bigger again. Cameron printed my word on a stencil. I pet the dogs. I tried not to watch Jessica prep her equipment. Not to think about blood or needles.

"Where on your body would you like your word?" she asked.

I faced a full-length mirror. Lifted my sweatshirt and ran my thumb along my upper ribs on my right side.

"I'm thinking, here." I looked at my torso, the freckles and moles I've had all my life, the abs I've never liked. "Eventually, I want a much longer piece, a bigger one, more involved. Lyrics from a song I love. But I need to see how the tiny one feels. What do you think?"

Jessica took the stencil from Cameron. Our eyes met in the mirror.

"When you mentioned the ultimate longer tattoo, you instinctively touched your left side. So I think we save that space. Let's do the little *bondi* on your upper right-side ribs. It'll take five minutes, max. I'll start with the dot above the *i*. And then I'll just go in and out with the needle, one letter at a time."

She gently shaved my upper rib area and placed the stencil on my skin. Even the stencil looked cool in the mirror. I reclined on one of the tables and pulled up my sweatshirt. Jessica instructed me to place my right arm behind my head.

"Okay, I'm just going to do the dot over the *i* first, all right?" she reiterated, then talked to Cameron about a poem. I heard the needle buzz. I felt a pinch but it didn't hurt.

"Good?"

"Yep." I closed my eyes and breathed.

A mere instant later, she said, "Okay, I just need to do the *b* and then we're done."

The buzz stopped. She wiped my skin, placed SecondSkin film over the wound and said it was okay for me to stand up.

I stood in front of the mirror. *So completely cool.*

Jessica sat on the couch and pet the dogs while Cameron handled payment and gratuity. I asked whether pieces of art for sale in a crate near the payment desk were Cameron's. They were. I bought one: a black skull levitating above a woman with dark hair lying on the ground, her skin rosied with strokes of pink paint.

I began babbling. "Thank you both so much. You made this whole experience so not scary. Now I want another one. I'm sorry I'm talking so much. I never talk this much."

Jessica laughed and explained, "You're going to feel a major adrenaline rush. I'm literally covered in tattoos, and I still get nervous before each one. And then a huge rush afterwards."

I thanked them again, clutched my art, and skipped home through a park. I stopped in a wine shop. I noticed a candle for sale with a label saying—coincidentally— "Bondi Beach." I bought it.

For days, every time I entered a bathroom—at home, at work, at a restaurant—I hiked up my shirt and marveled in the mirror at my tiny word.

I began plotting my next ink.

In the past, when I'd floated the idea of getting a tattoo to girlfriends, some would say, "Don't get something cliché like a U2 lyric. You'll totally regret it when you're eighty-five."

Whatever.

For two years, I'd been envisioning a tattoo of eleven words from U2's song "Bad." But in Italian. In fine-line cursive.

Using a website Jessica recommended, I surveyed hundreds of handwriting fonts. I narrowed the choices to two— *Attention* and *Notera*—then translated the lyrics into Italian. *Separation* became *separazione. Desolation* became *desolazione. Let it go* became *lasciarlo andare.* I didn't like how *isolation* turned into *isolamento*. I changed it to *solitudine*. My tattoo, my translation.

Three and a half weeks after my *bondi* tattoo, I returned to Haven Studio. At one of the tables, another female tattooer collaborated with a client on a design: a provocative peach. Jessica placed the stencil on my lower left abs—five lines of text, just above my hip bone. I climbed onto the table, placed my left arm behind my head, and closed my eyes.

Jessica talked and joked with the others as she worked. "Doing okay?" she asked every other minute or so. Then wiped my skin and continued. Some of the individual letters hurt. Deep slice, flash of pain, then instant relief. Other letters didn't sting at all. She noted the halfway point and when we had one line to go. The buzz of the equipment stopped.

I stood and looked in the mirror, T-shirt bunched into my pink bra.

"Look at you, badass, with a big ol' belly tattoo," Jessica murmured, standing next to me.

≈ ≈ ≈

My tattoos invited me to redefine my relationship with my body. At twelve years old, when this body started naturally changing, as adolescent bodies do, I cringed in shame instead of stepping into inquisitiveness or excitement about the meaning of womanhood. Adults—parents, teachers—provided zero clarity or reassurance.

Via casual quips conveying his exacting aesthetic standards, Trey critiqued this body—this precious frame that housed the brain and heart that desperately hungered for his approval—yet expected it to provide marital sustenance.

Forrest rejected this body.

Other men touched this body in ways I didn't like that much, but because I wanted so badly to be touched in *some* way, I didn't protest.

My tattoos helped me reseize agency. My choices: words, font, translation, placement. My body, my work of art.

I now accept how magical this body is. And from now on, I'm going to be more discerning about who gets to touch it and how.

The healing properties of words. And ink. Through a pen. Or a tattoo artist's hand. We shouldn't underestimate them.

7

a desert in california

Around Valentine's Day, my friend Michele proposed an adventure to celebrate her birthday and my tenure vote coinciding the same week: a quest to find U2's Joshua Tree. *The tree* from Dutch photographer Anton Corbijn's photo shoot that inspired the cover art of the band's 1987 album, an artistic exploration of America as "not just a country, but an idea."

I booked a flight to Los Angeles, figuring I'd need a getaway *either way*—whether the faculty's decision on my professional longevity at the law school was positive or negative.

The tenure decision was favorable, though stressful. I didn't celebrate the career milestone at home in New York at all. I boarded a plane, flew cross-country, and headed straight to an LA suburb to rendezvous with Michele and her BFF Renee.

With music videos as soundscape, we reminisced about trips to Dublin and other concert shenanigans. We plotted our weekend expedition over glasses of wine around Michele's outdoor firepit.

Our first research surprise: The tree is not actually in Joshua Tree National Park. Also, it's *dead*.

The tree fell in the year 2000 due to high winds. But its roots, trunk, and branches remain.

Pinning down the geographical coordinates of the fallen tree, we learned it rests in a desert along California's Highway 190 leading into Death Valley National Park.

Early morning, armed with lattes, road trip snacks, and a ten-hour playlist, we hit the freeway. We caught up on our respective lives, work projects, romantic starts and stops. We sang. We laughed so hard, our abs ached.

Three hours and six different versions of the song "One" later, we reached Route 190. The two-lane interstate resembled a cowboy movie set. Stark. Desolate. Cacti. Tumbleweeds. Prickly shrubs.

Reading step-by-step instructions from a U2 fan website, Renee relayed precise directions to the dead tree. We scoured the landscape for official mile markers, broken and rusted signposts few and far between. Using Michele's odometer to clock mileage instead, we finally spotted an unmarked half-moon turnout—described on the fan website—on a shoulder of the road.

We passed it. Michele pulled a U-turn and parked the SUV.

Standing on the side of the sunbaked asphalt, staring toward a mountain range, we saw nothing but sand, dried-out vegetation, and the occasional Joshua tree: succulents or yucca plants (not actually trees) with thorny trunks and twisty branches ending in clusters of spiky leaves. Reportedly, Mormon settlers crossing the Colorado River named the plant after the biblical character, Joshua, who led Israelites into the Promised Land after forty years wandering the desert.

We didn't see *our* Joshua tree.

We stepped from highway pavement into open expanse of desert. Sand and prickers infiltrated our boots. Sweating in February desert heat, I removed a bulky burgundy polyester *Joshua Tree* hoodie I'd bought out of necessity at a U2 show in Berlin on the album's thirtieth anniversary tour when rain poured and Bono sang "Singin' in the Rain" as a segue to "Bad." I tied the sweatshirt sleeves around my waist, grazing the bandage under my T-shirt protecting my still-healing tattoo—lyrics from "Bad"—on my abs. The tattoo remained my secret. Other than Jessica and her gals at the studio, no one had seen or touched it.

"Let's fan out," Renee suggested.

Michele veered left. I advanced straight. Renee aimed right. We scanned the panorama for signs of . . . anything.

Eventually, a shape. A contour. On the ground. We squinted into the sun. *Is it?*

We ran toward a shadow.

The tree.

It lay in a bed of sand, still somewhat in its original zigzag shape, its bark gray. We fell quiet. Surrounding the deadness, signs of *life*—of everyone who had journeyed to the site before us.

So much *life*.

Desert rocks configured to spell *Pride* (a track from the 1988 album, *The Unforgettable Fire*), U2, Love.

A weathered bronze plaque set in concrete by a fan in the middle of the night asking, "Have You Found What You're Looking For?"—paraphrasing another song title.

Two sun-dried guitars.

A cymbal left by fans from Belgium, perforated with holes spelling Larry Mullen Jr.'s name.

Drumsticks.

We noticed suitcases. Three pieces of silver luggage bearing labels of "U2" painted in black within pink hearts.

Should we open them?

Would it be irreverent to unseal them? A violation, somehow?

Michele played the song "With or Without You" on her phone. We stared at the tree. Dead but alive.

We opened the suitcases. Discovered notebooks. We paged through handwritten messages from prior pilgrims. Favorite lyrics. Wishes to future fans. Gratitude for the band. We took turns scribbling our own testimonials.

We explored the luggage contents. Photographs. Wristbands. Album covers. Love notes. Light bulbs—an icon from the 2015 iNNOCENCE + eXPERIENCE tour representing a memory from Bono's childhood bedroom. More travel light bulbs, runes I'm in the right place—for me.

Michele staged an album cover of our own—three girls in the middle of a desert paying homage to an ossified tree. Mountains looming. Sun radiating. Sand dusting.

We resettled the memorabilia in the suitcases. We left the tree as we found it, with slight additions: Our words in the notebooks. Our footprints in the sand.

We took a last look and backed out of the desert the way we came.

Four weeks later—ten days before my fiftieth birthday—the world closed.

8
split, croatia

A Croatian immigration officer photographed my vaccine card and waved me into the country. I nearly wept. A glorious moment after fourteen months riding out the pandemic in New York, staring longingly at my passport and travel graffiti photos, cleaning out junk drawers of leftover currency, ticket stubs, and matchbooks collected on past trips.

The March 2020 weekend New York City went into lockdown, I should have been merrily boarding a spring break flight to Rome to celebrate my fiftieth birthday. Obviously, COVID quashed those plans; Italy locked down before the rest of us.

Like many, I rapidly pivoted to working from home. I shifted my law school's writing program online, enrolled in crash courses on "best practices" in virtual education, and taught classes sitting cross-legged on my kitchen chair.

As an introvert who thrives working from my couch in comfy sweatpants, happily uninterrupted by office pandemonium, I fared pretty well emotionally—at first. I felt productive, wrote a lot, and once the stay-at-home mandate lifted, boxed with my trainer Lou in a nearby park. I met friends for dinners in pandemic-inspired outdoor restaurant structures jazzed up with battery-operated candlelight, artwork, and plastic ivy. I felt lucky to be employed, healthy, and surrounded by (almost) everything I needed. The promise of a vaccine—a license to travel internationally again—far-off, I made do.

As the pandemic raged on though, my daily laps around my neighborhood track and nightly Spanish Netflix binges (accompanied by Spanish red wine) no longer effectively tamped down the swirling angst I'd managed to ignore or subdue for months. Barbs of negativity from burned-out work colleagues and students overwrought by doom-and-gloom job market predictions knocked me out of hard-fought equilibrium. Whiplash of ever-changing COVID protocols and toxicity of American politics added strain. Lying in bed alone at night, I started freaking out I hadn't kissed anyone in over three years—a self-imposed dating moratorium after I'd chosen three sequential charmers who turned out to be penetratingly mean. An exile further protracted by germ-driven social distancing. *Have I aged out of a romantic life—at fifty?*

Realizing how much I'd used prepandemic freedom of movement as a stress-coping mechanism and one of my four pillars of well-being—travel, boxing, writing, U2—I began to feel trapped, landlocked, tethered.

The vaccine rollout brought a flicker of hope. I thought, *If I can just get through this spring semester, I'll tell my dean I need a real (long) break from my program director role. Then I'll go somewhere, someplace far away, and write.*

An American friend who'd relocated to Germany with his wife at the beginning of the pandemic texted me a photo of a cottage nestled in banana fields in Tenerife, one of Spain's Canary Islands off the coast of Morocco. He urged: You should go here and write your next book. A sweet Spanish lady named Marta rents out the cottage. It's awesome. Here's her number. Text her!

The notion of hatching and honing my next book in a bungalow on an island renowned for volcanic black-sand beaches sounded divine. One problem: Spain hadn't yet reopened to vaccinated travelers from the United States. To access Tenerife, I first needed to get into a European country accepting Americans, wait ten to fourteen days, then enter Spain. Battling insomnia, I stared at my phone at 3 a.m. each night, scrutinizing COVID rules for entry into Croatia and Greece—the only two European countries admitting Americans without quarantine.

I've been to Greece twice, but never Croatia!

As the spring 2021 academic semester wrapped up, I clicked *send* on a carefully crafted email to my boss I'd spent countless hours editing to strike the right tone, explaining my need for a serious break from my program director role because it was sapping every ounce of zest out of me. To my immense surprise, he offered a year-long sabbatical. Crumpling onto my living room carpet, I cried in relief. Then pounced into action.

I sent Marta a deposit to reserve her Tenerife cottage—Casa Plumeria, named after a fragrant flower—for a month, assuming I could get there. I booked a one-way ticket to Croatia via Amsterdam—an empowering and liberating financial transaction, signifying my first-ever international adventure with no end date or fixed itinerary. I reserved an apartment in the Croatian city of Split for eleven days—a sunny two-room, third-floor flat with a vestige of a Roman temple jutting from a bedroom wall.

Needing no COVID test to enter Croatia but a negative PCR molecular test simply to walk through Amsterdam's airport to switch planes, I located a testing site in New York promising twenty-four-hour turnaround for the more rigorous diagnostic's results (remarkably difficult to obtain in time to fly, and astronomically expensive). Then I made a pact with myself: *For at least the first phase of this sabbatical, you're not allowed to worry for a single minute about money. Every time you need to make a travel decision that will mitigate anxiety and stress, you will spend the requisite money to make that happen. Your savings will get you through this year. You've been saving for a rainy day for two decades. Let it rain.*

My entire adult life, I've had a guilt-and-fear-driven relationship with money, always irrationally worried I was one bad financial decision away from destitution, one exercise of poor professional judgment away from being stripped of all financial security, one self-indulgent expense away from debtor's prison. My mom's voice in my head: *You should move to New Jersey for cheaper rent. Your hair highlighting is awfully expensive. Dining out is a waste of money.*

I decided to approach the trip one segment at a time. Initial objective: Board the flight to Amsterdam. Switch planes. Get through immigration in Croatia.

Everything else will evolve from there.

I pulled Croatian *kuna* from an airport ATM. Retrieving my two suitcases from baggage claim, I noticed one bag's handle had broken, half its metal bracket abandoned somewhere along its journey from New York to Amsterdam to Split. Only a jagged edge remained. I gingerly rolled the luggage plus two carry-on bags down a hill to an open-air structure resembling a taxi stand. No cabs, no buses, no people in sight. The airport population had somehow vanished.

I contemplated options. I switched my mobile phone from airplane to active mode, checking to see whether my usual ride share app operated in Split. It did. But before I could input my rental apartment's address—situated in Diocletian's Palace, an ancient Roman ruin in Split's city center—a rusty sedan stopped curbside. The driver rolled down a window and asked me something in Croatian. I responded in English, "Hi. I'm looking for a taxi or bus to town?"

"I drive a taxi," he said. I glanced at the car's windows and dashboard, looking for any sign of officiality. "I'm off duty, but I can take you to the city center."

A dachshund hopped from the driver's lap, paws landing on the car window ledge, and barked. The driver smiled.

He didn't look like a serial killer.

"How much would that cost?" I asked.

"150 kuna."

Though I'd calculated the dollar-to-kuna conversion a whopping five minutes earlier at the ATM, I couldn't figure out the proposed fare.

The driver read my mind. "That's around twenty euros."

I pondered if this was a good idea or the last ride I'd ever take. The dog barked and wagged his tail. I nodded yes.

The driver placed my suitcases in his trunk, which I quickly scanned for anything nefarious. I climbed into the back seat with my carry-on bags and rolled down a window. The dog jumped into my lap. The driver apologized and coaxed the dachshund back into the front seat.

"It's okay. I love dogs."

I used my phone to calculate the driving time and route to Split. With visual confirmation we were headed the correct direction and not the opposite way toward some secret lair, I relaxed. I texted my apartment host, Zoran, to let him know I was in transit—in an unmarked taxi.

Thirty minutes later, the car delivered me to the port of Split. Palm trees. Catamaran ferries. A promenade of restaurants and coffee shops. Zoran—a friendly gentleman with archaeology professor vibes—and his teenage son awaited me in the taxi lot, vigorously waving hello. They helped the driver lift my bags from the trunk. I paid the fare in kuna and said thank you.

"How do you say *thank you* in Croatian?" I asked.

"Hvala," the driver said and smiled. The word sounded like a throatier version of *koala*.

Zoran and his son rolled my luggage along cobblestones through the arch of a stone portico, past market stalls selling jewelry, carved wooden donkeys (traditional modes of transport in Croatia's cultural heritage), and vials of olive oil. We ascended a staircase onto a concourse where black marble sphinxes guarded the entrance to a church. The Cathedral of Saint Domnius houses the mausoleum of Diocletian, a Roman emperor who reigned from 284 to 305 CE. During his tenure, Diocletian directed the move of twelve sphinxes from Egypt to Split. Today, a labyrinth of residential apartments, shops, and bistros exists within his former palace's walls.

We needled through a narrow alley, past another sphinx (headless), hooked a sharp corner, and arrived at a blue door. Zoran and his son carried my bags up two flights of stairs into a cheerful flat. I recognized a corner of an ancient marble structure poking through the bedroom wall from the apartment rental website photos I'd practically memorized while dreaming about release from pandemic travel purgatory. I asked Zoran if I could touch the stone.

"Of course," he chuckled. "That's the original wall of Jupiter's temple in Diocletian's Palace. It's held up for 1700 years." Zoran pointed to an opening in the bedroom's wooden flooring, embedded plexiglass providing an additional peep at reliefs cut into stone millennia ago. "We tried to preserve as much original architecture as possible as we updated the apartment."

I looked out the window and saw the remainder of the temple.

Handing me a set of house keys, Zoran offered to show me around Split and a nearby town called Trogir later in the week.

"My wife and I are licensed tour guides," he explained.

I showered, changed into a one-piece/one-shoulder swimsuit and a long sundress, and headed out. I traced the curve of the harbor promenade, passing catamaran terminals offering rides to nearby islands called Hvar and Brač. I reached Bačvice Beach, a pebbly inlet with a concrete boardwalk and ladders descending into the Adriatic Sea. I spread a yellow Turkish beach towel on the esplanade and checked the time: 4:09 p.m. I peered over the sharp ledge into seawater. Algae or seaweed clung to the rungs of a metal ladder. I noticed tube-like creatures wriggling—vertically. *Eels? Weird upright fish? Are my jetlagged eyes playing tricks on me?* I decided not to slip into the water, yet.

I pulled off the dress, bunched it into a ball to use as a pillow, stretched out, and willed my muscles to slacken, unclench. I didn't realize how much I'd been bracing to handle potential travel glitches. Everything had unfolded seamlessly: COVID protocols and paperwork, the flight connection through Amsterdam, Croatian immigration, airport transport, the apartment key handoff from Zoran. My body remained tense, steeled for nonexistent problems.

Today is the first day of a YEAR of sabbatical . . . writing, exploring, being . . . No pressure . . . No stress . . . No money guilt . . . No obligations. Just restoration. Rejuvenation. Rediscovery. Replenishment. Get your groove back, endeavor to break your lengthy man drought with someone fun, lighthearted, positive, romantic, sweet.

I half napped, half daydreamed, listening to Adriatic waves lap at seawalls, hearing locals speak Croatian as they walked past my towel aiming for the pebblier part of the beach. I sensed a shadow hovering over me, blocking the sun. I opened my eyes.

A shirtless guy in a yellow Speedo loomed above me. I sat up.

"Ciao," he said.

"Ciao," I responded.

He handed me a sprig of leaves and white flowers. "This is one of our native plants. I saw you from over there." He pointed to the far end of the cove. "I think you are beautiful and we should know each other."

He sat down next to me, half on, half off my towel. He was over six feet tall, manly, muscular but not chiseled, tan, rugged. Bushy brown hair, on his head and chest. He pulled my sunglasses off my face.

"I want to see your eyes," he said, in a Croatian accent. "I'm Drago. Welcome to my country."

I laughed. "How did you know I'm not from here?"

He laughed. "It's obvious from a kilometer away."

I squinted into the sun. "I just got off a plane from America, through Amsterdam. I feel like a dried apricot." Knee-jerk self-consciousness.

"You look like an angel. Let's go swimming," Drago suggested.

I pointed into the water. "What are those vertical things? Eels?"

"No eels here. Probably just seaweed. I'll show you a much better place to swim. A secret spot. I've been swimming there since I was a little kid."

He sprung from the towel, grabbed my hand, and pulled me from the ground. I gathered my rolled-up dress and beach bag, summoning two themes I'd established for this sabbatical: *Adventure. Flow.*

I wasn't sure what was happening but decided to roll with it. *You can bail if it gets weird.*

Drago and I walked along the boardwalk past a jungle gym of residents doing pull-ups and sit-ups on outdoor exercise equipment, toward a crag of rocks. Like with the taxi driver, I felt uncharacteristically calm, not catastrophizing worst-case *Law & Order: SVU* scenarios.

Drago pointed toward an opening between two boulders. We pressed through the gap to a small outcropping. Seawater sloshed against flat stones.

"Here, tuck your stuff in this space." He gestured at a divot in the rocks. He leaped from the landing into the sea, disappeared beneath the surface, then burst upward again, laughing and wiping his eyes. "Come in! Jump to me!" he beckoned.

I crammed my belongings into the crevice. I gripped the rough surface of the rocks with my hands, ragged edges scraping the skin of my hamstrings, snagging my swimsuit. I hesitated. Flash of fear. Of the ocean. Imaginary eels. Stranger danger?

Drago treaded water, grinning as waves slapped his cheeks and shoulders. "Come in! Don't worry, I won't let anything happen to you."

I stepped from the landing to a lower rock, its surface slippery with moss. I sat down and inched toward the precipice. Drago swam toward me. He grabbed my palms and wrists and slowly tugged me into the water, onto his chest, wrapping his arms around my waist, keeping me afloat. I pressed my knees onto his hips, crossing my ankles behind him.

Either this guy is going to drown me or make me feel like a mermaid.

I decided to let go. Of hang-ups. Of feeling tired, old, wrinkly from travel. Of self-consciousness about my body. Of overthinking. *Carpe diem.*

Arms gripping me, Drago kicked his feet, propelling us farther into the ocean. He located a rock beneath the surface and stood on it. I clung to him like a barnacle.

"I know these waters very well. We can stand on this stone here. I've got you, don't worry," he said.

I drifted my feet downward until my toes touched the rock, but the sensation creeped me out. I retangled my legs around Drago's hips. He trailed his hands down my spine to the small of my back. Kissed me.

He tasted of salt water, olive oil, a tinge of tobacco. We kissed as waves splashed our cheeks. He gripped my hip bones. I arched my back, leaning my hair into the water, relinquishing . . . tension, stress, control, the pandemic, everything. He pulled me back toward him, kissed my neck, then released one of his hands, pulling the single strap of my swimsuit off my shoulder, down my arm, over my elbow, my wrist, folding the material around my hips, exposing me to the sun, the water, the breeze, his hands, his mouth.

Okay, mermaid, it is.

I didn't feel afraid he would hurt me. I also didn't care how quickly this had turned physical. I wanted to be touched. Put an end to almost four years of initially self-mandated then pandemic-compounded sequestration.

Forget "rules" of appropriateness. There are no rules anymore.

"I'm worried you're getting cold," Drago murmured.

He turned, pulled me onto his back, and swam toward the rocks. He hopped onto the flat stone like an antelope and helped me out of the water, swimsuit bunched around my hips.

"You're the first person in the world to touch these tattoos."

"Lijep," he said. *Beautiful.*

We kissed on the rocks.

"I can't believe I've only been in Split an hour and *this* happened," I said, laughing at my toplessness.

"I'm glad it's only your first day here because we need to spend lots of time together. Are you hungry? Let's go to your place? Where are you staying?" he asked.

From there, things proceeded quickly, though in my brain felt like slow motion, like watching film clips from someone else's life. I dressed. Drago took my hand. We walked the curve of the cove toward its far end and retrieved a bicycle he'd locked to a post. He conversed with two men in Croatian. They responded in teasing tones. Drago stripped off his wet Speedo and changed into a white T-shirt and red shorts he pulled from a knapsack.

He held my hand, steering the handlebars of his bike with his free arm. We walked past ferry docks, through the harbor, under the arched entrance to Diocletian's Palace, past the sphinxes, through the narrow alley, to the blue door. He locked the bike to a utility pipe and followed me upstairs.

I felt relieved and happy I hadn't forgotten how to touch, how to kiss, how to move. When to pause, when to react, when to initiate, when to receive, when to slow it all down, when to speed it all up. The feel of someone's fingertips on my skin, their weight on my bones, their teeth catching my lip. Sensations I hadn't felt in ages. Drago manhandled me. Sturdy masculinity— a bit gruff at times, aggressive, not in a scary way but in an "I absolutely will have you this minute" way. It felt good to be desired after going so long without physical tenderness, corporeal touch.

We lay there, my hand in his chest hair, my cheek stuck to his shoulder. He played with locks of my hair, taught me Croatian words. Cathedral bells chimed so loudly, the belfry seemed inside the room.

"Let's order takeout," Drago declared.

"Mmm, hey, it's my first night in Split. I kind of want to be *outside* the apartment. Let's go to that cute restaurant we passed right down the alley. Starts with an *M* I think. Looks kinda romantic."

I'd noticed wooden tables and chairs resting on cobblestones beneath a Diocletian arch, adjacent stairsteps decorated with lanterns and colorful pillows, a chalkboard menu offering regional fare and wines.

He leaped from the bed and strode naked into the living room. I heard shower water tumble. I grabbed my phone and texted Clay and my four closest girlfriends: UM, I GOT TO CROATIA AND WAS HERE A MERE 45 MINUTES, MET A GUY ON THE BEACH, AND JUST GOT LAID! THE EPIC DROUGHT HAS FINALLY ENDED!!!

They responded within seconds. Messages like: YAYYYYY! HAVE SO MUCH FUN! BE CAREFUL BUT HAVE A BLAST! SO PROUD OF YOU! YOU ROCK! HAHAHA!

I rose from the bed, a bit wobbly, body recalibrating. I stepped into the living room. Drago sat naked on the couch checking his phone. I entered the bathroom. Every towel lay crumpled on the floor, wet. He'd used the toilet but hadn't flushed.

We left the apartment and walked to the restaurant—Mazzgoon. A sketch of a donkey with the caption "stubbornly different" decorated the placemats.

"This sounds like me," I joked to Drago, pointing at the words.

Conversing in Croatian with a server, he didn't hear me.

The server turned toward me. "The gentleman has already ordered for himself. The seafood stew. Would you like me to translate some of the menu for you?"

I looked at Drago. A pack of cigarettes had materialized. He smoked and fiddled with his phone. A ripple of disappointment at his bathroom and table manners washed through me. I shrugged it off, like a bull running toward a matador's red flag—as usual.

The server highlighted the popularity of donkey meat on restaurant menus in Split. I opted for tuna medallions with cauliflower puree and a glass of Croatian wine. The waiter brought us a basket of fresh bread and a slate plate holding rounds of creamy butter dabbled with black pepper. I sipped cold white wine tasting of green apple.

"I want to share with you that I don't have any money," Drago announced.

"Oh, that's okay, I have my wallet," I responded, thinking he meant he didn't have cash or cards on him, coming straight from the beach.

"No, I mean . . . I'm not poor, but I don't have any money. My training is agriculture. I raise olive trees. And strawberries. But I only have a part-time job right now," he elaborated.

"Oh. Okay. That's fine." I smiled. I really don't care what a guy does for a living, as long as he's reasonably self-sufficient.

I reached for another slice of spongy bread to spread with the soft butter. Drago had already consumed the entire loaf. The server delivered his bowl of stew. He ordered another basket of bread and ate all except one slice, which I quickly snagged.

My plate arrived with three chunks of rare tuna on dollops of mashed cauliflower, dots of orange and green sauces decorating the ceramic dish. The server reappeared with an enormous lemon and handed it to Drago. He set the whole lemon next to his pack of cigarettes and phone.

"Is that lemon for your stew?" I asked.

"No, I need it for something I'm cooking at home."

I frowned. *Did he just order groceries at a restaurant?*

The check arrived. The entire bill tallied barely a third of an average bar tab at home. A refreshing reorientation. I paid.

We drifted down the alley toward the apartment. At the blue door, Drago said, "I'm sad I have to work now. I ride for a bicycle food delivery app, and late evening is our busiest time. Would you like to go to a different beach with me tomorrow? I can pick you up around eleven?"

Happy to sleep alone, yet knowing I'd see much more of Split if I let a local show me its hidden parts, I said yes. We exchanged phone numbers.

A clanging carillon jostled me awake at 6 a.m. Chatty couriers rolling wheelbarrows across cobblestones in the courtyard below my windows added clamor. I shuffled to the kitchen, rummaged cabinets for coffee, and found an opened bag of grounds. I pressed buttons on a coffee machine labeled with unfamiliar Croatian words until the contraption started to rumble.

I stared into the bathroom mirror. Instead of shriveled skin I expected to see after sixteen hours of travel and less than optimal sleep, I saw glow. A cocktail of pheromones, friction against Drago's facial scruff, and Adriatic sunshine.

I carried a coffee mug to bed and listened to further sounds of Split waking up: shopkeepers chatting, dogs barking, bicycle bells jingling. A candle and a glass vase holding Drago's wilting sprig of jasmine sat on my nightstand. I lit the candle and wrote in my journal until hunger spurred me outside.

Hunting for an authentic, nontouristy place to eat breakfast in the interior footprint of Diocletian's Palace, I chose a restaurant in a bustling piazza, tables covered in funky textiles, chairs with button-tufted cushions. I ordered a bowl of granola, fresh yogurt, strawberries, and banana slices. I sipped coffee with milk and watched Croatians start their workday. Men smoking cigarettes, downing thimbles of espresso. Ladies wearing pandemic face masks, walking arm in arm, pulling miniature dogs on bedazzled leashes. Teenagers, also masked, school backpacks draped over shoulders.

Drago texted and asked me to meet him on the front steps of a church near the harbor for a late-morning excursion to his favorite beach. I'd assumed he'd be picking me up in a car, but when I reached the Monastery of St. Francis, he stood on a curb holding two beach towels and a knapsack.

"Do you have ride share apps on your phone?" he asked.

In that moment, I did three things. First, I decided I needed to write my first-ever ledger of ultimate relationship (or situationship) deal-breakers and include "doesn't pay for anything" on the list. Second, I gave myself permission to set aside temporary annoyance in pursuit of Day Two discovery. Third, I ordered the car. It arrived in forty-five seconds. We slid into the back seat. Drago bantered with the driver in Croatian. They joked like old friends.

"Do you guys know each other?" I asked.

"No," Drago laughed. "I just love talking to people." He put his hand on my knee.

"How do you say *mayor* in Croatian?" I asked.

"Gradonačelnik," he replied.

I laughed, not even attempting to pronounce the word. "You seem like *that*—of Split."

The driver dropped us at the perimeter of a parking lot bordering another pebbly beach. Drago grabbed my hand. "I want to show you the best spot in the world."

Still in his sneakers, he scurried along stones and sand past solo bathers and couples arranging towels. He darted onto a narrow pathway, trees on one side, sea on the other. Waves folded onto the stone walkway, dousing our shoes and feet as we plodded ahead. We stepped over branches tangled in sea-foam. As the path tapered, we could no longer walk side by side without one of us having to wade through water. He scooted ahead of me. I watched his calves and hamstrings propel him onward, a grown-up boy excited to be in his element.

He stopped near a curve of rocks. A clump of trees clinging to an embankment provided shade. He set down the towels and backpack.

"I'll be right back." He scrambled up the ridge like a mountain goat, disappearing into foliage. He returned seconds later with two puffy beach mats. He grinned. "I have a secret hiding place up there."

He positioned the mats side by side on the beach pebbles, rolled out the towels, and removed a package of strawberries and a bag of apples from his knapsack. He stripped off *all* his clothes. He grabbed a thin green bottle from a side pocket of his bag, removed a cork, and handed the vial to me.

"I grow my own olives and press my own oil on my land. I also grew these strawberries and apples. Will you rub oil on my back? By the way, we don't have to wear clothes on this beach. We have total privacy. No one knows about this spot. We can be free and do whatever we want here."

I'd only sunbathed naked twice in my life. Fifteen years earlier, as one of my unsuccessful efforts to fix my intimacy problems with Forrest, I'd agreed to sneak off to a "naturist" beach together during a family trip to an island in the Caribbean, a tax haven where his father and stepmother had retired and lived. Instead of kick-starting our sex life in the cabana we'd rented for the afternoon, Forrest disappeared to smoke weed with strangers.

Eight years after that, I signed up for an overly ambitious biking tour of the Canary Islands. Underestimating the physical rigor of the itinerary, I'd chosen the locale solely because the trip dates aligned with my winter break from teaching. Craving a solo afternoon away from the expert cyclists in the tour group, I'd visited my first black-sand beach. A sign noted a clothing optional area. I stripped to bare skin. The sensation of sun, breeze, and salt water felt rebellious, freeing. Like nature wanted to cherish what men in my life hadn't.

Drago lay face down on his mat. I knelt and poured olive oil into my palm. I rubbed the oil into his golden skin—shoulders, spine, backside, legs, calves.

"Your turn," he said, standing up, pulling sunscreen from his bag and me from my knees. "Your skin needs protection. No oil for you until you've soaked up months of Croatian sun."

He lifted the bottom hem of my tank top over my stomach, shoulders, and head and tossed the fabric onto the mat. He rolled my beach skirt to my hips, gave it a light push, letting it float to the ground. He untied each knot of my swimsuit, one at my neck, another at my vertebrae, two at my hips. The bikini tumbled to the towel.

After he covered me in SPF, we lazed in the sun eating strawberries.

Unable to sit still for long, Drago vaulted from the mat and hurtled into the rocky shallows, familiar with a layout of stepping stones easing the transition from bumpy terrain to sea. I tried mimicking his blueprint of steps, but sharp rocks poked at the soles of my feet. I stumbled. Noticing me faltering, he returned to shore, lifted me onto his back, and plunged into the water.

I glimpsed boulders below the water's surface, green seaweed undulating, schools of petite fish shimmering. I separated from Drago as he pushed farther out to sea. He turned and signaled for me to join him. I paddled toward him, keeping my head above water so I could see him—a buoy. I tried not to think about whatever creatures existed below me, between us. I focused on the sensation of the Adriatic against unencumbered skin, an undercurrent leeching the drama of the pandemic year from my body.

When I reached Drago, he stood on an underwater rock. He wrapped my legs around his waist, my arms around his shoulders.

"I've got you," he murmured. He kissed me. Our lips hinted of salt water, strawberries, traces of olive oil. "My American Aphrodite," he said.

We swam to shore. Forgoing towels, we let the sun dry our skin.

Drago loved being naked. He bounded from his mat again, trotted along the beach, collecting errant plastic bottles, trash, and detritus, scooping items into a garbage bag he'd brought. He fed me strawberries, slices of apple. He napped. He awoke, clutched my hand, one mat, and the bottle of olive oil, and led me up the embankment to a dirt alcove under a tree canopy. He settled the mat on the soil.

"I want to make love to you . . . here . . . now," he asserted.

Feeling floaty, completely transported from my regular life and persona, I let the scene unfold. I wanted the physicality to feel otherworldly, like four years of longing come to fruition. I told myself to be selfish, needy, draw everything into me that I'd survived without . . . through self-sentenced and pandemic-exacerbated separation, desolation, isolation . . . words from my tattoo.

Drago's gruffness, his coarseness, his unrefinedness, his own animalistic desire . . . began to hurt me, my body, a bit. I asked him to go a little softer, slower.

He didn't.

I winced, trying to focus on the parts that felt good. That's what I've always done.

Lying there, soil particles stuck in olive oil and sweat on our skin, sun spying on us through green leaves, surf hitting rocks beneath us, Drago feeding me a bite of red apple . . . Very Adam and Eve.

We fell asleep in the dirt.

I dreamed.

⚘   ⚘   ⚘

When girls in middle school began bragging about getting their periods and showing off their first bras, I cringed. The day our fifth-grade science teacher distributed a sex ed pamphlet entitled *Growing Up and Liking It*, I ran home and stowed it in a portable lockbox Mommom had given me for my birthday. Each night before bed, I prayed, "Please God, let me win the National French Contest and let me never get my period."

Other than handing me a mortifying stack of library books, my mom never explained menstruation, puberty, or sex to me. In sixth grade, I arrived home from school complaining about abdominal pain after my despotic gym teacher forced us to do sit-ups as part of the dreaded Presidential Physical Fitness Test. In front of my dad and brother, my mom announced, "You're probably getting your period." My face flushed crimson.

A year later, when I did get it—a maddening discovery in my art class restroom, and a stunning adolescent realization God indeed does *not* answer all prayers—I stuffed paper towels in my underwear. For the next five years, I pilfered maxi pads from my mother's bathroom cabinet. I never told her my coming-of-age news. She found out only when a doctor at an annual school physical detected blood in my urine and wanted to make sure I wasn't dying.

One afternoon after car pool, my mom swerved our mini-van into the parking lot of the discount store, Kmart. Shuttling my brother and me inside, she snatched three training bras from a "blue-light special" bin, paid for them, and tossed the bag to me in the car. My brother snickered in the back seat. I wanted to hurl the car door open and leap into oncoming traffic. Thereafter, my daily high school wardrobe involved dressing in oversized Boy George-style layers to hide visible bra straps from my father. (I also vowed that if I ever decided to have kids, my daughter's first bra-shopping experience would involve a magical girls-only expedition to a chic boutique in Paris.)

As a teenager, I didn't really know or understand what was happening to my body. The pamphlet lied; I was growing up, but I certainly wasn't liking it. I felt embarrassed, ashamed, like there was something unspoken wrong with me.

One Sunday at my grandparents' house after church, Mommom handed me yet another used copy of Judy Blume's book *Are You There God? It's Me, Margaret* she'd bought for a dollar at the library. I knew from my school friends that the storyline involved periods, maxi pads, bras, and "getting felt up" by boys. The last thing I needed was my parents seeing me engrossed in that piece of literature. I hid the book beneath a fake wood stove in my grandparents' living room. Now I wish I could go back four decades, sit down with Mommom out of earshot from

Mom and Dad, and have her explain puberty and sex to me, though perhaps she wouldn't have been any more informative than my parents. When the original *Top Gun* movie came out, in reference to a steamy scene involving Tom Cruise tongue-kissing Kelly McGillis, Mommom remarked, "You know, Heidi, people don't really kiss like that."

I'd already kissed someone like that. When I was fourteen, a sixteen-year-old boy I'd met at a school mixer invited me to the Homecoming Dance. Brody. My first-ever date. My father drove us and two other pairs to the chain restaurant TGI Fridays for dinner. For six teenagers to squish into our minivan, I had to sit either on Brody's lap or on the carpet covered in our St. Bernard's dog hair. Brody fastened a seat belt around both of us and wrapped his arms around my waist. When I exited the vehicle, my dad grabbed me by the shoulder, pinched my skin—hard—and whispered, "My daughter will not behave like that." My cheeks burned with shame, but I didn't exactly know what I'd done wrong. That night, in the school gymnasium, Brody and I slow danced to Prince's "Purple Rain" and Marvin Gaye's "Sexual Healing." He held my hand and led me around the back of the school building. He kissed me, my first French kiss, his silver-capped teeth bumping against my braces. I loved everything about that moment, the way kissing made my stomach flip upside down. Unfortunately, a teacher saw us through a window and narc'd me out to my parents the next day—early exposure to slut shaming based on the most innocent of adolescent exploration. Brody eventually dumped me because I wouldn't put out other than French kiss, which I believed I was quite excellent at. He lost his virginity to my best friend's sister.

In tenth grade, I started "going with" a boy from church I'd known for years. He kept pressuring me to give him oral sex in my mom's piano room. I didn't exactly know what oral sex entailed, remaining quite content to hover in the French kissing lane with perhaps some over-the-clothes touching. He ditched me for a more action-oriented cheerleader. My mom scolded me for not making it work with the "good Christian boy." I never enlightened her about why we broke up.

I didn't know what "normal" teenage girl feelings were, or how to act around boys, especially the guys at the boarding school where we lived. Mom implored me to dress up for breakfasts and dinners in the dining hall, sweep blush on my cheeks, wear clothes that "flattered my figure." But I received zero guidance on how to interact with the boys my figure actually enticed.

In my junior year of high school, a cute basketball player named Holden got restricted to the boarding school campus for violating curfew. Unbeknownst to me, his buddies dared him to date me (as a joke) because I—a faculty kid—lived *on campus.* When Holden began slipping romantic notes through the mail slot in our front door, I nearly died of happiness. When my parents went to choir rehearsal, I snuck him into our house, nicked one of my dad's cold beers for him, and kissed him in Mom's piano room. One day at my school, I sauntered into the student lounge and overheard the popular field hockey girls goofing around, laughing about a rumor that "Holden Harding is dating Heidi Brown as a joke because he's restricted to the boarding school campus and she's the only available girl. Isn't that hysterical?"

I ran to the cafeteria bathroom and sobbed. When I went home that night, I told my father what I'd found out, thinking he'd be upset on my behalf and want to protect me somehow, stand up for me. Dad shrugged. And did nothing. I avoided meals in the dining hall for a month. Finally, one evening, I yanked a black mock turtleneck dress from my closet, twisted my hair into a French braid, marched into the dining hall, found Holden, and said, "I am not a joke." I turned beet red and walked away. The year we graduated, he wrote me one last note: "I'm sorry I did you wrong."

My first college relationship—a thoughtful boy from my dorm—lasted nine months. Virgins, our physical experimentation strayed no further than curious-but-hesitant hands.

I spent the next twelve years with Trey, never truly under-standing *my* body, what makes *me* feel pleasure or stokes *my* desire. Sex was part of the marital contract—he had a strong, athletic sex drive; I presumed, and assumed, the role of trying to accommodate it. I never amplified my voice and articulated what I needed. Perhaps a mash-up of being raised to think I'm selfish if I express longings or yearnings that veer off script, and that my sexuality, my sensuality, is something to be ashamed of or embarrassed by . . . A self-demotion further incubated inside the hothouse of people-pleasing as a mode of survival, lest affec-tion and love be yanked away.

A brief foray into dating after the trauma of the divorce fol-lowed by eight years of sexual frustration with Forrest shrouded my thirties just as my body and inner feminine fury began to sync.

Throughout my forties, dating here and there, I confused the biochemical pyrotechnics of sexual intimacy with love, forging lightning-speed attachments to men I had no business liking. I let other men I didn't like that much take what they wanted be-cause it seemed easier to simply get it over with than resist or assert. After three particularly cruel discards by jerks, I'd locked myself in dating jail. Three years of self-decreed dating/sexual ab-stention, extended another year by the pandemic, served a pivotal purpose. It clarified six truths:

- I love (and deserve) intense, rewarding sexual intimacy.
- I need to monitor my tendency to (mis)equate sex with love (and it would be good for me to experience deep sexual sat-isfaction with a partner I trust—*without* necessarily falling/being in love).
- I deserve a sexual partner who asks, listens, reciprocates, and delights.
- I am 100% done with body anxiety.
- In fact, my body rocks.
- And my sex life is going to rock throughout my fifties, six-ties, and beyond.

❧ ❧ ❧

Drago and I dipped into the sea once more, a salty cleanse before packing up to go home. He restowed the beach pads in his
woodland hideout.

During our nap, the tide had rolled in, leaving little dry land
between the water and the embankment, the pathway already
flooded. Drago rushed ahead, gesturing at the best spot to place
each foot so I wouldn't get soaked by waves. He plucked dirty
soda cans from the terrain, muttering at human-made debris
littering his habitat. My sneakers wet and muddied from surf
and soil, I slowed my pace so I wouldn't trip on sticks and logs
hurled onto the sliver of shore by aggressive swells. The distance
between Drago and me widened. The sky turned gray. For an
instant, I imagined the trail completely washing away between
me and civilization, leaving me stranded and alone. What would
I do? Could I make it back to the Adam and Eve landing, to
safety on higher ground? Would the tide recede again before
dark, allowing me to exit? Or would I sleep alone in the elements? A forced rewilding. The possibility intrigued rather than
scared me.

My shoe caught on a branch stuck in the earth. A broken
tree bough tore a gash in my shin. Blood trickled to my ankle. I
ignored it. Kept going. Drago hadn't turned around. Normally,
the sensation of even temporary abandonment or unpriority
would have rankled me. Perhaps I already knew this time I'd be
the abandoner.

The path finally broadened, transitioned from sand to concrete, then to a sidewalk leading to the parking lot. Drago bus-
ied himself distributing trash he'd collected into appropriate
recycling bins. The wilderness we'd just emerged from seemed
a stark contrast to authoritative signposts barking rules in Croatian about acceptable and unacceptable garbage cataloging.

"Can you order us a ride?" Drago pressed.

Blood from my shin mixed with muck on my sneaker.

When our transport entered the parking lot, Drago asked the driver to drop him at his apartment on the outskirts of town but ferry me into the city.

"Beautiful, I need to work for the food delivery app for a few hours, but I'll come to your place when I'm finished, and we can spend the night together," Drago explained en route.

As we neared his street, he kissed me goodbye and leaped from the car.

The driver delivered me to the port. As I passed sphinxes and heard ear-splitting cathedral bells clang, a desire for solitude coursed through me. I didn't regret what had transpired between Drago and me, but I hadn't had much time to breathe since I left New York.

I showered off blood and beach grime, rinsed my muddy sneakers, and tended to my ripped shin. I planned to send a text message later thanking Drago for the exploratory and sensory-filled day but informing him I wanted to sleep alone.

I returned to Mazzgoon for dinner, sat at the same table, reordered the fish dish I'd eaten the night before, this time with a basket of bread and salty butter all to myself. The waitress brought tastings of different Croatian wines—white and red. She lit a candle on my table. Taught me Croatian words. I ate bites of tuna and sipped white wine tingling of apricot and pear, then red wine bursting with pepper and earth.

My phone buzzed. A message from Zoran offering to give me a walking tour of Split in the morning, then drive me to the nearby historic town of Trogir. I quickly responded: YES, WHAT TIME?

I paid my check, again pleasantly surprised at the inexpensiveness of Croatian dining. I looped streets, alleys, and squares I recognized. A quiet night in Split. With most foreign tourists still deterred by erratic COVID rules, I barely encountered another human. When I approached the apartment building, I found Drago leaning against the blue door, talking on his phone.

"My father says hello!" he laughed. He hung up and hugged me. "I'm going to bring my bicycle inside. Better than locking it up out here."

He began carrying his bike inside the building and up the first flight of stairs. I didn't have the energy or the nerve to insist on sleeping solo. I knew I'd have to affirmatively communicate my preferences to him sooner rather than later; telepathy wasn't exactly cutting it. But I didn't yet have the words to say *I want to be alone* without sounding rude.

Am I ever going to stop indulging others' desires at the expense of my own?

"Um, it's okay if you spend the night, but I kind of need you to have the bike out of the apartment by 10:30 tomorrow morning because the flat owner is coming to take me on a tour of Split, and I don't want him to charge more money or city taxes or whatever if he finds out more than one guest is staying here. That happened to me once in Italy," I said. A hotelier in Rome had charged me a pile of extra fees and taxes upon discovering Luca had entered my room in the middle of the night.

"This is Croatia. No one cares about rules like that," Drago responded.

"Well, I kind of care. So, if you don't mind, let's be out of the apartment by 10:30, okay?"

He parked the bike next to the kitchen table, took a shower, used all my towels again, then ate a box of crackers with butter and jam left by Zoran as a welcome gift, plus an apple and a banana from a fruit basket. He devoured all but one piece of candy resting in a bowl near the living room couch.

I didn't feel like fooling around. I felt annoyed. My body hurt. The cut on my shin stung. I wanted to fall asleep, and I wanted him to leave. But I said nothing. We slipped into bed. He drifted to sleep. I spent most of the night pondering why I constantly let men obtain what they want but I feel bitchy stating what I want. Drago snored, rolled around, and tugged covers off me.

At 6 a.m., cathedral bells howled, shaking the bedroom windows. Drago grumbled, turned over, pulled my body into his, my back to his chest. Somatically, it felt good to be held tightly like that, though I wished I could summon romantic, or even appreciative, feelings toward the offeror. Instead, I sensed initial kindlings of an urge I knew would only continue to smolder hour by hour until it ultimately erupted: the irrepressible compulsion to flee.

The cathedral bells tolled at 7 a.m., again at 8 a.m., once more at 9 a.m. Finally, at 10 a.m., when Drago still made no forays toward getting out of bed and getting the fuck, I mean the bike, out of the apartment, I got up, brewed coffee, and began opening all the apartment shutters—loudly. He emerged from the bedroom—naked, naturally—a sleepy bear stumbling toward the coffee pot, poured a cup, gulped its contents, spilled droplets on the floor. He sat—naked, naturally—on a kitchen chair and checked his phone, with leisure. The bike stared at me.

"Hey, I realllllly would like the bike to not be in this apartment when Zoran shows up. And I need you to put some clothes on, and . . . please go. I'm trying not to be bitchy but . . . this is sort of stressing me out."

I really hate being ignored.

He buttered a cracker. Ate it, sprinkling crumbs all over the table. Poured another cup of coffee. Drank it. Unwrapped the last piece of candy.

Finally, at 10:35, he dressed, kissed me goodbye, carried his bike down the two flights of stairs, tire marks smudging walls as he descended, and left.

I know how to make a deal-breaker list. I don't know how to enforce it. How do I say "rudeness is a deal-breaker for me" if I'm worried about sounding rude?

🌰   🌰   🌰

Zoran met me outside the blue door. As we walked, he narrated historical highlights of Diocletian's Palace, explaining the sphinxes' Egyptian provenance and themes embedded in intricate woodwork in the Cathedral of Saint Domnius—a martyred Christian beheaded at the direction of Emperor Diocletian. Ironically, Domnius's namesake cathedral occupies the same footprint as his executioner's mausoleum.

At the base of a twenty-eight-foot-tall bronze sculpture of Gregory of Nin, a medieval Croatian bishop, Zoran pointed out scuff marks on a giant golden toe. Apparently, Gregory of Nin defied the Roman Catholic Church by calling for the use of national languages instead of Latin in religious services so worshippers could better comprehend the scripture. Gregory of Nin made me think of Bono converting scripture to rock lyrics and me trying to convince my parents U2 shows are like church services with no secret password for inclusion.

Zoran shared a piece of Croatian lore. "Make a wish, rub Gregory's big toe, and your desire will come true," he urged. "But you have to be *really* specific."

Okay. I wish to find a hot, edgy, sweet, cool, caring, affectionate, creative, fun, smart, worldly, communicative, reliable, consistent, nonanxiety-producing dude who cherishes every inch of my body, mind, and soul, tells me so, prioritizes me, and lets me do the same for him.

I rubbed the toe.

Next stop: Trogir, a coastal village approximately twelve miles from Split. Established by Greeks, ruled by Venetians, occupied sequentially by Hungarians, French (under Napoleon), and Austrians until the birth of Yugoslavia in 1918, the town boasts a rich and layered architectural history. (Croatia eventually declared independence from Yugoslavia on June 25, 1991.)

Zoran led me through a maze of boulevards, canals, and squares, sharing his knowledge about UNESCO (United Nations Educational, Scientific, and Cultural Organization) sites. He noted carved friezes over doorways depicting religious parables, and architectural innovations like air-conditioning in the form of holes drilled through beams and cinder blocks.

He gestured at a simple sketch on the side of a building. Brownish ink, a boat shaped like a pirate's vessel, five oars on one side, a few sails, a cross topping a mast.

"You mentioned you love street art," Zoran said. "This is ancient graffiti. It's literally seventeen hundred years old, the same age as the corner of Jupiter's temple in your bedroom."

Street art and graffiti texturize my travels. I love seeing unscripted colors, shapes, and shades juxtaposed against formally commissioned icons like commemorative monuments, statues, and museums. Like tattoos, a message delivered through art tagged on topographical places that aren't "supposed" to have fonts or forms splashed on them. Similar to tattooers, I like that graffiti and street artists don't need fancy provenances or pedigrees. I admire self-made.

Zoran drove me back to Split. As I entered the apartment, my phone reconnected with the Wi-Fi signal. Nine missed calls and ten texts from Drago asking when he could come over again.

I'd only been in Croatia three days, but it felt like a month. I wanted to gracefully extricate myself from the Drago situation, garner a few days of true mental and physical rest alone, and explore the Dalmatian Coast beyond the city center of Split.

I sent Drago a text:

CIAO BELLO. I'M JUST GETTING BACK TO SPLIT FROM MY TOUR OF TROGIR AND HAVE A BAD HEADACHE.

True.

I'M GOING TO SLEEP EARLY BUT I'LL TEXT YOU IN THE MORNING. I'M MEETING UP WITH A FRIEND IN HVAR TOMORROW FOR THE DAY. GOOD NIGHT!

True—if I count myself as a friend. Which I do.

I snuck out of the apartment, hoping Drago was somewhere other than my neighborhood and I wouldn't bump into him on the street, and ducked into a grocery store. I bought green spinach-flavored spaghetti, a can of what I thought was tomato sauce, a package of something resembling ground turkey, though I couldn't decipher the Croatian words indicating the precise genre of meat, a plastic tub of shaved parmesan cheese, and a bottle of red Croatian wine, a donkey on its label. I peered around corners, scanning for Drago's bicycle, and scampered back inside my building.

Elated I figured out how to work the apartment's convection stovetop, I boiled water for the noodles and sautéed the meat substance. I opened the can I'd presumed was tomato sauce, but dipping my finger into orange goo, I realized I'd purchased sticky pimento cheese paste. I chucked the full can in the garbage bin.

I toted a bowl of pasta tossed with ground meat, parmesan, olive oil, and black pepper, plus a glass of spicy Croatian red wine, into the bedroom. Eating forkfuls of my concoction, I checked catamaran schedules for journeys between Split and the nearby island of Hvar.

After booking a 7:30 a.m. ferry, I slept ten solid hours until the cathedral bells hollered at dawn.

I boarded the ferry as Split began to awaken. Bands of lavender and orange streaked the sky. Church bells chimed from disparate locations around the city. Seagulls swooped in figure eights over the Adriatic. Only two other passengers stepped onto the early-morning ferry with me. I purchased a coffee and a bottle of pear juice from a barista and chose a window seat.

Hopping off the ferry at Hvar's harbor, I set off to explore the island. Most establishments remained shuttered, either for COVID or awaiting the official start of summer. I passed an outdoor boxing gym, yellow punching bags hanging from beams. A pathway hugging the coastline led me to a deserted pebble beach. I pulled a towel and a book from my tote bag. Small waves curled onto the shore, then receded. I sat alone for an hour until a guy in shorts and a tank top appeared and strode directly toward me on the beach. He approached, grinning.

"Hello," he began. Croatian accent. He sat down in the silt and stones near my towel. Another friendly and forthright

Croatian dude. "What does your tattoo say?" He pointed at my abs. "Teach me about it."

I responded politely for a few minutes, but he inched closer. I checked the time, said, "Nice to meet you, but I'm late for lunch," packed my stuff, and moved on. Lying to a stranger still seemed nicer, or safer, than saying "Respectfully, I'm not into this."

Wandering the desolate town, I peeked into a few cathedrals open to tourists, snapped photos of painted boats bobbing in the harbor, and found a rustic restaurant tucked into an alley. Two waiters fussed with linens and arranged bottles of olive oil and white wine vinegar on café tables. I asked if I could sit for lunch.

A server showed me to a table with a view of Hvar's port through a trellised archway. He brought me an aperitivo in a glass ampoule: honey grappa. The liquid warmed my every molecule. He set a bowl of shaved raw cabbage, cucumbers, and tomatoes on the tablecloth and showed me the right ratio of olive oil and vinegar to dress the salad. He returned with a plate of grilled whole bream, skin uniformly charred and crispy, resting on a bed of sautéed Swiss chard drizzled with olive oil, topped with two slices of lemon. The grappa buzz, the zesty taste of the fish and vegetables, the sounds of boatsmen greeting one another in Croatian . . . I felt happy I'd trusted my travel instincts and chosen the perfect country to springboard my sabbatical adventure.

I spent the afternoon sunbathing on rocks. On the ferry back to Split, I pulled a notebook from my bag. I began playing around with a "mind map," a visual depiction of the narrative arc of my new book project—*The Flourishing Lawyer: A Multi-Dimensional Approach to Performance and Well-Being*—the third volume in my well-being trilogy. I drew bubbles and clouds around potential chapter titles on notebook pages, scribbling in white space between them, busying the page. When I'd boarded the flight from New York to Amsterdam, onward to Split, declaring my sabbatical themes of *adventure* and *flow*, I'd also set a resolute intention for my manuscript: *Take the first five days in Split to rest and rejuvenate, then start writing Page One of the new book on May 15.*

As an Aries, I'm stubborn and methodical. I like establishing a definitive start date to writing projects, ideally the first or fifteenth of a month. I assign myself a daily quota of two hours of writing every morning (no days off, no excuses) until I complete the first (awful) rough draft. When I'm away from home, writing provides structure. Each day, if I write for two hours, then work out, I feel accomplished; anything else that happens that day is a bonus. This European adventure—starting in Croatia, hopefully segueing to a month in Tenerife, ideally finishing in Rome if Italy opened and I could use my hotel credit from my canceled fiftieth birthday trip—would serve as a six-or-seven-week writing retreat, removed from the pressures of New York, life, job, pandemic drama, everything. I knew if I stuck to my writing regimen, the pages would accumulate.

Back at the flat, feeling upbeat after the Hvar excursion, I booked a catamaran ticket for another morning trip to the island of Brač. I needed to stem the constant stream of text messages from Drago. My body still hurt. I felt no romantic connection toward him. Plus, I'd hopefully depart for Spain in exactly seven days, assuming I could figure out Split's COVID PCR testing situation. I apologized to him over text and indicated I wasn't sure when we could see each other again as I'd be traveling along the Croatian coast (the Dalmatian Coast, named for a now-extinct Greco-Roman tribe called Dalmatae) for some "research and writing work" for the next few days. I silenced my phone and fell asleep.

I woke up to the cathedral bell racket, sipped coffee, drafted the preface to my new book, then scurried to the ferry terminal.

Brač was rainy, deserted, and uninspiring. But I enjoyed the fresh air and solitude. The most interesting site in Brač: Zlatni Rat, often referred to as the Golden Cape or Golden Horn—a beach shaped like an ice cream cone, or a thin wedge of pie. The length and width of the pointy land mass fluctuate with changes in wind, tide, and current, like Whitehaven Beach in Australia

I'd visited with Jenna. I trudged through white pebbles and sand to Zlatni Rat's needle-like point. Then I noticed the only human I'd encountered all day besides the catamaran operators: a man watching me from an interior triangle of dense woodlands within Zlatni Rat. I hugged the periphery of the beach, hustled back to the port, and took an earlier catamaran home.

The next morning, I wrote, then set out to hike a hill in Split called Marjan. I started up a staircase fringed by row houses leading into a forest park with trails, lookout points, botanical gardens, and a petting zoo.

As sweat flecked my cheeks, I realized I was ruminating . . . foreboding problems with upcoming travel logistics. I'd determined my best possible itinerary to Tenerife involved a flight from Split to Vienna, Austria, with a connecting leg to Barcelona, Spain; one night in a hotel; then an afternoon budget airline hop to the Canary Islands. I needed a PCR test in Split with seventy-two hours of validity to cover entry into all three jurisdictions. I began to worry: *Will I find a PCR testing facility in Split that will guarantee results in time to fly? Will the results stay valid until I land in Tenerife, or will I need to find another place to retest in Barcelona? Will either airline charge me astronomical fees for my overweight suitcases full of research books? Maybe this whole trip is too self-indulgent. Nobody else is taking this much time "off" to rest and write.*

I walked smack into a scent cloud of honeysuckle so strong I nearly choked. A song lilted over the stone wall of someone's garden. *It's a beautiful day.* A stranger's radio blasting U2's song, "Beautiful Day." I laughed out loud. *Don't let it get away.*

Okay, it's a beautiful day. Don't let it get away by worrying about travel glitches that are not likely to happen because you are good at researching and planning. Don't let it get away by feeling guilty or ashamed about taking time to recover from this raucous year and work on a writing project you're excited about and you know needs solitary focus to get done. Trust your process. You deserve this time. Hike this hill. Inhale Croatian honeysuckle air. Listen to distant

Adriatic waves tumble onto rocks. Put one foot in front of the other. This trip, and this writing project, are about you. Everything else is a side show. Now, move it.

I climbed another stone staircase to a platform offering panoramic views of Split. The port. Basilica steeples. Beach coves. A Croatian flag flapped overhead in a light breeze. I descended a twin staircase on the far side of the viewing deck and followed a paved road through thick woods, alone except for the occasional ambitious cyclist. I briefly considered if it was unnecessarily risky to walk solo through the forest. But an older couple with walking sticks appeared as I crested a hill, two dogs running circles around their feet. We exchanged hellos—theirs in Croatian, mine in English.

The forest canopy provided shade. Scents of cypress and pine trees permeated the air. Legs tiring from scaling hills, I spotted a welcome sight: a sign for Kupalište Bene, roughly translating to "Well Bath," a public swimming hole. Families lounged around picnic tables. Children bounced on trampolines. Seeking a less populated nook to take a dip in the water, I wandered toward a shallow inlet. I pulled a towel from my day pack, spread it on flat rocks, and stripped off jean shorts and my tank top. A pair of crabs—pincers opening and closing—shuffled along the stony edge. I peered into the water. More crabs. Sea urchins with spiky needles clung to underwater rocks.

On second thought . . . maybe I'll just read on the deck.

I retraced my steps to the apartment, scuttled inside my blue door without bumping into Drago along the way, and hunkered down for an evening solidifying travel plans. I booked the flight to Barcelona via Vienna, one night at the W Hotel, and air transit to Tenerife. I found a website for a medical clinic in Split guaranteeing PCR test results for foreigners within twenty-four hours and offering on-site English translation of the certificate.

Early morning, I confirmed a seat on a four-hour ferry to the Croatian city of Dubrovnik and reserved a cheap room for two nights, shrugging off a twinge of guilt over paying for Zoran's place at the same time but not sleeping there. At sunrise, I boarded another near-empty catamaran. As the ferry threaded islands along the Dalmatian Coast, my fingers pressed laptop keys; the quiet rocking of the ferry nudged me along as words accumulated on the screen and I met my writing quota for the day.

I arrived in Dubrovnik's port and walked two miles from the harbor, through arcades of an old fortress buttressed by high stone walls, past coffee shops and nautical restaurants, up a long staircase bordered by fruit orchards. Everything smelled orange. I opened a metal gate and entered a courtyard with a swimming pool framed by lemon trees and murals of 1950s and 1960s American movie stars like James Dean and Steve McQueen. A blonde woman my age—tan skin, gray-blue eyes—greeted me.

"I'm Kristina," she said. She handed me a key to a poolside room and gestured at an olive-green door. "You can pay me in two days when you check out."

Bookshelves teeming with novels in multiple languages lined the walls of a sitting area inside the doorway. A mural of Ernest Hemingway smoking a cigar and holding copies of his own books decorated the wall behind a double bed. I hid my laptop under a pillow and headed back outside.

I returned to the fortress—the focal point of Dubrovnik's city center—in search of lunch. I chose a restaurant with outdoor tables wrapped in pretty linens and ate another grilled fish doused in olive oil and lemon. I climbed a series of stone staircases to reach an upper walkway looping the fortress with plunging views of the sea and land below. Feeling twitches of vertigo on the narrower paths—nothing between me and a deep drop to the sea except thigh-high stone walls—I slowed and gripped the rock balustrade to regain equilibrium. I stopped for coffee and orange juice at a lookout point, a café with a sweeping Adriatic view, and noticed Dubrovnik's calming effect on me. Work demands, pandemic burnout, the Drago fling, had started to fade into ephemera.

I slept well the first night, Hemingway and his books watching over me. In the morning, my own words flowed onto the page. For lunch, I ate bites of feta cheese mixed with fresh chunks of cucumber and tomato with a touch of olive oil. I visited a Salvador Dalí exhibit, my friend Kelly's favorite artist. I photographed a Dalí painting—a kaleidoscopic horse wearing a crown—and sent it to her. We often text one another the crown emoji as a reminder: "You rule."

I crossed a drawbridge and stopped to glance at the Adriatic splashing against wooden posts supporting a dock below. Small boats in various states of repair lay askew on the shore. I glimpsed a single letter and number spray-painted on a metal grate next to a boat resting on pilings. The letter and number said: *U2*. I laughed. Another bizarrely placed message of encouragement from the universe.

Early afternoon, I found a cove called Banje Beach. I rented a lounge chair with a soft cushion and basked in the sun. Flecks of green and gold glinted in the sand. Sea glass. I plucked broken bottle pieces pounded by waves for months, maybe years, and collected a mound on my towel. I ordered a bowl of fresh mussels from the beach bar and ate them with my fingers, dripping garlic and lemon juice on my legs. I swam in shallow, clear water, toes and heels imprinting soft sand as I entered and exited. No craggy rocks assaulting my feet like Drago's beach in Split. I floated in the waves, beginning to feel liberated—from expectations, external control, any sense of urgency to figure out my life. An entire year of sabbatical, to write, to *be*.

At sunset, I tucked into Banje Beach's bar to pay for the snack and use the restroom to wash my hands, sticky with mussel juice and sunscreen. Inside the restroom, on the wall, a mural of Muhammad Ali stared back at me, one arm defiantly hooked in a victory gesture. More karmic cheerleading. *Hvala, universe. Thank you.*

The next day, a morning of writing logged, I rode a small ferry to Lokrum Island, a nature reserve ten minutes by boat from Dubrovnik. Benedictine monks settled the island in 915 CE.

When the ferry berthed at Lokrum, the few other passengers darted toward a gift shop. I hinged the opposite direction, desiring to explore the island alone. Dirt paths carved through thickets of plants and palm trees. Wild peacocks strutted ahead of me, occasionally spreading paisley plumes in dominance as I infringed their territory. A sign intrigued me: *Nudističko Kupalište.* Nudist beach.

A rough-hewn path opened to a span of silvery rocks. I stepped onto a boulder. Then over a small crevice to another one. The terrain looked moonlike. I found a flat spot facing the sea, protected from view on either side by large stones. Nothing in front of me except the vast Adriatic. No people. I took off my shorts and T-shirt. Then my swimsuit. At first, I felt jittery, on high alert, the slightest sound causing me to jolt upright and glance around for witnesses, interlopers, judges, censors. But soon, I settled. Closed my eyes. Let the sun warm my body, the breeze explore my skin. Moon rock. Sun. Wind. Waves hitting stone. No artificial barriers between body and element. Intense sensuality. Sexual, even. *Rewild. Be wild.* An interesting twist—beginning to treasure the body I'd had for five decades yet never liked that much because I'd listened to other people—my mom, men—implying it should be different. The misunderstood changing body I'd been ashamed of as a teenager. The twenty-five-year-old body Trey had nitpicked yet I'd conferred access to. The thirty-five-year-old body Forrest had rejected.

Now, at fifty-one, a stronger authentic body.

Time passed. I sat up. Took a selfie, sunlight dancing like glitter on my skin, wind wisping hair around my face, the borders of the frame a bit fuzzy. I liked what I saw on that moon rock—an airiness, a lightness, a mermaidness, an Aphroditeness I was beginning to genuinely feel.

I redressed, skipped along the rocks back to the dirt path, and followed a peacock around the other side of the island, passing cactus gardens and tide pools. The peacock escorted me to the dock. The next boat carried me back to Dubrovnik's shore.

I found the PCR test center in Split after accidentally waiting in the vestibule of a Botox MedSpa and sipping the cappuccino they graciously offered me before we all realized I was in the wrong place. I obtained the test results in English three hours later, uploaded them to the airline website, and within minutes received a QR code for entry into Barcelona Airport. *Step one of Operation-Get-to-Tenerife: complete.*

The day of my departure, Zoran and his son arrived at the apartment with printouts of my travel documents—PCR test results, QR code, boarding passes—and helped tote my luggage to the harbor. They secured me in a taxi to Split Airport and waved goodbye until I was out of sight.

Not even half a smile passed the pursed lips of the Austrian Airlines agent who checked and rechecked my passport and COVID documents. She weighed my luggage, declared it overweight, and ordered me to lug the suitcases to another part of the terminal to pay an extra 580 kuna (around eighty dollars) to check both bags.

Remember the plan. Do not feel guilty about spending money to streamline travel logistics on this trip. Whatever it takes. Pay the fee and go.

After being scolded by a flight attendant for wearing a cloth mask on the plane instead of a European FFP2 mask, I made a mental note not to ignore any more authoritative emails in German assuming they were spam. I deplaned in Vienna. Every expansion and contraction of my heart's chambers seemed audible as an Austrian border patrol officer scrutinized my passport, COVID paperwork, and second boarding pass. He asked how many days I'd be spending in Barcelona.

"Just one night. I'm trying to get to Tenerife," I stuttered.

His embosser hit my passport with a satisfying *th-thunk*. He returned my swath of papers and waved me through.

On the 140-minute flight from Vienna to Barcelona, I worried. *What if I have to go through immigration again but somehow I missed a Spain entry rule? What if they detain me for not having an exit flight from Tenerife yet because I don't know if I'll be flying home or if I can finally get into Rome if Italy opens next month?*

I landed in Barcelona and wrested my two suitcases from the baggage claim conveyor belt, trying not to shred my palm with the cracked handle of the smaller bag. Bracing for the moment when I'd hit yet another paperwork checkpoint, I rolled my luggage toward signs for . . . *Salida.* Exit.

I burst outside. Outside! In Barcelona!

Wait. No immigration or COVID checkpoints? Am I done?

I inhaled humid salty air and hailed a taxi.

"W Hotel, *por favor*," I said to the driver. I rolled down the window and grinned.

The W Hotel in Barcelona is shaped like a boat's sail. Mirrored glass windows reflect blues and greens of the Mediterranean Sea. The building sits on a promontory at the end of a long beach bordered by a promenade called La Barceloneta where residents and tourists take boxing lessons, ride skateboards, and drink cocktails.

In the hotel lobby, club music vibrated the floor. Sexy musk from the W's signature candles commingled with stylish patrons' colognes and perfumes. I watched the desk clerk magnetize my room key. Adrenaline pumped through my limbs as I realized: *I did it.* I got myself from New York to Amsterdam, to Split, to Vienna, to Barcelona in one piece. Luggage (mostly) intact. Zero logistic hiccups. Just one short flight left to make my month in Tenerife a reality.

I walked the Barceloneta boardwalk in moonlight, searching for a place to eat. I found an outdoor tapas bar, Gallito, tucked into a corner of the hotel's footprint at sea level. I sat at a wooden table, surf sounds intermingling with Spanish voices, a mélange of dialects I couldn't understand. Thick cigarette smoke threatened to unleash a tension headache I'd managed to keep bridled all day. I ordered a glass of white Rioja by accident, thinking I'd requested red, but I drank it anyway. A waitress brought a salad of avocado, arugula, and shaved parmesan, then a ceviche of fish, fresh lime, and crispy plantain chips.

That night, I slept deeply. Sumptuous bedding. Air-conditioning set to icebox temperatures. No raucous Croatian cathedral bells tolling at the crack of dawn.

My flight to Tenerife wasn't until 4 p.m., so I had several hours to rove Barcelona. I'd been to the city once before, for a U2 show with Clay. We'd explored two of Spanish architect-designer Antoni Gaudí's modernist masterpieces: a house he was commissioned to build, the Casa Milà, and a garden, Park Güell. Both landmarks incorporate structural designs, curves, and textures depicting plants and animals in fantastical colors. Clay and I hadn't had time on that trip to visit the Sagrada Familia (meaning *Holy Family*), a still-unfinished basilica originally designed by Spanish architect Francisco de Paula del Villar in 1882; construction began the same year. Gaudí took over the project in 1883. When he died in 1926, hit by a tram at the age of seventy-four on his way to his local parish for daily confession, his disciple, Domènec Sugrañes i Gras, assumed leadership of the architectural initiative. Ten decades later, infrastructure and artistic work persists. Experts projected a 2026 completion date—one hundred years after Gaudí's death. I like the concept that a 140-year-old structure can still be a work in progress.

After a quick *café con leche* at the hotel, I strolled the beach, kicking off my shoes so my feet could touch a new body of water—first the Adriatic in Croatia, now the Mediterranean. I listened to guitarists strum tunes for morning yogis and meditators. A three-mile walk led me to the Sagrada Familia. Its silhouette conjured memories of drip castles my brother and I had constructed from buckets of sand and Atlantic ocean water as kids. Stained glass windows, playfully engineered shapes, whimsical fonts of letters attached to doors and spires, and colorful orbs resembling holiday ornaments give the edifice a fantasy vibe. Chaotic, yet cheerful. Not somber, grim, or sanctimonious like many churches I'd seen in my life. I wondered if the atmosphere of its religious services reflected a similar lightness. Even if the house of prayer weren't closed for COVID, I had no time to find out. Eyeing the time, I sheered toward the shoreline.

Nearing the W, I noticed a surf school sign, its tagline: *Disconnect from what keeps you away. Reconnect with what keeps you alive.* A good mission statement for my upcoming Tenerife adventure.

Hungry, I entered Gallito for a quick bite. A waitress indicated the restaurant wasn't yet open for lunch.

"I can bring you coffee and juice though," she offered.

I sat on a bench at a long communal table facing the ocean. The waitress brought a café con leche, a glass of fresh-squeezed blood orange juice, and a flat round sandwich: fresh salty bread, thin slices of *jamón* (Spanish ham), shaved Manchego cheese. She apologized it was all she could provide. Without hyperbole, it was the most delicious sandwich I'd ever eaten. I paid my check and bopped back to the hotel room.

The Barcelona Airport authorities accepted my Croatian PCR test; sixteen hours remained on its seventy-two-hour validity clock. The low-cost airline personnel first questioned whether I'd paid enough fees to check my two heavy suitcases, but when a large group of boisterous travelers approached the ticket desk with none of their COVID documentation in order, an agent hustled me to a different line and took both bags off my hands without further inquiry.

As the plane descended toward Tenerife's airport on the northern part of the island, I glanced out the window. Black sand. Green vegetation. A volcano called El Teide.

I stepped off a mobile air staircase onto a tarmac. I showed my COVID paperwork at two checkpoints inside the airport terminal. The Croatian PCR test withstood final scrutiny.
Done.
My heart, abloom.
I made it to Tenerife.

Because of Marta's cottage's remote location in a banana grove far from public transportation, I needed to rent a car. Living in New York City, I don't own a vehicle; I ride the subway or walk everywhere. The last time I'd sat behind the steering wheel of an automobile was prepandemic Thanksgiving when I'd flown to Norfolk, Virginia, rented a cheap compact car, then driven another two hours to visit my family at my brother's house in North Carolina's Outer Banks.

At the Tenerife airport, I slid my driver's license and credit card through a half-moon opening in a glass barrier between an Autoreisen clerk and me. I tried to exude cool competence, like I operate motor vehicles in foreign countries all the livelong day.

He handed me keys to a Citroën.

I found the white hatchback in its designated parking spot, heaved my suitcases into the trunk, nestled into the driver's seat, and murmured a quiet *thank you* to my dad, who taught me to drive stick shift on a beat-up, rusted-out Volkswagen Beetle when I was sixteen. Learning how to drive a car with a manual transmission, a temperamental clutch, and sticky gears armed me with at least one helpful tool for getting to my Tenerife sanctuary in one piece. I activated GPS and entered Casa Plumeria's address. Marta had sent me precise latitude and longitude coordinates, but I thought, *Why on earth would I need those details if I have the house number and street name?*

I shifted into first gear, listened to my phone's GPS Americanize the Spanish names of map markers, and unclenched my shoulders.

Yayyyyy. Almost to my writing retreat! For a whole month!
I navigated a curvy two-lane highway away from the airport
fine, watching orange sun set over green mountains. I practiced
downshifting and upshifting through the motorway's arcs, getting a feel for the car. GPS led me to a roundabout. Instructed
me to take the third exit.
Uno. Dos. Tres. Wait, which one's the third exit?
The Citroën circled the roundabout again. I recounted,
prayed I chose the correct route, veered onto a smaller byway,
then found myself on an even narrower *one-lane* passageway
flanked by stone walls. No visible street names or house numbers. Only banana trees, tropical vines, cactus plants, and me—
feeling initial pangs of panic.
What if another vehicle comes from the opposite direction?
My GPS started speaking Spanish, then English, then told
me I'd passed my destination.
But there is nowhere to turn around?
The road funneled farther toward the ocean, deeper into
fields of banana trees. The sky purpled. The pavement broadened
slightly to reveal a parked pickup truck, Technicolor windsurf
boards stacked in the flatbed, and four guys sitting on the ground,
chilling, drinking beers. I slammed the brakes so I wouldn't plow
into them. The car stalled.
I decided to input the actual latitude and longitude coordinates of the house into the GPS, which immediately admonished me to backtrack. I restarted the Citroën and orchestrated
a five-point turn to aim back up the hill. The guys waved. After
a few hundred feet, the GPS declared, *You have arrived at your
destination.*
*I HAVE NOT ARRIVED—I AM IN THE MIDDLE OF A
BANANA FIELD!*
My heart knocked at my ribs. I inched the car up the hill,
stalled again, gently restarted the engine miraculously without
rolling the vehicle backward into a concrete wall. I wound my

way around twists and bends in the asphalt and ended up back at the main junction.

Do not freak out. Turn around and try again. It's okay if you're lost. You're not going to be stuck in the middle of a banana farm forever. You'll eventually find where you're supposed to be. You have no deadline.

I maneuvered the Citroën in the correct direction and slowly descended the serpentine hill once more. I recognized a heart-shaped cactus leaf I'd passed twice already, and suddenly noticed a bamboo gate between two white terra-cotta planters. The entrance to the property I'd seen in Marta's photographs! No house number in sight. I pulled into the driveway. Marta—gorgeous, tan, chic, smiley—awaited and opened the mechanized gate, waving happily. I exhaled.

Dude, you made it.

Marta administered a brief tour of the property, handed me a map with instructions on how to find the nearest grocery stores, and said she'd check on me the next day. I surveyed the refrigerator: empty.

Desiring a glass of wine to take the edge off my thirty-hour journey from Split, and knowing I'd want coffee, milk, and some sort of breakfast item in the morning, I steeled myself for another quick trip in the car to the closest food mart. I opened the property gate with a key fob, shifted the Citroën into reverse, slowly threaded the vehicle between the massive twin plant pots, looked both ways four times for oncoming traffic, and scooted along twisty lanes back to the highway. I counted two exits, veered onto a ramp, and saw the name of a market Marta recommended. I steered the Citroën into a parking spot, tested the door locks, and followed Canarians inside.

I love shopping for groceries in foreign countries. Seeing the names of fruits, vegetables, meats, and milks in other languages soothes me, as if the workaday task of stocking a refrigerator means I *belong* there and I'm not just passing through.

I filled a plastic basket with mystery cheeses, packages of jamón, bottles of wine with yellow canaries on their labels, a bag of coffee grounds, a carton of almond milk, and a small sack of dried apricots. I wanted to get home before the sky turned completely dark so I wouldn't get lost again. I joined a checkout line. When I reached the clerk, I didn't understand anything she said to me. She gestured and spoke at me, but none of my items began moving along the conveyor belt toward any sort of bag. I thought a year's worth of binge-watching Spanish Netflix shows would have armed me with at least some Tenerife vocabulary, but I comprehended nothing. Finally, a man behind me—the first in a growing line of waiting shoppers—handed me a burlap shopping bag from a stack beneath the conveyor belt.

Oh. I need to buy a reusable bag.

"Gracias," I said to him. "Gracias!"

I made it home without missing any turns or encountering any other drivers on the one-lane corridor. I poured a glass of Canarian wine and opened a sliding door, stepping bare feet onto veranda tiles. I surveyed my view for the next thirty days. Wicker daybed built for two with red-and-white striped cushions. Stone fountain with a spout trickling water into a square plunge pool. Metal sculpture of a fish resting on a plinth. White privacy fence. Lush foliage. Atlantic Ocean in the distance. Orange sun dunking into it.

I sat on the travertine trim of the pool and dipped my toes in the water. I watched six-inch lizards engage in standoffs with sweet-looking cats as butterflies and dragonflies darted across the daybed. My heart rate slowed. I smiled.

I did it.

I'd figured out pandemic protocols from New York, to Amsterdam, to Split, to Vienna, to Barcelona, to Tenerife. I'd deciphered three different airlines' luggage rules. I'd hauled my belongings—notwithstanding one busted suitcase handle—through six airports. I'd broken my man drought. I'd started my new book manuscript and accumulated fifty pages so far. I'd

driven a car for the first time in eighteen months, untangled confusing geographical directions, felt lost, kept going, and found
the property.

I'd stuck to what I thought, no, what I *knew*, would make
me happy: finding a place to write, to rest, a location where not a
lot of Americans would be, where I'd be forced to hear and learn
unfamiliar languages, to sample new foods, to rediscover myself.
A locale with no daily agenda or expectations. Just writing, exercising, exploring, recuperating. A raw and wild location—in the
middle of nature. Volcanoes. Tropical flora. Black sand. Lizards.
Canaries. Cats. Dragonflies.

Croatian reboot complete.

Let the Canarian rewilding begin.

9
tenerife, canary islands

Canaries chirped.

Disoriented, I opened my eyes, struggling to discern shapes. I unlatched a window, pushing wooden shutters into darkness. Imagining an army of lizards and tropical bugs scooting over the sill, I reclosed the glass panes, leaving the shutters ajar.

Roosters crowed.

Rewilding.

I padded barefoot to the kitchen to punch buttons on yet another foreign coffee contraption. I'd slept deeply, relieved the Barcelona-Tenerife flight, the Citroën rental, the settling into Casa Plumeria, had gone so smoothly. Staring through a sliding glass door onto the cottage's veranda, I caught my reflection. My brain flashed to every horror movie I'd watched at teenage slumber parties. I blinked, canceling a mirage of a hatchet-wielding human staring at me from outside.

You'll get used to this . . . these new, remote surroundings.

I carried a mug of coffee to bed and lit a red candle I found in a cupboard, dust particles snap crackling in its flame. I scribbled journal pages. Morning light peeked through palm leaves, like a photograph developing in an untamed darkroom.

Opening the sliding door, I stepped onto the terrace. Canaries cheeped. Roosters cawed. A car honked a gentle warning as it leaned into a blind turn on the one-lane road bordering the property fence. Wind rustled fronds of palm trees and tropical plants blanketing the land between bungalows. I heard but couldn't see distant waves striking rocks, multiple tiers of land and vegetation between the sea and me.

Laptop in hand, I sat on the sunbed, setting my coffee mug on a glass trolley. A willowy orange cat leaped onto the chaise, rubbing his ribs against my shin. I'm a dog person, not usually on Team Cat, but this creature—sleepy eyed, prickers stuck in his fur—quickly wooed me. He melded his lanky body to my hip bone and fell asleep.

I wrote the day's book pages, orange cat snoozing next to me, occasionally waking up to unfurl his legs dramatically, tiny claws impaling my skin. A gray cat poked his head beneath a white privacy screen surrounding the terrace, crouched at the edge of the plunge pool, stared at a red dragonfly doing aerial tricks over the water. I heard odd squeaks, a racket emanating from a pair of lizards stretching and sighing on a concrete spout dumping fresh water into the pool. The gray cat eyed them. He meowed but kept his distance. *Introvert.* The extroverted, flirtier orange one burrowed farther into my abs.

Finished with my writing, I calculated the distance to El Bollullo, the black-sand beach closest to Casa Plumeria. Three miles round-trip. I changed into exercise clothes, stepped out of the property gate, and turned left onto the one-lane road. Cinder-block walls lined the narrow lane, protecting private dwellings from public view. Shards of broken glass—shattered beer and wine bottles—jutted from layers of mortar topping property barriers, warding off intruders, human and animal. One yellow flower drooped over a partition, a single bloom from a green cactus leaf.

I started jogging down the steep hill. Gaps between fences revealed endless rows of banana trees, clusters of green fruit drooping toward soil. Roosters with cartoonish plumes pecked at fallen branches and sunbaked stalks. Green-brown lizards crisscrossed the street, inches from my sneakers. I ran past water cisterns resembling aboveground pools. The road twisted and coiled, descending toward sea level, banana trees as far as I could see. The pavement roughened. Potholes. Gravel. The soles of my sneakers struggled to grip the abrupt decline and uneven surface. My knees already ached.

Maybe jogging isn't gonna work here.

I decelerated to a walk. I glanced downward toward the ocean, distinguishing stria of topography. Curvy asphalt. Orange and pink blossoms spilling over privacy walls. Hundreds of banana trees. Irrigation reservoirs. Green and yellow vegetation covering black craggy rocks—the gradation closest to the dark Atlantic.

My third ocean in twelve days.

The road torqued around a sharp turn. A red door of a white cottage opened. A dapper Spanish couple stepped onto a porch, the first humans I'd encountered all morning. COVID masks obscured their faces. I realized I'd forgotten my mask. Before I'd left home for Europe, New York had finally lifted its outdoor mask mandate, as had Croatia, though many residents of Split continued wearing them. Canary Island authorities still enforced an outdoor face covering rule. I tugged my T-shirt collar over my nose and mouth as the couple passed me. We nodded.

"Buenos días," they said.

"Buenos días," I replied.

I heard surf thrashing rocks. I stopped to peer over a stone wall. A dizzying drop to sea level. El Bollullo's black-sand beach. Waves smashed a trio of dark rocks protruding from earth like waterlogged charcoal. White foam detonated into the air with each collision. I headed toward a staircase of switchbacks cascading to the cove. I nodded at a security officer leaning against a beach access sign, face mask bunched below his chin, making me feel less disobedient without mine.

Loose piles of stones offered the only barrier between the narrow footpath to the stairs and a cliffside plunging to black sand below. No guardrails. Feeling a flutter of vertigo reminiscent of walking the upper ramparts of Dubrovnik's fort, I trailed my hand against a dirt embankment on one side of the path. *Take it slow. You're fine. Eyes to the right. Don't look left. Don't look down.*

The staircase doubled back toward the coastline, dropping altitude fast. Lizards chased one other down stone steps. I passed a blue wooden box with painted letters spelling *Virgen del Carmen*—the patron saint of the sea—storing bouquets of dead flowers and burned-out votive candles. At sea level, I stepped onto a pathway of smooth lava rocks leading to a shuttered beach shack café. I passed a large yucca plant resembling a Joshua tree. Behind it, a red flag rippled from a pole in a breeze, its color signaling rough surf. No swimming today. "Red Flag Day," a U2 song, once again the imaginary soundtrack to my adventures.

I hopped off one last boulder into soft sand, sneakers sinking into black silt. I kicked off shoes and socks and aimed toward the ocean, the beach deserted except for one man—shirtless in red swimming trunks—striding the line where surf met shore. I noticed the word *salvavidas* on his shorts. *Lifeguard.* Fit, tan, long blond hair, cocky gait, he looked like he'd been patrolling that beach for thirty years. We nodded hello.

I sat in the sand, watching waves batter boulders resembling large chunks of coal. I sifted black sand granules through my fingers. Velvety. No pebbles. No seaweed. No shells. No sea glass. Just magma once on fire, spewed from a volcano, cooled over time, shattered into particles by persistent surf.

I felt like I'd been summoned to Tenerife to *rewild*, to get in touch with nature after fourteen months homebound. Other tropical locations certainly would have been easier to get to. Mexico. The Caribbean. But this island lured me. Volcanoes imply wreckage, but they make me think of change. Like the Tower card in tarot: perceived chaos leading to transformation. Like Kali, the Hindu goddess of destruction *and* liberation from ignorance.

I like change. Even if it's messy. Maybe *especially* if it's messy.

I returned to the bungalow, sweat drenched. I stripped, leaving a trail of clothing—sneakers, socks, shorts, T-shirt, bra, sunglasses—on veranda tiles, slipping into the plunge pool. Lizards squeaked from the waterspout. The gray cat studied me from the shade of a patio table. I emerged from the pool and flopped onto the sunbed. I liked not feeling compelled to drag on a swimsuit. Part of the rewilding I sought included appreciating my body—in all its fifty-one-year-old glory—a reframing Croatia had initiated.

Voices from other cottages flitted over privacy fences and foliage. I loved hearing foreign words, evidence I wasn't the only human occupying the remote tropical footprint, though I happily inhabited Casa Plumeria alone.

After an hour letting Tenerife sun seep into my skin, I showered, dressed, and out of habit grabbed a stick of eyeliner from my makeup bag. *On second thought.* I set the eye pencil down. *Thirty days in the jungle. Au natural. Let's do it.* My skin deserved a break from products I'd slathered on it for a year in a constant attempt to look virtual-meeting ready. I left my hair in tousled mayhem.

The prospect of driving the Citroën again and encountering an oncoming vehicle on the narrow road still freaked me out. If I came face-to-face with another car, one of us would have to reverse up or down the twisty tarmac, maneuvering stick shift and clutch, avoiding drop-offs into unmarked irrigation ditches. But I knew I needed to get over my trepidation to maximize my Tenerife adventure.

I inserted the key in the Citroën's ignition. *Please God, let me get to the main intersection unscathed.*

Over the years, my parents have assumed I don't have a relationship or conversations with God. I do. I rarely pray for God to *give* me tangible stuff or make specific dreams a reality. To manifest big goals and desires, I write in a daily journal called "Nude Gratitude" one of my former students created; per her instructions, I jot "I am grateful for . . . ," then list future events or achievements as if they've already happened. That process works for me. I've manifested book contracts, acceptance to a master's degree program, and fruition of various creative projects that way. But when I'm supernervous or afraid, or need a situation expedited, I cut out the conduit and go straight to the source.

I upshifted and downshifted around curves, reaching the first junction without drama. I paused at a stop sign, cruised left onto a two-lane avenue, circled a roundabout, and dashed up a long hill to La Orotava, a village established in 1502, six years after Spain conquered Tenerife, the last of the Canary Islands (formerly inhabited by an Indigenous population called Guanches) to be colonized.

I figured I'd park the Citroën and explore La Orotava's historical sights before finding another grocery store. I quickly nixed that plan. Car horns blared each time I slowed on a hill (toggling brake, clutch, accelerator, and turn signal) to gauge whether I could squeeze into an open parking spot. I turned the wrong way down a one-way street, reversed onto a boulevard (another riot of honking), and nearly flattened a lady pushing a shopping cart through a crosswalk (a torrent of angry Spanish). I decided cultural exploration could wait. I aimed the Citroën downhill and jagged the vehicle into the parking lot of a grocery store called SuperDino. I sat—gripping the steering wheel— until my heart stopped ricocheting. I stocked up on packages of raw meats, cartons of fresh juices, yogurts, lemons, lima beans, and two bunches of not-yet-ripe Canary Island bananas. Safely back in my bungalow after a thankfully uneventful drive home, I dumped the car keys in a bowl on the kitchen counter and declared a three-day driving hiatus. Exploring the coast by foot seemed less heart attack inducing.

Midafternoon, I felt the urge to write. I rarely write twice in one day. I do my best creative work in the morning and often tempt a headache if I try to push past two hours of intense focus. But sitting on the sunbed, canvas umbrella providing respite from heat and glare, orange cat spooning my hip, lemon slices floating in a carafe of cold water on the glass trolley, four more pages materialized. I'd always romanticized the life of "real" authors journeying to writing retreats in faraway places, an artistic sequestration to get serious work done. Now I remind myself: *You're writing your seventh book; you are a real author.* Croatia had kick-started my eagerness to construct, to shape, to craft something from nothing again . . . to pull words out of my own brain and arrange them on a blank page. Less than twenty-four hours in Tenerife, pandemic fog had further lifted, making space for new ideas.

I closed my laptop, craving a dip in the plunge pool. Edging into the water, I noticed a lizard resting at the bottom. I paused, wondering if lizards bite. *Do they have teeth?* I pulled my feet from the water, wrapped myself in a Turkish towel, decided it was happy hour, and went inside to pour a glass of wine.

I cooked steak and lima beans and ate dinner on the veranda, listening to the island wind down after a perfect first day. Cats meowing, dogs baying, waves whorling. A stark contrast to the evening hubbub of Diocletian's Palace in Split.

Sunlight segued to dusk, then darkness. The orange cat disappeared into the palm grove. In moonlight, I checked the bottom of the pool. The lizard hadn't moved. I closed the sliding glass door, settled under a chenille throw blanket on the couch, grabbed my computer, and typed, "How long can lizards remain alive underwater?"

Morning to-do list: *Deal with my first dead jungle creature.*

Easing into bed, I extinguished the bedside lamp. Two seconds later, I clicked the light back on, jumped up, and checked the room for geckos, spiders, and other citizens of Tenerife.

I woke up to chirping canaries and tapping raindrops. I set my laptop on a desk in the living room facing the terrace and inched the sliding glass door open. The orange cat—wet, waiting on the veranda tiles—sauntered inside, toured the kitchen for food scraps, hopped onto the writing table, rubbed his ribs against my computer screen, curled onto a sheaf of papers, and fell asleep. I stepped outside into raindrops and stared into the pool.

That lizard is definitely dead.

I'd noticed a pool skimmer poking from underbrush near the patio table. I shook dry leaves out of its mesh basket and submerged the netting into the pool. After a few attempts, I scooped the lizard's lifeless body and situated his little corpse on a mulch pile on the other side of the privacy fence.

Dabbing raindrops from my shoulders with a kitchen towel, I noticed a metal sculpture standing on a pedestal near the couch—a square of iron, eight twisted steel strips curling outward, like a welded matchbook. It reminded me of 9/11 beams salvaged from the World Trade Center and memorialized by artists in installations placed around New York. I messaged Marta:

HOLA! EVERYTHING IS WONDERFUL AT CASA PLUMERIA. I LOVE THE SCULPTURE IN THE LIVING ROOM. WHO'S THE ARTIST?

She responded immediately:

I'M SO GLAD YOU ARE LOVING THE COTTAGE! THE ARTIST IS PEPE ABAD, ALSO KNOWN AS JOSÉ ABAD. BY THE WAY, PLEASE DON'T FEED THE CATS WHO ROAM THE PROPERTY. SOME GUESTS ARE BOTHERED BY THE CATS SO WE DON'T WANT THEM TO BECOME DEPENDENT ON HUMANS FOR FOOD. IT'S BEST IF THEY STAY OUTSIDE. ALSO, IF YOU HAPPEN TO SEE OR SMELL A SMOKY SCENT, IT'S DUST FROM THE SAHARA DESERT THAT MAKES ITS WAY TO THE CANARY ISLANDS. WE CALL IT CALIMA.

I glanced at the orange cat . . . in my lap. Oops. I'd already named him Larry Mullen Jr.

Larry stretched his skinny legs, prickers sticking to fur around pink paw pads, sharp claws pressing the skin of my thighs.

I wrote pages, then started a load of laundry—mounds of gritty clothes I'd worn in Croatia and Barcelona—in a miniature washing machine hidden in a cabinet beneath the bathroom sink. I scribbled a list of items to purchase on an outing to a coastal village called Puerto de la Cruz I'd scouted on a map. I needed bug spray. Mosquito bites already dotted my shins and shoulders. I also wanted to find a citronella candle to repel jungle flies persistently buzzing around my face and laptop. A growing indoor ant population also required urgent attention.

I nudged sleepy Larry back outside, locked the cottage, and glanced at the Citroën, noticing rain-spattered rust-brown Saharan *calima* dust on its doors and windows. I opened the property gate and stepped onto the one-lane road.

Casa Plumeria sits in an enclave of Tenerife called El Rincón, three miles up the coast from the village of Puerto de la Cruz. I descended the twisty hill toward the ocean. Instead of turning right toward El Bollullo Beach, I turned left onto a staircase carved into a ravine.

A man in cycling attire carried a racing bike up the steps.

"Buenos días," he said as he passed.

"Buenos días," I echoed.

Lizards played tag inches from my feet. I traversed a valley, its landscape carpeted with stones, cacti, and spiky shrubs. I climbed another staircase leading to tiers of rock walls partitioning agricultural plots—Machu Picchu-style. The pathway narrowed, pulling me into dense banana fields bordered by wire fencing. Roosters and hens foraged soil. Weighty fruit bunches in various color stages between green and yellow bent toward the ground. I momentarily questioned the safety of walking the trail alone— like the twitch I'd felt in the Marjan forest in Split and along the docks of the Liffey late-night in Dublin—but soon heard voices in Spanish. Workmen with tools hacked at banana clusters, harvesting fruit into sacks. They smiled and waved. I rounded a turn and nearly crashed into three ladies in exercise clothes and face masks, speed walking.

I pressed up a hill and entered a short tunnel, an underpass with graffitied walls, COVID conspiracy theories stenciled in Spanish. I emerged onto a coastal promenade and passed a pair of paragliders adjusting red parachutes. They leaped off a ledge into open air, floating toward surf far below. I heard dogs barking, tenants of a cliffside animal shelter. I entered a residential neighborhood. Coffee cups clinked saucers as homeowners read newspapers on whitewashed balconies. A female voice led a fitness class behind a mosaic wall, instructions in Spanish mixed with rhythmic music. Honeypots and beehives painted on a garage door marked a beekeeper's abode.

I turned onto a street called Camino San Amaro. The word *amaro* reminded me of the Italian herbal liqueur I like. The word means *bitter* in Italian, but makes me think of the verb *amare*, to love. A single vowel converts bitterness to love, and vice versa.

Ornate gates guarded swanky hillside residences. A café interrupted the flow of fancy real estate. Its chalkboard listed treats like *apfelstrudel* in German handwriting. The principal language in Tenerife is Spanish, but German appears on numerous restaurant menus. A well-coiffed lady in blue linen pants and an embroidered tunic sat at a table with two men sipping espressos. She stood to greet me.

"Guten morgen," she said.

I studied German in kindergarten, but I can't remember anything besides "die Katze." *The cat.*

"Un café con leche y un strudel, por favor?" I attempted in Spanish.

The lady ushered me inside the café and pointed at an assortment of pastries housed in a glass case. I ordered a cherry strudel and coffee and sat at an outdoor table.

The coffee arrived in a clear glass with a metal handle, accompanied by a triangle of strudel—pastry dough bulging with marinated cherries, soaking in a pool of vanilla sauce.

Camino San Amaro transitioned into a staircase with Agatha Christie book titles painted on colorful steps, some translated into Spanish: *Tres Ratones Ciegos.* Three Blind Mice. *Los Elefantes Pueden Recordar.* Elephants Can Remember. More encouragement from the universe: *You're here to write too.*

Following yet another lengthy staircase sloping to sea level, eventually I reached a shopping district. Boutique windows advertised macramé swimsuits, aloe vera soaps, books in Spanish and German. I entered a grocery store, browsed the home goods section, and found a candle the color of pomegranate with an image of a dead fly and the words *geranio* (geranium) and *stop mosca* (stop fly) on its label. I bought two—one for the veranda and one for the living room.

At the edge of the shopping arcade, I discovered a cove called Lago Martiánez. A jetty forged a protected crescent for surfers and swimmers. I kicked off my running shoes. Black sand scorched my bare feet. I ran toward a spot where waves cooled the terrain. I stripped to my swimsuit. Multiple shapes and sizes of rocks posed an obstacle course between sand and sea. I wobbled. I slipped. I slid. Finally, my feet touched soft underwater sand. I dove into a wave, surfaced, took a breath, dunked again, coolness saturating my hair. I floated on my back, then paddled to shore, grappling with the rock blockade once more before reaching flat ground.

I sat on a Turkish towel and removed my bikini top once I noticed most of the women on the beach were topless. The mature. The young. The curvy. The thin. Collective body language suggesting comfort and confidence in their individual skin. Some solo. Some with partners massaging sunscreen into backs and bare shoulders. I liked the vibe at Lago Martiánez. *Everyone, welcome. Everyone, beautiful.* I felt beautiful. Usually on beach vacations, my skin fries in blazing sunshine. Even coated in SPF 50, I freckle and turn an alarming shade of watermelon. But the Tenerife sun felt nourishing, expelling pandemic anxiety and stress from my pores. Thirteen days away from home, my body already felt leaner, stronger, healthier.

After an hour at Lago Martiánez, famished, I followed a shoreline promenade into the city center of Puerto de la Cruz. A sun-bleached church overlooked a tide pool where sunseekers lounged on rocks and dipped into swimming holes flooded by sea waves. I learned the word *heladerías*—gelato shops. Vendors manned carts displaying skin care products made from aloe vera grown in the wild and on farms throughout the Canary Islands. I wandered a city square, flower beds circling a fountain, a sculpted swan rising from its basin. I traced the arc of a harbor, past families eating boiled shrimp, discarding beady-eyed heads and tails into baskets on picnic tables.

A small uncrowded restaurant with garden seating enticed me.

I said to a hostess, "Lo siento, no hablo español muy bien. Pero quiero probar." *I'm sorry, I don't speak Spanish very well. But I want to try.*

She handed me two tapas menus—one in Spanish, another in English—so I could learn new vocabulary. I ordered *queso asado*: a square of grilled white cheese, a circle cut from its middle and placed separately on the plate. Inside the square's hole, the chef poured half-moons of red sauce (*mojo picante*) and green sauce (*mojo verde*). On the circle cutout, the chef drizzled *miel de palma* (a sap from palm trees) and dusted *gofio* (a light-brown Canarian flour). Savory + sweet.

Happy at how the Puerto de la Cruz day evolved, I structured each Tenerife day the same way: Allowed chirping canaries to serve as alarm clock. Wrote in my journal. Devoted two hours to book writing by the pool, orange cat glued to my hip. Changed into exercise gear and walked the hills to El Bollullo or Lago Martiánez. Sunbathed, swam, and read books, earmarking quotes and concepts to incorporate into my *Flourishing Lawyer* manuscript. Ate lunch at local restaurants, trying Canarian specialties, practicing Spanish terms and phrases. Sought out cultural experiences through art galleries, historic architecture, and craft shops. Meandered along the coast toward home. Wrote by the plunge pool for another hour or two. Cooked dinner, thin slices of beef or chicken, sautéed spinach or steamed lima beans. Sipped wine at sundown with the orange cat until he abandoned me to night stalk in his palm grove. Watched Spanish Netflix, sometimes with Italian subtitles to joggle my brain. Slept when I felt tired, words in multiple languages narrating my dreams. I noticed I didn't feel the slightest bit lonely.

Sunning on a Turkish towel one afternoon on the black sand of El Bollullo Beach, as research for my manuscript, I read a book by Stanley Rosenberg called *Accessing the Healing Power of the Vagus Nerve.* The vagus nerve is a tributary within our nervous system starting at our brainstem, stretching into our chest and abdomen, touching and impacting many of our organs. Its name derives from the Latin *vagus,* meaning *vagrant* or *wanderer.* According to Rosenberg, our vagus nerve helps us modulate our fight-flight-freeze response to perceived danger or threats to our safety. Staring at aggressive waves pounding the shoreline, I contemplated my reflex reaction to harsh criticism by family, work colleagues, men. First, I freeze. Once I thaw, my instinct is to flee. I realized travel though—*my* wandering, my *vagus*—has helped me build a track record of successfully riding out anxiety-producing or scary experiences, neither freezing nor fleeing, instead staying grounded yet fluid in the moment. Riding on the back of Luca's motorcycle in Rome . . . participating in *two* sweat lodge experiences, in Mexico and Vanvouver . . . climbing Montaña in Peru . . . snorkeling with the reef shark in Australia . . . driving the Citroën in Tenerife's hills. Boxing lessons also have taught me to recognize the panicky sensation and reject the false belief that I can't breathe and my heart might stop. I'm able to remember I've developed the resources—physical, mental, and emotional—to handle the situation, to keep moving rather than turning to stone. "Inhale. Exhale. Work it out. Move your head. Move your feet," my trainer Lou reminds me. "The fighter who stays still gets hit."

The gray cat watched me fish another dead lizard from the depths of the plunge pool. I surmised he was the lizard killer. (Never underestimate the quiet ones.) I lit geranium *mosca* candles, warding away aggressive flies. I tried using bug repellant to deter a caravan of ants crawling the four corners of my writing desk, but they persisted. I bought the wrong mosquito zapper; liquid citronella pods I'd purchased didn't fit the diffuser.

I gave up and decided to coexist with my creatures.

On daily excursions, I made countless language and food mistakes. I have a complete mental block about the difference between octopus and squid. I always thought *calamari* in Italian or *calamar* in Spanish meant octopus but, of course, it's actually squid. *Polpo* in Italian, or *pulpo* in Spanish, is octopus. An octopus has a round "mantle"—the part holding its organs—whereas a squid's is longer and triangular. Both have eight arms; an octopus's arms are covered with suction cups; squids' are not necessarily suction-y. A squid has two tentacles with hooks. Octopuses live an exclusively solitary life, while some species of squid live in schools. Maybe I'm more octopus than squid. Thanks to my terminology blurriness, I tasted seven different versions of *calamar* and *pulpo*, loving each iteration: fried tentacles with lemon wedges; grilled slices sprinkled with paprika; roasted chunks dipped in spicy aioli. I also tried fish croquettes, bug-eyed shrimp, and *albóndigas* (meatballs).

I alternated between El Bollullo and Lago Martiánez. I loved the charcoal lava rocks framing Bollullo's descent to silky black sand. Bollullo's transition from beach to sea proved easy on the feet—no wobbly rocks or itchy seaweed to wade through. But the surf refused to stop roiling long enough for safe swimming. The blond lifeguard scolded anyone who ventured into the water beyond knee level. There, I sunbathed, read books, listened to the Atlantic hammer rocks, and watched sexy Spaniards with man buns juggle soccer balls with bare feet. When thirsty, I climbed a short staircase to the beach shack café and ordered ice-cold Estrella beer handed to me by a friendly server who exclaimed, "Sí! Vamos a practicar!" (*Yes, let's practice!*) every time I repeated, "Lo siento, no hablo español muy bien. Pero quiero probar," apologizing for my bad Spanish but indicating a desire to learn.

I adored Lago Martiánez for opposite reasons—the long walk through my Canarian Machu Picchu . . . along the coast . . . past the paraglider ledge, the animal shelter, the beekeeper's house, the German strudel café, the Agatha Christie steps, finally arriving at the cove—the beach, my reward for ninety minutes of physical exertion. The rocky hurdle between hot black sand and cool water threatened a knee or hip dislocation each time I craved a swim. I looked like an awkward baby deer . . . no limb control, trying not to twist an ankle as intrepid surfers leaped past me belly diving onto boards. Eventually, I'd splash into the water and float a bit, then hobble back to a towel. I captured a single decent selfie: lying on volcanic sand, hair splayed like blonde Medusa against black terrain, mouth smirky, chilled out, feeling the *me*-est version of me. I didn't want to be anywhere else. I didn't miss home. I wasn't worried about my job. My book manuscript was chugging along. I felt no urgency to meet a new guy.

On each coastal exploration, my legs served as mode of transport up and down the hills, through banana fields, to and from beaches, cafés, and favorite heladerías. When my knees and hips ached, I MacGyvered a makeshift foam roller, wrapping a cheap beach mat around a wine bottle, securing the edges with masking tape. I placed the contraption on the veranda tiles, pressed my quadriceps and thighs into the foam, and rolled hip to knee and back again, curious cats and lizards watching.

I kept *rewilding*. Swimming in salt water. Sinking feet into volcanic sand. Making zero effort with my hair except rubbing coconut oil into it after showers. Avoiding skin products other than rose oil and sunscreen. Letting the orange cat press pink footpads into my belly, the lizards squeak at me, the ants march around my laptop. Sleeping whenever my eyes drooped. Waking to canaries and roosters.

My body rebooted. My period appeared for the first time in eight months, perhaps a somatic cleanse after my long man drought and mojo kick start with Drago. When the Sahara's *calima* dust initiated a mild headache—and infused my sun-dried laundry with an unpleasant sulfur scent—I realized I hadn't had a single migraine since landing in Tenerife.

Every third or fourth day, I'd force myself to use the Citroën for a grocery outing or to explore a different part of the island. I set out to find a coastal town called Taganana. Pumping the

Citroën's brakes around coils of mountain curves, I feared the car would nose-dive off a bluff if I paused for a millisecond to savor the view. Gas trucks, sporty roadsters, and tour vans careened around me. Surviving the descent to sea level, I squeezed the vehicle into an impossibly tight parking spot, ate tuna steak on a bed of roasted potatoes, then, with an entire restaurant's clientele watching, extracted the car from its wedge between bumpers of two vans, like playing the children's board game, *Operation.* Relieved I didn't sheer off a side-view mirror or scrape lines in anyone's door paint, I catapulted the Citroën up the mountain, dipped into a familiar valley, and deposited the car at Casa Plumeria before sundown, vowing—once again—not to touch the vehicle for three days.

Sometimes when a strange thump on the cottage roof roused me in the middle of the night and I had trouble falling back asleep, I listened to podcasts about "attachment theory" in relationships. *Anxious* types like me (distinct from *avoidant* or *secure* types) are drawn to romantic dynamics fraught with inconsistency, vacillation, conditionality, and unreliability. If we haven't fully worked through childhood trauma or conflict, we choose adult bonds that mirror unhealthy, "push-pull," manipulative patterns we experienced growing up. I learned that I'm typically attracted to avoidant types because I'm accustomed to trying to extract unconditional love from people ill-equipped to reciprocate. Emotional chaos equals familiarity, i.e., comfort. I confuse anxiety with love. When I'm into someone, I crave feeling like I've been hit by a Mack truck. If there's no roller coaster of uncertainty, I quickly grow bored. The relationship registers bland. Monochrome. Grayscale. Flatlined. I'm addicted to intoxicating sparks, jolts of connection, lightning strikes of infatuation.

I felt proud I'd extricated myself from two long-term pairings that had sliced off layers of my self-worth, though I took the heat and publicly shouldered most of the blame—and the shame—for both breakups. But I wasn't quite sure how to choose better in the future, how not to feel *meh* around nice guys, yet smitten with those who stoke desperation, clinging, and unease. Intensity feels tantalizing but I know it ain't love. Next time, I need to remind myself, *This isn't love pumping through your arteries; it's a fraud you're perpetrating on yourself.*

🏔 🏔 🏔

Nearing the end of my second-to-last week in Tenerife, I pushed myself into two final road trips. First, I ascended and descended El Teide, the island's dormant volcano, navigating a motorway cutting through Mars-like red-rock terrain and Sahara-windblown vegetation. Second, I drove to Parque Rural de Anaga, an environmentally-protected region in the northern part of the island with scenic drives through mountains and forests with lookout points and walking paths. The greenway through the woodlands, though corkscrew, didn't feel as precarious as the coastal byway with its steep gullies. Tree canopies offered peekaboo views of foothills. I stopped the car at a few turnouts, snapping landscape and seascape photos, swatting bees buzzing my face. Spotting a visitors' center in a hamlet called Cruz del Carmen (again dedicated to Virgen del Carmen, patron saint of the sea), I parked the Citroën and ambled toward a pair of picnic tables, looking for a place to buy a bottle of cold water. I entered a gift shop and noticed a small bar with a menu handwritten in Spanish. The only word I recognized was *hamburguesa*.

I placed an order and sat at a banquette inside the gift shop, noticing diners at outside tables swishing flies and slapping mosquitos nipping their shoulders. A waiter brought an artisanal burger on a piece of slate—thick grilled patty, tri-colored lettuce, roasted tomatoes, melted Canarian cheese, on a crunchy sunflower seed bun—plus hand-sliced potato rounds dipped in hot olive oil. I ate the burger with knife and fork, cheese dripping over the slate and crispy potatoes. The simple yet complex meal made my taste buds cartwheel.

I paid the check and studied a map tacked to a bulletin board, noticing a forest trail nearby called the Path of the

Senses—*El Sendero de los Sentidos*. As the waiter cleared my plate, he pointed across the parking lot toward the walking path's entrance.

Wooden planks led into an arch of tree branches. A signpost offered instructions in Spanish, German, and English, suggesting how to experience the nature path through multiple senses:

If you close your eyes and walk in silence, a door will open in your mind which will put you in close contact with nature in this special area . . . Walk in silence; go deep into the vegetation . . . Gently feel the texture of the logs . . . Softly touch the surface of the most delicate elements, like leaves and moss.

The boardwalk guided me deeper into the woods. I noticed a marker with a carved image of an eye, the sense of *sight*. I paid attention to what I could see. Nascent flower buds poked from stems. Gnarled knots peered from fallen bark. A green lizard curled around a log.

I moved on. Another placard held an etching of a nose, the sense of *smell*. I inhaled. Dampness. Mist. Mulch. No headachy sulfur scent of the Sahara *calima*.

Another board depicted an image of a hand whittled into wood. The sense of *touch*. I traced concentric circles in a nearby tree stump.

I saw signs bearing another nose, another eye, but never an ear or a mouth. I paused anyway to listen, to hear. Chirp of canaries. Footfalls of other humans. Smack of a couple's kiss. Wind stirring leaves. Squeak of a lizard, perhaps trying to communicate. Avoiding any potential catastrophe from *tasting* a leaf or flower, I licked my lips. Salt from my last potato chip. Rose lip balm. I thought about how the *mouth* icon could also imply speech. I liked realizing how few English words I'd uttered in three Tenerife weeks.

👤 👤 👤

That evening, as I browsed Netflix for a Spanish or Italian TV series to watch, my phone vibrated. News alert: *Italy officially welcomes vaccinated Americans traveling from the United States or any European Union country.*

Giddy, I immediately emailed the proprietor of the Rome hotel called Chapter Roma which, loving its literary name, I'd booked for my fiftieth birthday fifteen months earlier, a plan rudely disrupted by COVID. I'd originally prepaid for a non-refundable hotel reservation, figuring *nothing* could possibly prevent me from spending my big birthday in my favorite spot in the world. Except, of course, a global pandemic.

Initially, the hotel staff provided limited options to recoup my derailed reservation—nontouristy time blocks in low-season winter months. But when I gently reminded them about the extraordinariness of the circumstances—I hadn't flaked on my own holiday plans or whimsically changed my itinerary—eventually they conceded, "Yes indeed, please come as soon as you are able!" For 460+ days, I'd fantasized about Italy reopening to Americans. The moment had arrived.

Chapter Roma responded immediately: "Cara Heidi, non vediamo l'ora di darti il benvenuto!" *Dear Heidi, we can't wait to welcome you!*

My body tingled with anticipation. I booked a flight from Tenerife Norte airport to Rome, connecting through Madrid. In my haste, I overlooked one tiny glitch. I scheduled the journey for a Monday, the last day of my thirty-day stay at Casa Plumeria. Which meant—to comply with Italy's within-twenty-four-hours-of-boarding COVID testing rule—I needed to obtain a rapid antigen test in Tenerife on a *Sunday*—when most businesses, shops, and medical centers were *closed.*

I felt like I was one credit shy of earning a PhD in figuring out complicated COVID travel logistics. Testing rules, transit policies, accommodations, airline luggage parameters, country-specific passenger locator paperwork, vaccine attestations translated into English, face mask mandates—all just quirky puzzle pieces to reconfigure each time I moved to a new locale.

With a couple clicks on the internet, I found a clinic in
Puerto de la Cruz run by an American doctor and his Spanish
wife who offered COVID testing for expat travelers, including
Sundays for a slight (i.e., price-gauging) fee. I emailed the doctor
to request an appointment before my Monday departure. He replied: "All set for 6:30 p.m. Sunday. We look forward to assisting
you with your travels."

My last day in Tenerife, on the trek through Canarian Machu Picchu I'd walked at least twenty times in thirty days, I noticed two tall, thin cacti for the first time. Twin twisty green
columns with spiky yellow needles. They reminded me of the
Twin Towers, just like the shapes of the reflecting pools in *real*
Machu Picchu had invoked mental images of New York's 9/11
memorial pools. I thought about how the violent attack on New
York's World Trade Center had been a "tower moment" (in tarot
language): a time of uproar, turbulence, and change in the form
of collective pain, suffering, and grief—on top of the still-raw
trauma wounds I was trying to suture and mend from my divorce. I recalled a quote from author Michelle Tea's book, *Modern Tarot: Connecting with Your Higher Self Through the Wisdom
of the Cards*: "When all the debris and rubble are cleared and the
smoke fades from the sky, the Tower offers you a way of living
that is much more in accordance with your heart and mind."
Surviving 2001 definitely set me on a different course . . . healing . . . writing . . . no longer taking the marvel of my life for
granted.

I trudged through the banana groves, reached Camino San
Amaro, passed the strudel café, descended the Agatha Christie
steps, and arrived in Puerto de la Cruz. Light rain deterred one
last detour to Lago Martiánez. I ducked into a boutique offering
eco-friendly and sustainable products and bought a straw fedora.
I purchased a candle with a scent described as *poesía*. Poetry. A
gift for Marta. I approached a restaurant I'd passed a dozen times
on the promenade. Chose a table with an ocean view. Ordered
pumpkin soup and salmon filet with roasted peppers. I reflected

on my month in Tenerife, so happy I'd enjoyed my time alone in the wild, yet realizing how excited I felt about returning to Rome and rekindling my romance with the gritty city.

I checked my watch: 6 p.m. I paid the bill and headed to the clinic.

The doctor and his wife welcomed me, administered the swab test, and fifteen minutes later, handed me authoritative paperwork in Spanish and English. I rushed along the seafront, wanting to make my way back home before rain and nightfall darkened the path; I'd never walked the banana fields after dusk. As I left urban sidewalk, folding into the banana grove for the last time, I noticed a new piece of graffiti sprayed on the underpass walls: a man and woman kissing through face masks, a caption, "Los besos que no te di." *The kisses I didn't give you.* Maybe the image constituted a political statement, but I considered perhaps the words implied regret. Like, had someone been too stubborn to kiss? Because of anger? Insecurity? Fear of taking a chance? Intimacy phobia? I thought about whether I'd ever held back kissing someone for any of those reasons. Nope. I have many flaws, but restraining myself from telling people I love or desire them, or showing them through physical touch, is definitely not one of them.

I took a final glance around Casa Plumeria, beginning to *wist*, not wanting to leave this special place but also feeling energized to get to Rome. Each component of this journey seemed to jettison old, outdated, tired, inherited DNA, supplanting it with new genetic code I actively assembled myself, drawing a fresh world map from scratch. With each jaunt, my body chemistry, my personality, my soul's infrastructure shifted, adjusted, reconfigured . . . like Whitehaven Beach in Australia and Zlatni Rat in Croatia morphing into new shapes as sand interacted with winds and tides. I smiled at the thought that, thanks to travel, maybe my fifty-one-year-old body possessed a completely new DNA configuration from the bones and flesh I inhabited at thirty.

As I folded Casa Plumeria's chenille blanket and set it on the couch for the last time, a lizard darted along a sofa cushion and took a flying leap at the wall. *A lizard. Inside the cottage.* I stared at the little guy, neon-green suction-cup feet clinging to paint.

Okay. Enough rewilding. Time for urbanity.

I went to bed, hoping the lizard would stay glued above the couch all night. I woke up with the canaries. I loaded the suitcases into the Citroën and drove to Tenerife Norte airport, watching sky transmute from black to orange to blue. I pumped a fist in victory as I delivered the vehicle back to its original parking spot in the rental lot, not a single scratch on doors or bumpers after thirty days navigating one-lane roads and volcanic hills. I rolled my luggage into the terminal and delivered the car keys to the Autoreisen clerk with a relieved smile. I entrusted my bags to a handler, navigated airport security without a hitch—COVID paperwork once again intact—and relaxed into a café chair with a gooey Nutella croissant and a final café con leche.

Waiting at the gate to board the stopover flight to Madrid, I caught a glimpse of my reflection in a mirrored wall panel. Sun-drenched skin. Wild hair peeking from straw fedora. Blue-green eyes. A silver tote on one shoulder (the recycled paper one I'd bought in Bondi Beach) holding a laptop containing two hundred book manuscript pages.

I grinned.

Andiamo.

10
roma, roma

Each time I land at Fiumicino Airport (*Fiumicino*: *little river*), my body untwists. It fills space differently. Like it's reinserting where it belongs. As if I were born in Rome in a past life, or lives. My organs sync with Rome's heartbeat, its respiration, its sensuality.

After my first trip to Rome in 2013 when I met Luca, I'd returned to Italy's capital over fifteen times—to write, to teach English legal writing to Italian lawyers, to do book talks at law conferences, to see a U2 show, to roam, to *be*.

I'm in love with the city's textures, scars, folds, and shades.

Lugging my two suitcases, the one handle still broken, and two carry-on bags, I hailed a taxi to the city center. The driver informed me—in hyper Italian—I'm the first American he's transported in fifteen months.

The cab looped the Colosseum. Historical narrative etchings on a column dedicated to Emperor Trajan (who died on 9/11 in the year 117) blurred as we curved around Monumento Nazionale a Vittorio Emanuele II— a large national monument tourists say resembles a white wedding cake. Vittorio Emanuele II, formerly the King of Sardinia (the island in the Mediterranean), became the first monarch of a unified Italy in 1861, the culmination of *Risorgimento*, the *Resurgence*, a political and social movement against centuries of foreign domination. Distinct Italian states, republics, and principalities consolidated into a single kingdom under Vittorio Emanuele II for the first time since the sixth century.

Inhaling Roman air, I already felt like this third segment of my sabbatical—after Croatia's reboot and Tenerife's rewilding—represented my own resurgence. No more subjugation to external domination (familial or relational). Instead, prioritization of *my* growth, needs, wishes, desires, goals.

We passed Capitoline Hill, one of Rome's seven hills, famous for two prominent sets of steps. One gradual staircase called the Cordonata, designed by Michelangelo, ascends to the Capitoline Museums. A steeper one leads to the Basilica of St. Mary of *Ara Coeli* (the *altar of heaven*), a church completed in 1348 allegedly to celebrate the end of Italy's bubonic plague. I planned to jog both staircases after consuming the piles of rigatoni with guanciale (the world's best bacon) I'd been dreaming about since the onset of 2020's plague.

As the cab zipped past Teatro di Marcello, I caught a glimpse of my three columns—the trio of pillars lingering from Tempio di Apollo Sosiano that, without fail, supercharge my electrical grid. Two sharp right turns channeled us onto Lungotevere, a thoroughfare tracing the curves of the Tiber River. Two additional corners. A screech of the taxi's brakes. A halt in front of Chapter Roma.

The hotel doors burst open. A pair of men in excellent shoes and blue linen jackets scurried to grab my luggage from the taxi's trunk. "Benvenuta!" they said.

"Finalmente!" I responded. *Finally.*

I entered the lobby, an artistic and sensory shock to my system after a month in Tenerife's wilds. Green velvet curtains cinched with gold rope tassels. Spiral staircase with fleur-de-lis patterns embedded in an iron railing. Graffiti mural filling a wall between stone architectural arches: a woman peeking through wispy hair, violet lipstick accentuating provocative lips. A silver sculpture of a barefoot guy in suit jacket, tie, and boxers, sitting on a pedestal.

Palming a heavy brass room key, I pressed into a narrow elevator with my luggage and a porter who showed me to a corner suite, a belated birthday upgrade from my original reservation. Brick walls. More velvet: white velvet comforter, mustard-yellow velvet armchairs, moss-green velvet curtains. A vintage bar with cocktail glasses, metal stirrers, shakers, and crystal bottles holding hues of brown liquor. Brass lampshades hanging from cords wired into the ceiling. Antique telephone. A bathroom with a rainfall shower, plush white towels, a soft robe. Windows with shutters overlooking terra-cotta roof tiles.

I love shutters—*scuri* in Italian. The act of closing and opening them, to me, evokes transitions from privacy, coziness, solitude, or romance at night to reconnection with the world in the morning.

The porter shut the door, then returned five minutes later with an ice-cold prosecco—bubbles effervescing in a goblet—and a delicate saucer holding two warm *madeleines,* small yellow sponge cakes imprinted to resemble seashells.

Travel grunge showered away, I plopped my Tenerife straw fedora on my head and exited the hotel into Rome's dusk heat.

I walked cobblestones along Via del Portico d'Ottavia, the main street in Rome's Jewish Ghetto district, passing gelato shops, cafés, and kosher restaurants advertising carciofi alla giudia (fried artichokes). I reached the ruins of Portico d'Ottavia, descended a pedestrian ramp, and meandered through fallen pillars until I reached my columns. I gazed at the three and felt the lightning strike I always experience standing at that precise junction of latitude and longitude.

Rome always makes me feel seen.

I commenced my ritual first-day-in-Rome walkabout. Crossing a small park called Piazza Benedetto Cairoli, I window-shopped along Via dei Giubbonari, eyeing trendy leather jackets and boots in a shop called Empresa and funky casual wear in my favorite store, Niña Loca, its Spanish moniker meaning *crazy girl.* I entered Campo de' Fiori, deflecting dramatic offers of marriage from flirty guys positioned outside each restaurant. "No, grazie!" I smiled. They clutched their chests, feigning heartbreak. Vendors

swept flower petals and lemon rinds into garbage bags, decon-
structing market stalls as evening approached. The familiarity
of the scenes recalibrated me. I felt happy the pandemic hadn't
dulled Rome's energy. In fact, with fewer tourists congesting
the spaces between columns and porticos, Rome's heartbeat
thumped even louder.

I crossed a main thoroughfare, Corso Vittorio Emanuele II,
and entered Piazza Navona, excited to reconnect with the three
fountains—Fontana del Moro (the Moors), Fontana dei Quattro Fiumi (four rivers), and Fontana del Nettuno (Neptune).
Couples sipped orange Aperol spritzes at trattoria tables. Kids
blew soap bubbles on sidewalks, popping airy orbs with tiny
fingers. I stopped at the Fountain of the Four Rivers, the bulging
muscles of the sculpted horse and lion captivating me as always,
the rippling calf and arch of the Danube River God's foot mes-
merizing me.

I turned a corner, passing a mime pretending to be a windblown businessman—coat hanger wire hidden in his tie and
the flaps of his jacket, giving the impression the fabric had been
swept into the air by strong gusts. I cut across an avenue where a
line of carabinieri officers safeguarded their station, and I poked
through an alley depositing me in Piazza della Rotonda. I stared
at the letters spelling *Agrippa* across the Pantheon's pediment.
I felt the building's palpable, reassuring energy. The sky turned
purple and orange as I stepped into the rotunda's shadow, like
Agrippa recognized me and said, *Yo, welcome back.*

I scanned the piazza for a street musician. On past visits, I'd
listened to a busker with a guitar hooked to an amplifier sing
Coldplay, Bob Dylan, and Bruce Springsteen songs in an accent
that sounded Spanish or French, not Italian, and if I was really
patient, he eventually cycled through his repertoire to his one
U2 track: *I can't leeeeve weeth or weethout you.*

No music today.

I pushed onward, scooting through Piazza di Pietra (*pietra
= rocks*), past eleven forty-eight-foot-tall Corinthian columns

of Emperor Hadrian's temple, chunks missing from each stone
pillar as if mafioso machine guns had once riddled them with
bullets. I crossed another main road, Via del Corso (a former
fifteenth-century racetrack for an annual running of riderless
horses during Roman Carnival), scanned vendor carts of used
books in multiple languages, stepped around spray-paint artists
wielding canisters of colorful ink to craft images of the Colosseum for onlookers, snapped a quick photo of a ubiquitous soap
shop to send Clay as a joke (he can't stand the syrupy aroma wafting from the international chain store), and eventually reached
Fontana di Trevi. The usual heap of tourists deterred by COVID,
I had nearly a private viewing of the fountain. I hopped down
a short flight of stairs typically overrun with couples and families posing for selfies tossing coins over their shoulders into the
reflecting pool. I fished in my bag for an embroidered change
purse I'd bought six years earlier on a forty-fifth birthday trip to
Lisbon. I foraged one leftover Croatian coin and made a wish:
Let's keep this reboot, rewilding, and resurgence going. I lobbed the
kuna into the fountain.

Starving, I backtracked toward Chapter Roma, letting fresh
graffiti lure me onto unfamiliar side streets. I noticed an unscripted theme of *eyes*: sketches of women in headscarves peering
over COVID masks . . . dark eyeliner accentuating eyes peeking
through window shades . . . a grandmother's eyes surrounded
by crinkly wrinkles. I stumbled into a courtyard I'd never previously explored. Vicolo degli Osti, *osti* meaning *hosts*. A Vespa the
color of raspberry sherbet leaned against another piece of street
art: a profile of a woman's face, curly hair piled in sinuous tresses
on top of her head, like Medusa.

I've always been intrigued by the story of Medusa, though it
starts off rough. Assaulted by sea god Poseidon. Her amber hair
transformed into a tangle of writhing snakes by Athena (goddess of wisdom, war, and handicraft). Ultimately beheaded by
Perseus (a purported hero to the Greeks because he slayed monsters). Legend has it, Medusa's head and blood retained magical

properties in her afterlife. She could turn bad men to stone, re-vive the dead, and cure ailments. Now, Medusa represents female agency, a call to arms to reclaim our identity. French feminist theorist Hélène Cixous advocates in her essay "The Laugh of the Medusa" that we can do this through writing.

I snapped a photo of the pink Vespa and its spray-painted backdrop. Turning around, I noticed a restaurant called Osteria del Gallo. Six empty wooden tables occupied a triangle of cob-blestones. A server with a cropped blonde bob leaned against a doorjamb, smoking a cigarette. A yellow placard bearing a rooster, a *gallo*, swayed in the breeze.

"Posso?" I asked the server, pointing at a table.

"Certo!" She flicked the cigarette to the ground, extinguish-ing it with her shoe, and handed me a menu.

I'd decided to force myself to speak only Italian as much as possible for ten days or until I finally felt ready to go home to New York. Racking my brain to remember Italian nouns and verb conjugations after wrestling with amateur Spanish for a month in Tenerife, I explained to the server I'd been dying to get back to Rome since my last visit the summer before the pan-demic, and how happy I was that Italy finally reopened to tour-ists. She concurred, lamenting how the lack of foreigners had decimated Rome's restaurant business. She brought me a glass of ruby Chianti. I ordered *polpette al limone con funghi*. Meatballs in lemon sauce with mushrooms. A side of steamed *cicoria*, chic-ory—like spinach but bitter-er. I ate each bite of meatball with a leaf of *cicoria*. Sweet, sour, zesty. Couples and families began nestling around the other tables. The server lit votive candles.

I cleared every dab of lemon sauce from my plate, declined an after-dinner coffee and *un dolce* (dessert), sipped a second Chi-anti instead, listened to guests exchange details of their days in melodic Italian, paid my bill, and walked home through Piazza Navona. I traversed Campo de' Fiori, now quiet—market ven-dors gone home—and discovered a band setting up instruments and microphones in Piazza Benedetto Cairoli near my hotel. I

joined an intimate crowd gathering on the park's pebbles—the
first live music I'd heard since U2's Sydney shows three months
before the pandemic struck. The sound of fingers sliding along
electric guitar strings. Percussion of sticks hitting drums. Chatter of merry spectators swaying to American song lyrics sung by
Italian musicians. I closed my eyes.

   Rome. Breathe me.

Vespas zoomed. Shutters clacked. Italian voices argued . . . or
passionately agreed; half awake, I couldn't tell the difference. I
inched to the far end of the hotel bed and tugged a velvet curtain aside. A gentleman in an undershirt leaned out his apartment window and bellowed to a delivery guy on a bicycle at
street level, loaves of bread strapped to handlebars. I forced myself from bed, quickly dressed in running clothes, and bounded
down the spiral staircase.

   "Buongiorno, signorina!" A dark-haired concierge greeted me.

   "Buongiorno!" I responded, placing the heavy brass room
key on the counter. I exited the building into a punch of sunlight and headed toward the Tiber River.

   Ponte Fabricio is the oldest bridge in Rome, built in 62 BCE.
Stepping onto 2082-year-old cobblestones, I paused at a square
pillar, four sides bearing faces eroded by time, or tourists like
me pressing a palm against the cold stone. I learned this type
of column topped with a head is called a herm. Twin herms on
opposite sides of the bridge depict visages of Janus, a Roman
god who fathered (via a nymph named Camasene) Tiberinus for
whom Rome's river is named. As the god of beginnings, endings,
doorways, passages, gates, and duality, Janus is often portrayed
through two faces—one gazing at the past and one peering into
the future. I thought about how my travels have enabled me to
reflect on, process, write about, and make sense of my past. *Perhaps it's time to let it all go. Lasciarlo andare. And visualize my
future.* I stared at the four-paneled herm, trying to differentiate

past from future so I could touch the optimal Janus effigy each time I passed the post.

Ponte Fabricio connects Via Portico d'Ottavia to Isola Tiberina, a small island plunked in the center of the Tiber housing a gelateria, a café, and a hospital. I crossed another bridge, Ponte Cestio, into the *rione* (district) of Trastevere. Two baristas bearing morning facial scruff brewed cappuccinos in a coffee kiosk at the top of a flight of stairs descending to a running and cycling path hugging the curves of the Tiber. I waved at them and followed men carrying bicycles down the steps to the exercise trail. I jogged along the river, under ancient bridges, past walls tagged with vibrant graffiti. The brown-green tint of the Tiber—the color of matcha tea—reminded me of the paint palette of Italian artist, Giorgio Morandi, a contemporary of Picasso.

When I'd moved back to New York from California, still processing two losses—my relationship with Forrest and my dog Rowan—I'd enrolled in a painting class in Manhattan's Tribeca neighborhood. The teacher introduced me to Morandi's art. She arranged *natura morta* (an Italian phrase directly translating to *dead nature* but meaning *still life*), compositions of glass jars, pitchers, and fruit on a table, and urged, "paint your angst." Morandi's soothing colors—buttery yellow, cloudy gray, milky chocolate—allowed canvas to wrest sadness.

Bicyclists jangled gentle warning bells, or perhaps greetings, as they passed me on the Lungotevere. I ran a mile and a half, past a barge floating near the spot where Luca and Roberto took Mia and me on our double date eight years earlier. I ascended a stairway to street level at Castel Sant'Angelo, a mausoleum built for Emperor Hadrian. I turned right onto Ponte Sant'Angelo, a bridge flanked with sculptures of angels bearing ominous Latin inscriptions and equally jarring accessories. *In flagella*

paratus sum: angel with whips. *Aspicient ad me quem confixerunt:* angel with nails. *In aerumna mea dum configitur spina*: angel with crown of thorns.

Another memory swirled.

When my parents decided to sell the one-bedroom condo in Rehoboth Beach they'd owned since Chris and I were in high school, they prodded me to rent a car and drive from New York to Delaware to clear out boxes of adolescent memorabilia before the real estate closing; otherwise, everything would end up at Goodwill.

I obliged, rented a car, drove four hours, and sat on the floor of the condo where I'd penned dreamy diary entries about unrequited crushes on boys. Trent: a football player I kissed at high school volleyball camp. David: a sous-chef I met at a summer job busing tables who introduced me to Bob Marley music and Captain Morgan's rum. Michael: a college classmate who once held my hand walking me home from religion class. I sifted through boxes of *Nancy Drew* and *Bobbsey Twins* books, Baudelaire poetry collections like *Les Fleurs du Mal*, cassette tapes of songs by David Bowie, Tears for Fears, Depeche Mode, and Frankie Goes to Hollywood. A Nirvana album, reminding me how singer Kurt Cobain died by suicide four days before I married Trey.

I reached blindly into a packing crate. Something sharp sliced a gash in my hand. I peered into the box, blood dripping. A literal crown of thorns. Mom's startling Easter decorations.

My days in Rome somewhat mimicked my Tenerife routine. Morning coffee brewed downstairs in the hotel lounge and carried back to my room. Two hours of book writing. A late morning walk across Ponte Fabricio, then Ponte Cestio, a quick wave to the barista guys, a three-mile jog along the Tiber to Castel

Sant'Angelo and back. After each run, I climbed the steps to the coffee kiosk where the baristas served me *caffè americano con un po' di latte* (American-style coffee with a little milk) and *una spremuta* (fresh-pressed orange juice), commending me for exercising in Rome's sticky June humidity. I practiced my Italian with them, conversing about the city's recovery . . . and our personal revival . . . after pandemic isolation.

Afternoons, I wandered, purposefully disorienting in mazes of *viali, vie,* and *vicoli.* Some days I explored unfamiliar nooks of Trastevere, other days backstreets in a hilly *quartiere* called Monti near the Colosseum. I experimented with new restaurants, choosing outdoor tables with cheery decor: handwoven tablecloths, placemats bearing poems in loopy fonts, jewel-toned flasks of olive oil, silverware resting in painted flowerpots. I requested menus in Italian, not English, explaining to each patient waiter, "Devo praticare." *I need to practice.* I felt refreshed, calm, inspired.

My culinary quest to roam beyond unadventurous pasta and pizza exposed me to novel flavor combinations: chickpea soup topped with shaved artichoke; ricotta cheese with honey and jam; eggplant meatballs. I sat at each trattoria, writing in my journal, tasting food fusions, listening to Italians converse tête-à-tête, Romans sharing excitement at their city's resurgence—risorgimento—after being closed to the world for over a year. Cuisine, accents, gritty sexy scent of the city—caressing, alluring.

I visited a gallery showcasing work by the famous, elusive street artist Banksy. I popped into my favorite clothing boutique, Niña Loca, and spoke Italian with friendly clerks who seemed— or perhaps pretended—to recognize me from my last stock up of casual clothes during my prepandemic summer trip to Rome. I updated my wardrobe: a resupply of linen-cotton T-shirts, button-fly jeans with low-set rear pockets, and drawstring pants in Morandi's shade of brown. I felt artsy, creative, replenished. I realized once again how happy I am traveling alone. I don't want to speak English; I want to absorb others' dialects, upbringings, perceptions. At night, I curled up in my Chapter Roma bed watching Italian movies with Italian subtitles on my laptop, repeating words aloud as they emerged from actors' lips.

I knew it was nearing time to go home to New York. I didn't want to. I didn't want the bubble of my seven weeks of travel to burst. The sensory blur of Croatia. My triumphant trek—Split via Vienna to Barcelona, onward to Tenerife, to Casa Plumeria. The Citroën. The black sand. The banana groves. The roosters and canaries. The cats. My writer flow. Finally making it to Rome—a taser jolt to my soul.

Mornings, I tried converting fluid feelings into concrete words in my journal: *I want to live here. Stay here . . . forever. I love who I am here. I love how my insides feel. Peaceful. Upbeat. Go-with-the-flow. Positive. Motivated. To write. To learn. To exercise. To expand.*

Moping, I forced myself onto Delta's website to figure out a flight home. One-way prices were exorbitant. On a whim, I checked round-trip rates: Rome to New York, then back to Rome—the opposite of my usual route. Half the price! I booked a return flight to Italy in late summer. Like the rebellion I'd felt purchasing my one-way ticket to Croatia, buying round-trip transit back to Italy immediately adjusted my mindset: Mild aching, my action verb of *wisting*, allowed, but Rome would await my return. *Ti aspetto. I am waiting for you*, as Italians say.

I texted Clay:

I'm coming home!!! Can't wait to see you. Let's make this summer and this next year the best one ever. And let's help each other reboot our love lives. New mantra: If they don't repulse us—physically and politically, haha!—let's make ourselves date them!

Researching preflight COVID test protocols to get back to New York, I discovered Rome pharmacies offered rapid testing for a reasonable twenty-two euros. I learned a new word—*tampone* (*swab*)—and obtained one in a white outdoor tent on which a vandal had scribbled, *Il COVID non esiste. Il terrorismo psicologico! COVID doesn't exist. Psychological terrorism!* Someone else had scratched red ink through the *non* (*doesn't*). In twenty minutes, the technician certified me travel ready—the least stressful and least expensive international testing experience of my pandemic life.

As I left the pharmacy, documents secured, I passed a "slow food" restaurant, part of a movement launched in Italy in 1986 to promote traditional and regional cuisine, small businesses, and sustainable food system practices. As I stopped to investigate the menu, someone grasped my elbow.

"Ciao, sei bellissima!" *Hi, you're beautiful,* said a cute, dark-haired guy in a server's apron. He pulled sunglasses off my face. "Voglio vedere i tuoi occhi . . . " *I want to see your eyes.*

He removed his apron, stuffed it into a backpack slung over his shoulder, and grabbed my hand.

"Sono in pausa pranzo. Lascia che ti mostri il mio posto preferito a Roma." *I'm on a lunch break. Let me show you my favorite place in Rome.* His pickup line sounded remarkably similar to Drago's in Split.

I'd literally just told Clay our new motto is: Let's put ourselves out there and give guys a chance.

Am I rolling with this?

His name: Antonio. Maybe twenty-five or thirty years old. He spoke at warp speed—not a single word of English. I understood about half what he said. We walked toward the river, his hand clutching mine. We reached Ponte Sant'Angelo, the bridge with the ominous angels. He stopped at a staircase descending to the Lungotevere and kissed me on both cheeks. He scampered down the steps, tugging my hand. I followed. Initially.

As earnest and playful as he seemed, the situation felt off. One lesson I'd learned from all the attachment theory podcasts I'd listened to in Tenerife: I have a bad habit of misinterpreting lightning-speed affection and intimacy as cosmic connection. The new, rebooted, rewilded me had made a pact to stop confusing fast-tracked fire—"love bombing"—with genuine interest or care.

Attention from an attractive younger guy is flattering, yes of course, but why had he really chosen me? Am I that easy a mark?

For once, I heeded internal alarm bells. Standing on a landing near the S&M angel bridge, I hesitated. Antonio launched into a speech—in Italian—about how life is an *avventura*, how encounters like these are all that matters, how we should live in the present. He pressed his body against mine and tried to slide his hand up my shirt. I decided *carpe diem*—at least this time—wasn't worth the risk of getting shivved and shoved into the Tiber. I pulled away. I said I needed to meet someone for lunch but I'd be happy to exchange numbers and have a drink sometime. Anger shaded his face. He pushed past me, rushed up the stairs, and left without a glance.

I walked home, foggy, glad I'd interrupted the momentum.

I still felt like I had no idea what I was doing. How, at fifty-one years old, did I not know? I felt like Goldilocks. Nonchalance makes me cling. Full-court press sends me running. What am I supposed to like?

Either way, I guess it's a sign it's time to go home.

On the flight from Fiumicino to New York, I reflected . . . *Eight airports. Four pieces of luggage. Four COVID tests. Intimacy and sex, finally. Pages and pages written. Volcanoes and mountains driven. Banana hills climbed. Three oceans touched. Five languages heard and spoken. Rebooted. Rewilded. Resurged. This is just the beginning. Be patient and see where a year of sabbatical travel . . . of adventure . . . of writing . . . of self-love and self-discovery . . . takes you.*

Entering my Manhattan apartment after seven weeks away felt odd but comforting. My art. My books. My American coffee machine. My thirsty plants. New additions: Sack of sea glass I collected at Dubrovnik's Banje Beach. Black lava rock plucked from Tenerife sand. Rome journal imprinted with the word *giallo* (yellow).

For the next month, I edited my book manuscript, reconnected with my trainer Lou at the park for sweaty sparring lessons, and dined outside with friends all over the city.

Soon though, media pundits began fomenting rumors about Europe closing to American tourists again, even vaccinated ones. I gritted my teeth and counted the days until my return trip to Italy.

I boarded the flight to Fiumicino, a ball of anxiety, agitated by constantly changing pandemic travel protocols: Monday, tests required. Tuesday, allegedly no tests required anymore. Wednesday, tests required again. I swatted away a smack of guilt over blowing money on Rome apartments as my New York one sat empty. I overrode the miserly nag in my head, the progeny of an ultra-frugal upbringing.

This is what sabbatical is for. Get on the plane and go.

JFK Airport. Wheels up. Listening to flight attendants speak Italian around me, my heart rate stabilized. My shoulders unhunched. By the time the plane landed at Fiumicino, I'd mended, my body like magnetized puzzle pieces clicking together after breaking apart at home. Toting less luggage than my last visit, I boarded the Leonardo Express train to Termini Station, slid into a taxi, and relayed my apartment address to the driver: Via di Sant'Angelo in Pescheria (*fish market*, memorializing Portico d'Ottavia's role as a meetup for fishmongers in the Middle Ages through the late 1800s).

I opened a door decorated with mosaic tiles and flung every shutter open to flood the flat's interior with light. I gazed around my new home for the next few weeks. Curtains with handwritten words in French. A writing desk. Faux fireplace in the bedroom. Ceiling fan.

This space feels creative. I definitely can write here.
I activated my daily comfort routine: Write. Run. Roam . . .
Rome holding my hand again, our fingers intertwined, pulling
me along cobblestones toward discovery and surprise.

One night, lying in bed, grazing on dried apricots, fresh
mozzarella, and prosciutto, relaxing and watching Italian Netflix, I researched Italian language schools in Rome. I found one
in the rione of Monti near the Colosseum. I emailed the course
coordinator and asked if I could join a class. She wrote back immediately: "Classes run from 9 to noon on weekdays. Come
tomorrow at 8:45 a.m. I'll do a language assessment test when
you arrive. We'll place you in the right course for your compre-
hension level."

In the morning, I packed a legal pad and a snack of apricots
into a tote, plopped my Tenerife fedora on my head, and trotted
through alleys toward Piazza Venezia. I felt excited that, on a
late August Monday morning, passing Trajan's Column . . . the
Colosseum and Roman Forum within view . . . I was on my way
to my first language class in Rome. A student again. My favorite
persona. Growing up, excelling at math, French, and writing
garnered me positive attention from adults who weren't my parents. I'd loved college too, studying subjects like anthropology,
psychology, Italian, a semester of Russian. Getting good grades
symbolized a ticket to eventual freedom to explore the world.
Entering law school at twenty-one though, my usual system
faltered; I read and studied but didn't understand the language
of law, the secret cipher everyone else seemed to possess. Law
school was the only educational experience of my life in which I
felt dumber than everyone else.

I walked to Monti, past Romans sharing morning coffee,
smokes, and stories around café tables, dogs on leashes asleep
at their feet. Waiters—COVID masks drooping below noses—
served *cornettos* (Italian croissants), chocolate-hazelnut Nutella
oozing from flaky dough onto pretty plates. Delivery guys carted
crates of fresh oranges to be pressed into spremuta. Chic women

on pastel Vespas zipped along cobblestones, linen trousers billowing in the wind, dark hair flecked with blonde highlights peeking from helmets. Men in cobalt-blue blazers and stylish shoes drained last drops of espressos, extinguishing cigarettes, embracing before parting.

Opening the door to the language school, I heard Italian spoken in a dozen accents. An instructor in a flowered smock, her nose and mouth visible through a clear COVID face shield, welcomed me and handed me a two-page quiz. I squished into a chair with a small desktop attached to it, like a kindergartner. I breezed through the first nine questions: simple vocabulary and verb conjugations in present, past, and future tenses. But at Question #10, I started guessing. I'd studied advanced verb tenses—imperfect, conditional, imperative—but I'd forgotten everything. Rather than waste everyone's time pretending, I stopped and handed the pages to the proctor.

"Livello 2A," she said, and pointed down a hall.

I entered another classroom and chose a desk near an open window, the building's air-conditioning putting forth lackluster effort, my face perspiring beneath my mandatory COVID mask. A teacher entered the classroom and introduced herself. *Aurelia.* Aurelia asked us to recite our names, our countries of origin, our jobs, and why we wanted to learn Italian. A blond tennis player from England explained that his employer—an accounting firm—encouraged and paid for language lessons. A Russian girl planned to marry an Italian boy in a month. A Cuban girl quit her marketing job in Chicago and relocated to Rome for a year. A French lady's grandchildren lived in Rome. A quiet Slovakian girl shared she'd taken a break from her paralegal job to travel to Rome—her first solo trip—to study Italian. A shy Catholic priest visiting the Vatican from Burkina Faso whispered a barely audible response. A feisty German woman with shoulder tattoos and artsy jewelry indicated she just needed "smart fun." I said, "I'm learning Italian because I want to live in Rome someday." I'd never said that out loud to anyone.

Aurelia led us through a grammar lesson, written exercises, and conversation games. An hour and a half passed quickly. We paused for a coffee break. Every student and professor left the building, reconvened at a nearby café, downed espressos while chatting in Italian, then returned to school. For another ninety minutes, we plowed through a syntax tutorial and a vocabulary quiz.

On my commute to the language lab each day, I felt less like a temporary tourist and more like a Roman resident. I checked in with my three columns. I filled my water bottle from gargoyle spigots. I waved *buongiorno* at restaurateurs placing empty wine bottles in recycling bins, art gallery owners propping doors open for morning shifts, salt-and-pepper-haired ladies sweeping their balconies.

I loved being a student again, doing homework, raising my hand to answer questions in Italian, searching for vocabulary, conjugating verbs in my head and on paper before experimenting with them aloud. A few things about the teaching methodology, however, quickly started getting on my nerves. Extroverted classmates—the grandmother and the bride-to-be—refused to wait their turn, ignoring classroom norms and vibes. They blurted answers to every question, dominating each exchange. The teacher did nothing to ensure quieter students like the paralegal and the priest got a chance to participate. (Introverts like to think before speaking and hate interrupting people.) Further, with each idiom we learned, the more layers of explicit sexism, ageism, and offensive stereotyping jumped out from the teaching and the textbook. One exercise expressly asked us to list words typecasting individuals from Vietnam, Africa, and Lebanon. My American political correctness started going haywire. One accidental phrasing mistake at a law school podium can get a professor canceled on social media. This Italian classroom was inappropriateness on steroids.

Another day, a male substitute teacher replaced Aurelia. He cracked a joke about a band popular with youth worldwide, then singled me out, saying—in Italian—"Heidi probably doesn't recognize the name of that band because she's *vecchia*." *Old.*

Once I got over my initial embarrassment (and my biologically reactive blush), I seethed.

Bro, I've been to over forty U2 shows in five countries. I'm not vecchia. I rock.

In another awful exercise ostensibly designed to help us practice using numbers, the teacher prompted each student to guess the age of the person sitting next to them. The priest sized me up and murmured to the class, "Sessanta." *Sixty.* I nearly burst into tears at the nine-year tack on to my actual age. Later, once I calmed down, I reasoned a devout missionary hailing from a different continent perhaps doesn't have a ton of experience calculating the correct age of a fifty-one-year-old American woman wearing a COVID mask. Why would (or should) *anyone*, for that matter? Nonetheless, the overestimation hurt.

On our coffee break, the Russian girl asked, "Heidi, how old are you *really?*"

"*Cinquantuno.* Fifty-one."

"Wow. In Russia, once a woman hits forty-five, her life is basically over. You're brave to travel and learn new things at your age."

She probably meant her comment to be complimentary, but three sequential age references stung. Most of the time, I forget I'm in my fifties. I *never* regard aging as a negative, on anyone. There's literally nothing we can do about age anyway except embrace it and constantly strive to be as awesome as possible in our own skin. Lou helps me with that. To him, age means nothing. Attitude, consistency, and work ethic mean everything. Whenever I thank him for treating me like a "real" fighter, he always responds, "You *are* a real fighter." He's right about age. I'd much rather have the body I have now than the body I had in my twenties, thirties, or forties.

I decided not to return to the language school. Instead, I made Rome my classroom again. I practiced my Italian with

coffee baristas, grocery clerks, and strangers. I infused vocabulary lessons into every meal, ordering only from Italian menus,
not English. I found a health food shop and spoke Italian with
the owner as he blended avocado, pistachios, apples, and almond
milk into a smoothie for me. I ate gazpacho, chicory prepared
numerous ways, fig and mozzarella pressed between salty focaccia
rounds—learning words for less familiar ingredients.

I tended to my creative marrow. I searched for art in the
wild: street art, graffiti, ancient ruins juxtaposed against modern
splashes of color and texture. I noticed a sign in the window
of a poster shop: "I am a real artist." I snapped a photo to remind myself, *I AM a real artist*, then noticed another sign: "No
photos!" I edited my book manuscript and clocked daily miles
running by the Tiber. I felt a million miles away from America,
my job, ongoing pandemic politics. I felt revived, remotivated,
resurged.

My fall calendar began filling up with requests for book-re-
lated speaking engagements in the States. Clay texted: COME
HOME! I MISS YOU!

I knew I probably should go home soon. Before I began
to *wist*, I reminded myself how fall and winter are my favorite seasons in New York City. I love the glorious moment each
October when I realize I've gone an entire twenty-four hours
without sweating from my face. Leaves on trees around my
neighborhood track turn gold, orange, red, then tumble to the
tarmac. I forage in my storage unit for plastic tubs housing winter clothes—soft sweaters I haven't seen in seven months; biker
boots to pair with jeans; cozy wool scarves, hats, gloves. I love
the autumn romance of dining outside, the scent of firewood
wafting from more affluent New Yorkers' brownstone chimneys.

Wait, I don't have a return flight home! The budding rebel
in me got excited about buying another round-trip ticket from
Rome to New York, back again to Italy. Reverse commute. *No
need to wist. You'll be here again soon.*

I booked a flight home with a return ticket to Rome a few days before Christmas, invigorated to see my sabbatical turning into a hopscotch of trips.

My last day in Rome, I treated myself to a final meal of *rigatoni alla gricia*—pasta with my beloved guanciale, pecorino cheese, and black pepper—and a side of *cicoria* sautéed in red pepper olive oil. A waitress brought a bottle of Cesanese—Roman red wine—for me to taste. The Cesanese tasted strange, richer than my usual preference, lush and silky. Wine aficionado Madeline Puckette describes Cesanese as "the ichor of wild boar." (*Ichor*: "the fluid that flows like blood in the veins of the gods.")

Raindrops plunking on an awning overhead sounded like fingers pressing typewriter keys. Vespas whizzed past my table. The server delivered my check with a plate of taralli—crackers I'd learned to make in my 2013 cooking lesson in Puglia—dusted with cinnamon and sugar. A true vecchia, a silver-haired *nonna* (*grandmother*), stood at a window on the third floor of a building across the street, red velvet curtain drawn aside, watching me. I imagined myself standing at the window of *my* Roman apartment when I am her glorious age.

Wanting an amaro as a nightcap to help me sleep—and to capstone another sensual tryst with Rome—I walked to an enoteca, potted plants bracing its doors open. Patrons draped barstools, wine barrel tables, and a couplet of entryway stairs.

I sat on the steps among gorgeous Romans, sipping amaro, feeling its molecules warm my soul, like a somatic changing of the vowel *o* in *amaro* (*bitter*) to *e* in *amare* (the verb, *to love*).

Rain misting my hair and cheeks, I thought, *People are like cities*. I don't want to be perfect like Capri or Positano. I don't want to be fancy like Como, or sophisticated like Milan. I want to be grit and sex and diesel and edge and she-wolf like Rome.

epilogue

Most of my life, I've followed the maps other people have drawn for me—parents, grandparents, teachers, boys, bosses, men. Other people's demarcations, rules, interpretations, limitations, expectations, definitions, demands. The boundary lines, or lack thereof, around my body. Where I can or can't go. The way I'm supposed to look, talk, think, feel, behave.

Maybe that's why I have such a bad sense of geographical direction. My internal compass is underdeveloped.

Many times, I've let people—dates, partners, professional superiors—convince me I want something I don't. In those moments, I tried asserting myself, but it didn't come out the right way, or I was too vague or wishy-washy, or I blushed and they didn't take me seriously. Often, it just seemed easier to do what they wanted, or let them do what they wanted, to get it over with. Instead of setting standards, crafting and enforcing deal-breakers, I settled for scraps. Ceded power. Satisfied others' needs. Forgot I even had any of my own.

I've written books; given speeches to hundreds, sometimes thousands, of people; earned money and a master's degree on top of a law degree; and juggled eight thousand balls in the air, in the highest of heels, backward and upside down like a circus performer, all with a lipsticked smile on my face to please whoever is telling me to just be happy because it's unpleasant for them when I'm not.

I'm done with all that.

I am done following other people's maps.

The trips in these pages empowered me to rip up the old atlases, burn them in a bonfire, scatter the ashes in the Hudson River . . . and the Tiber.

I'm drawing my own map from now on.